Qualifications and Credit Framework (QCF)
AQ2013
LEVEL 2 CERTIFICATE IN ACCOUNTING

TEXT

Processing
Bookkeeping
Transactions

2015 Edition

For assessments from September 2015

A NOTE ABOUT COPYRIGHT

Dear Customer

What does the little © mean and why does it matter?

Your market-leading BPP books, course materials and e-learning materials do not write and update themselves. People write them on their own behalf or as employees of an organisation that invests in this activity. Copyright law protects their livelihoods. It does so by creating rights over the use of the content.

Breach of copyright is a form of theft – as well being a criminal offence in some jurisdictions, it is potentially a serious breach of professional ethics.

With current technology, things might seem a bit hazy but, basically, without the express permission of BPP Learning Media:

- Photocopying our materials is a breach of copyright

- Scanning, ripcasting or conversion of our digital materials into different file formats, uploading them to facebook or emailing them to your friends is a breach of copyright

You can, of course, sell your books, in the form in which you have bought them – once you have finished with them. (Is this fair to your fellow students? We update for a reason.) Please note the e-products are sold on a single user licence basis: we do not supply 'unlock' codes to people who have bought them secondhand.

And what about outside the UK? BPP Learning Media strives to make our materials available at prices students can afford by local printing arrangements, pricing policies and partnerships which are clearly listed on our website. A tiny minority ignore this and indulge in criminal activity by illegally photocopying our material or supporting organisations that do. If they act illegally and unethically in one area, can you really trust them?

BPP LEARNING MEDIA'S AAT MATERIALS

The AAT's assessments fall within the **Qualifications and Credit Framework** and most papers are assessed by way of an on demand **computer based assessment**. BPP Learning Media has invested heavily to ensure our materials are as relevant as possible for this method of assessment. In particular, our **suite of online resources** ensures that you are prepared for online testing by allowing you to practise numerous online tasks that are similar to the tasks you will encounter in the AAT's assessments.

Resources

The BPP range of resources comprises:

- **Texts**, covering all the knowledge and understanding needed by students, with numerous illustrations of 'how it works', practical examples and tasks for you to use to consolidate your learning. The majority of tasks within the texts have been written in an interactive style that reflects the style of the online tasks we anticipate the AAT will set. When you purchase a Text you are also granted free access to your Text content online.

- **Question Banks**, including additional learning questions plus the AAT's sample assessment(s) and a number of BPP full practice assessments. Full answers to all questions and assessments, prepared by BPP Learning Media Ltd, are included. Our question banks are provided free of charge online.

- **Passcards**, which are handy pocket-sized revision tools designed to fit in a handbag or briefcase to enable you to revise anywhere at anytime. All major points are covered in the Passcards which have been designed to assist you in consolidating knowledge.

- **Workbooks**, which have been designed to cover the units that are assessed by way of computer based project/case study. The workbooks contain many practical tasks to assist in the learning process and also a sample assessment or project to work through.

- **Lecturers' resources**, for units assessed by computer based assessments. These provide a further bank of tasks, answers and full practice assessments for classroom use, available separately only to lecturers whose colleges adopt BPP Learning Media material.

This Text for Processing Bookkeeping Transactions has been written specifically to ensure comprehensive yet concise coverage of the AAT's **AQ2013** learning outcomes and assessment criteria.

Each chapter contains:

- Clear, step by step explanation of the topic

- Logical progression and linking from one chapter to the next

- Numerous illustrations of 'how it works'

- Interactive tasks within the text of the chapter itself, with answers at the back of the book. The majority of these tasks have been written in the interactive form that students can expect to see in their real assessments

- Test your learning questions of varying complexity, again with answers supplied at the back of the book. The majority of these questions have been written in the interactive form that students can expect to see in their real assessments

The emphasis in all tasks and test questions is on the practical application of the skills acquired.

Supplements

From time to time we may need to publish supplementary materials to one of our titles. This can be for a variety of reasons, from a small change in the AAT unit guidance to new legislation coming into effect between editions.

You should check our supplements page regularly for anything that may affect your learning materials. All supplements are available free of charge on our supplements page on our website at:

www.bpp.com/about-bpp/aboutBPP/StudentInfo#q4

Customer feedback

If you have any comments about this book, please email nisarahmed@bpp.com or write to Nisar Ahmed, AAT Head of Programme, BPP Learning Media Ltd, BPP House, Aldine Place, London W12 8AA.

Any feedback we receive is taken into consideration when we periodically update our materials, including comments on style, depth and coverage of AAT standards.

In addition, although our products pass through strict technical checking and quality control processes, unfortunately errors may occasionally slip through when producing material to tight deadlines.

When we learn of an error in a batch of our printed materials, either from internal review processes or from customers using our materials, we want to make sure customers are made aware of this as soon as possible and the appropriate action is taken to minimise the impact on student learning.

As a result, when we become aware of any such errors we will:

1) Include details of the error and, if necessary, PDF prints of any revised pages under the related subject heading on our 'supplements' page at: www.bpp.com/about-bpp/aboutBPP/StudentInfo#q4

2) Update the source files ahead of any further printing of the materials

3) Investigate the reason for the error and take appropriate action to minimise the risk of reoccurrence

A NOTE ON TERMINOLOGY

The AAT AQ2013 standards and assessments use international terminology based on International Financial Reporting Standards (IFRSs). Although you may be familiar with UK terminology, you need to now know the equivalent international terminology for your assessments.

The following information is taken from an article on the AAT's website and compares IFRS terminology with UK GAAP terminology. It then goes on to describe the impact of IFRS terminology on students studying for each level of the AAT QCF qualification.

Note that since the article containing the information below was published, there have been changes made to some IFRSs. Therefore BPP Learning Media have updated the table and other information below to reflect these changes.

In particular, the primary performance statement under IFRSs which was formerly known as the 'income statement' or the 'statement of comprehensive income' is now called the 'statement of profit or loss' or the 'statement of profit or loss and other comprehensive income'.

What is the impact of IFRS terms on AAT assessments?

The list shown in the table that follows gives the 'translation' between UK GAAP and IFRS.

UK GAAP	IFRS
Final accounts	Financial statements
Trading and profit and loss account	**Statement of profit or loss (or statement of profit or loss and other comprehensive income)**
Turnover or Sales	Revenue or Sales Revenue
Sundry income	Other operating income
Interest payable	Finance costs
Sundry expenses	Other operating costs
Operating profit	Profit from operations
Net profit/loss	Profit/Loss for the year/period
Balance sheet	**Statement of financial position**
Fixed assets	Non-current assets
Net book value	Carrying amount

UK GAAP	IFRS
Tangible assets	Property, plant and equipment
Reducing balance depreciation	Diminishing balance depreciation
Depreciation/Depreciation expense(s)	Depreciation charge(s)
Stocks	Inventories
Trade debtors or Debtors	Trade receivables
Prepayments	Other receivables
Debtors and prepayments	Trade and other receivables
Cash at bank and in hand	Cash and cash equivalents
Trade creditors or Creditors	Trade payables
Accruals	Other payables
Creditors and accruals	Trade and other payables
Long-term liabilities	Non-current liabilities
Capital and reserves	Equity (limited companies)
Profit and loss balance	Retained earnings
Minority interest	Non-controlling interest
Cash flow statement	**Statement of cash flows**

This is certainly not a comprehensive list, which would run to several pages, but it does cover the main terms that you will come across in your studies and assessments. However, you won't need to know all of these in the early stages of your studies – some of the terms will not be used until you reach Level 4. For each level of the AAT qualification, the points to bear in mind are as follows:

Level 2 Certificate in Accounting

The IFRS terms do not impact greatly at this level. Make sure you are familiar with 'receivables' (also referred to as 'trade receivables'), 'payables' (also referred to as 'trade payables'), and 'inventories'. The terms sales ledger and purchases ledger – together with their control accounts – will continue to be used. Sometimes the control accounts might be called 'trade receivables control account' and 'trade payables control account'. The other term to be aware of is 'non-current asset' – this may be used in some assessments.

Level 3 Diploma in Accounting

At this level you need to be familiar with the term 'financial statements'. The financial statements comprise a 'statement of profit or loss' (previously known as an income statement), and a 'statement of financial position'. In the statement of profit or loss the term 'revenue' or 'sales revenue' takes the place of 'sales', and 'profit for the year' replaces 'net profit'. Other terms may be used in the statement of financial position – eg 'non-current assets' and 'carrying amount'. However, specialist limited company terms are not required at this level.

Level 4 Diploma in Accounting

At Level 4 a wider range of IFRS terms is needed, and in the case of Financial statements, are already in use – particularly those relating to limited companies. Note especially that a statement of profit or loss becomes a 'statement of profit or loss and other comprehensive income'.

Note: The information above was taken from an AAT article from the 'assessment news' area of the AAT website (www.aat.org.uk). However, it has been adapted by BPP Learning Media for changes in international terminology since the article was published.

ASSESSMENT STRATEGY

Processing Bookkeeping Transactions (PBKT) is the first of two bookkeeping assessments at Level 2.

The assessment is normally a computer based assessment (CBT) and students will be required to respond to CBT tasks in a variety of ways, for example using multiple choice, true/false, drag and drop, drop-down lists, text select, linking boxes and gap fill tools.

The PBKT assessment consists of 10 tasks in one section.

Competency

For the purpose of assessment the competency level for AAT assessment is set at 70%. The level descriptor in the table below describes the ability and skills students at this level must successfully demonstrate to achieve competence.

QCF Level descriptor	**Summary**
	Achievement at Level 2 reflects the ability to select and use relevant knowledge, ideas, skills and procedures to complete well-defined tasks and address straightforward problems. It includes taking responsibility for completing tasks and procedures and exercising autonomy and judgement subject to overall direction or guidance.
	Knowledge and understanding
	▪ Use understanding of facts, procedures and ideas to complete well-defined tasks and address straightforward problems
	▪ Interpret relevant information and ideas
	▪ Be aware of the types of information that are relevant to the area of study or work
	Application and action
	▪ Complete well-defined, generally routine tasks and address straightforward problems
	▪ Select and use relevant skills and procedures
	▪ Identify, gather and use relevant information to inform actions
	▪ Identify how effective actions have been
	Autonomy and accountability
	▪ Take responsibility for completing tasks and procedures
	▪ Exercise autonomy and judgement subject to overall direction or guidance

Task	Learning outcome	Assessment criteria	Maximum marks	Title for topics within task range
1	1, 2, 4, 5	1.2, 2.2, 2.3 (implied) 4.3, 5.2	15	Make entries in an analysed day-book
2	2, 8	2.2, 2.4 (implied) 8.1	15	Transfer data from day-books to ledgers
3	6	1.3 (implied) 6.1, 6.2	20	Make entries in a three column cash book
4	8	8.1	15	Transfer data from a three column cash book
5	1, 7, 8	1.1, 7.1, 7.2, 7.3, 7.4, 8.1	20	Make entries in and transfers from an analysed Petty cash book
6	8	8.3	20	Prepare an initial trial balance
7	3, 5	3.1, 3.2, (implied) 5.1, 5.3, 5.4	15	Check supplier invoices/credit notes
8	1, 2, 3, 4	3.1, 3.2 (implied) 1.1, 1.3, 2.3, 4.1, 4.2, 4.4	15	Prepare sales invoice or credit note Check the accuracy of receipts from customers
9	1, 4, 8	1.1 (implied) 4.5, 8.2	15	Prepare a statement of account from an account in the sales ledger
10	2	2.1, 2.3, 2.4, 2.5, 2.6	15	Understand the double entry bookkeeping system

AAT UNIT GUIDE

Processing Bookkeeping Transactions (PBKT)

Introduction

Please read the information below in conjunction with the QCF standards for the unit.

Purpose of the unit

This unit is designed to introduce students to the double entry bookkeeping system and associated documents and processes. The student is taken to the stage of extracting an initial trial balance, before any adjustments are made.

This unit is the first of two bookkeeping units at Level 2. It will help the student to better understand the computerised accounting unit at the same level and be an important foundation for the financial accounting units at Level 3.

The practical nature of this unit will help students develop vital skills that are valued in the workplace and will make AAT students attractive to future employers.

Those who have achieved this Level 2 unit will not only benefit employers through the relevant knowledge they have acquired but also through the practical skills they have gained, enabling them to carry out accounting and accounting-related tasks confidently. They will add value to a business organisation with their up to date knowledge of business practices and the motivated and willing approach that AAT students develop during the learning process.

Learning Objectives

This unit will enable students to develop an understanding of a manual double entry bookkeeping system to the initial trial balance stage.

Students will develop the necessary knowledge and skills to deal with documents that are sent to and from organisations. They will need to know how to make entries in sales, purchases and returns day books using account codes, and to transfer those totals to the sales, purchases and general ledgers. The Cash Book and Petty Cash Book are also dealt with in this unit, making entries into both and transferring totals to the ledgers.

Candidates will learn how to make appropriate checks on supplier invoices and credit notes, reconcile supplier statements with the purchases ledger account and calculate payments due to suppliers. They will also learn how to prepare sales invoices and credit notes and check receipts from customers.

The skills and knowledge detailed above are reflected in the eight learning outcomes included in this unit.

Learning Outcomes

Processing Bookkeeping Transactions consists of eight learning outcomes each of which has two or more assessment criteria:

Learning Outcome	Covered in Chapter(s)
1. Understand the principles of processing financial transactions (three assessment criteria)	3
2. Understand the double entry bookkeeping system (six assessment criteria)	6
3. Understand discounts (two assessment criteria)	2
4. Prepare and process financial documentation for customers (five assessment criteria)	1, 3, 4
5. Process supplier invoices and credit notes and calculate payments (four assessment criteria)	3, 5
6. Maintain the cash book (two assessment criteria)	7
7. Maintain petty cash records (four assessment criteria)	10
8. Process ledger transactions and extract a trial balance (three assessment criteria)	6, 7, 8, 9, 10, 11

Delivery guidance

The guidance is structured in skills areas relevant to processing bookkeeping transaction and then matched to the relevant assessment criteria.

The six broad skills areas which will be tested are as follows:

1   Books of prime entry, including: Sales/Purchases Day Books and Returns Day Books; three-column analysed Cash Book; Petty Cash Book

2   Understanding coding within a double entry bookkeeping system

3   Double entry bookkeeping

4   Trial balance

5   Trade, bulk and settlement discounts

6   Document preparation and checking

Each skills area relates to assessment criteria in one or more of the above learning outcomes.

1 Books of prime entry

1A Sales and Purchases Day Books and Sales and Purchases Returns Day Books

Students will be required to make entries in at least one day book, that is Sales, Sales Returns, Purchases and Purchases Returns Day Books, using given data or source documents. The day books will include total, VAT net and analytical columns and a column for customer or supplier account codes.

Students will also be required to transfer data from at least one of the day-books listed above to the sales or purchases ledger and general ledger.

Assessment criteria for skills area 1A:

1.2 Explain the purpose and content of the books of prime entry

2.2 Outline how the books of prime entry integrate with the double entry bookkeeping system

2.3 Describe the function of a coding system within a double entry bookkeeping system

2.4 Describe the processing of financial transactions from the books of prime entry into the double entry bookkeeping system

4.3 Enter sales invoices and credit notes into books of prime entry using suitable codes

5.2 Enter supplier invoices and credit notes into books of prime entry using suitable codes

8.1 Transfer data from the books of prime entry to the ledgers

1B *Three-column analysed Cash Book*

Students will be required to make entries into one or both sides of the Cash Book using given data or source documents reflecting different methods of payment, eg cash, cheques and automated payments. Numerical columns could include cash, bank, discounts, VAT, trade receivables, trade payables, cash sales, cash purchases, income and expenses.

Students should be prepared to total the columns and balance the Cash Book or answer questions on the cash and bank balances.

Students will also be required to transfer data from the Cash Book to the sales, purchases and general ledgers. They must understand that the Cash Book can be a book of prime entry and part of the double entry bookkeeping system or a book of prime entry alone.

Assessment criteria for skills area 1B:

1.2 Explain the purpose and content of the books of prime entry

1.3 List the ways in which customers may pay an organisation and an organisation may pay its suppliers

2.2 Outline how the books of prime entry integrate with the double entry bookkeeping system

2.4 Describe the processing of financial transactions from the books of prime entry into the double entry bookkeeping system

6.1 Enter receipts and payment details from relevant primary records into a three column analysed Cash Book

6.2 Total and balance the Cash Book

8.1 Transfer data from the books of prime entry to the ledgers

1C *Petty Cash Book*

Students should be prepared to make entries for payments and the reimbursement of petty cash in an analysed Petty Cash Book from given data or source documents and to identify the subsequent entries in the general ledger. Students should be prepared to total the columns and balance the Petty Cash Book. They must understand the imprest system, and that the Petty Cash Book can be a book of prime entry and part of the double entry bookkeeping system or a book of prime entry alone.

Students will be asked to conduct a simple reconciliation of the cash in hand with the Petty Cash Book balance, which may involve calculating the individual and total amounts of notes and coins from a given list.

Whilst students will not be asked to prepare a petty cash voucher they should be able to identify the purpose and content of a petty cash voucher.

Assessment criteria for skills area 1C:

1.1 Outline the purpose and content of a petty cash voucher

1.2 Explain the purpose and content of the books of prime entry

2.2 Outline how the books of prime entry integrate with the double entry bookkeeping system

2.4 Describe the processing of financial transactions from the books of prime entry into the double entry bookkeeping system

7.1 Enter petty cash transactions into an analysed Petty Cash Book, accounting for tax where appropriate

7.2 Total and balance the Petty Cash Book

7.3 Reconcile the Petty Cash Book with the cash in hand

7.4 Enter the reimbursement of the petty cash expenditure in the Petty Cash Book using the imprest system

8.1 Transfer data from the books of prime entry to the ledgers

2 Understanding coding within a double entry bookkeeping system

As well as entering codes in the sales and purchases and returns day-books students will be required to understand the function of coding. Codes include customer and supplier account codes, general ledger codes and product codes. Students may be required to create codes that are consistent with the organisation's coding policy. They may also be asked to enter codes when preparing sales invoices and credit notes.

Assessment criteria for skills area 2:

2.3 Describe the function of a coding system within a double entry bookkeeping system

2.4 Describe the processing of financial transactions from the books of prime entry into the double entry bookkeeping system

4.3 Enter sales invoices and credit notes into books of prime entry using suitable codes

5.2 Enter supplier invoices and credit notes into books of prime entry using suitable codes

3 Double entry bookkeeping

Students should be prepared to answer questions relating to processing transactions throughout the double entry system from books of prime entry to ledgers. Tasks may include questions or calculations relating to the accounting equation and the dual effect of transactions. Students should be able to define capital and revenue income and expenditure as well as classify such transactions. They should also be able to classify assets or liability accounts.

It is important that students learn how to balance T accounts, clearly showing the totals of each side of the account and the balance carried down and brought down.

Assessment criteria for skills area 3:

2.1 Explain the accounting equation and how it relates to a double entry bookkeeping system

2.4 Describe the processing of financial transactions from the books of prime entry into the double entry bookkeeping system

2.5 Define capital income and capital expenditure

2.6 Define revenue income and revenue expenditure

8.2 Total and balance ledger accounts, clearly showing balances carried down and brought down

4   **Trial balance**

Students will be asked to transfer given account balances to the appropriate column of an initial trial balance and total both columns. The trial balance may be in alphabetical or random order, or may follow the structure of final accounts.

Assessment criterion for skills area 4:

8.3 Extract an initial trial balance

5   **Trade, bulk and settlement discounts**

Students will need to be able to explain and calculate trade, bulk and settlement discounts together with the appropriate VAT amount. They may be asked to produce a sales invoice or credit note including some or all of these discounts or identify discrepancies in receipts from customers involving incorrect discounts taken. They should also be able to check discounts, and identify discrepancies, on invoices and credit notes from suppliers.

Assessment criteria for skills area 5:

3.1 Explain the difference between settlement, trade and bulk discount

3.2 Describe the effect that settlement discount has on the sales tax (VAT) charged

6   **Document preparation and checking**

Students must understand the purpose and content of petty cash vouchers, remittance advice notes, sales and purchases invoices and credit notes and statements of account to be sent to customers. They must also be able to prepare and code sales invoices and credit notes, including VAT and trade, bulk and settlement discounts, referring to quotations, discount policy, customer orders, delivery notes and price lists as source documents. They should also be able to prepare statements of account with varying formats.

Students must also be able to check the accuracy of receipts from customers by referring to sales invoices, remittance advice notes and the sales ledger and be able to identify discrepancies for example, under or over payment or incorrect discount taken. They should be aware of the different methods organisations use to make and receive payments.

Students must be able to use purchase orders, goods received notes and delivery notes to check the accuracy of invoices and credit notes from suppliers and identify discrepancies such as non-delivery of goods, incorrect type or quantity of goods, incorrect calculations and incorrect discounts. They must be able to reconcile statements from suppliers with the purchases ledger account and calculate payments due from given data and source documents.

Assessment criteria for skills area 6:

1.1 Outline the purpose and content of petty cash voucher, invoice, credit note, remittance advice, statement of account

1.3 List the ways in which customers may pay an organisation and an organisation may pay its suppliers

2.3 Describe the function of a coding system within a double entry bookkeeping system

3.1 Explain the difference between settlement, trade and bulk discount

3.2 Describe the effect that settlement discount has on the sales tax (VAT) charged

4.1 Use source documents to prepare invoices or credit notes

4.2 Calculate invoice or credit note amounts reflecting any trade discount, bulk discount, settlement discount and sales tax

4.4 Check the accuracy of receipts from customers against relevant supporting documentation

4.5 Produce statements of account to send to credit customers

5.1 Check accuracy of supplier invoices and credit notes against purchase orders, goods received notes, delivery notes

5.3 Reconcile supplier statements to purchases ledger accounts

5.4 Calculate payments due to suppliers

Note on VAT

From 1 April 2015 changes to UK legislation will affect the way all businesses account for VAT when offering a prompt payment (settlement) discount. Suppliers will no longer be able to account for VAT on the discounted price but must account for VAT on the consideration actually received. However, as there are a number of valid accounting treatments for the new situation and none has so far emerged as standard practice, this change in legislation will not be reflected in this unit until September 2016 at the earliest.

chapter 1:
BUSINESS DOCUMENTATION

---

chapter coverage 📖

This opening chapter briefly introduces the world of business and then looks at the types of business documentation that are encountered. The topics covered are:

✎ Introduction to business

✎ Types of transaction

✎ The purpose of accounting

✎ Invoices

✎ Credit notes

✎ Remittance advice notes

✎ Petty cash vouchers

✎ Statements of account

✎ Coding systems

INTRODUCTION TO BUSINESS

A business exists so that its activities make a PROFIT for its OWNER (the person who has invested money in it). The business makes a profit if its INCOME is more than its EXPENSES. Its activities involve using its ASSETS (items that it owns, such as cash and equipment). In doing so it normally incurs LIABILITIES, which are items that it owes such as loans and overdrafts.

We shall see how these terms link together in more detail in Chapter 6.

The simplest type of business is that of a SOLE TRADER. A sole trader is someone who trades under their own name and who owns the business outright. Many businesses are sole traders, from electricians through to accountants. The owner is not necessarily the only person working in the business as he or she may employ a number of other staff. But, in most cases, the sole trader is in charge of most of the business functions such as buying and selling the goods or performing the services.

The owner of the business is the one who initially contributes money or CAPITAL to the business, although it might also have a LOAN, either commercial or from friends. The owner is also the only one to benefit from the profit of the business, normally by taking money or goods out of the business (known as DRAWINGS).

TYPES OF TRANSACTION

Businesses tend to carry out the same types of business transaction, although on different scales depending on their size.

Typical transactions that businesses will undertake include:

- Selling goods or services
- Buying goods to resell
- Paying money into the bank
- Withdrawing cash from the bank
- Paying expenses from the bank account or from small amounts of cash
- Paying the owner's drawings
- Paying taxes such as VAT

Each and every one of these transactions must be correctly recorded in the business's accounting records, and this is what will be covered in this Text.

The accounting system provides valuable information to the owner:

- How much money is owing to the business and from whom: its customers or TRADE RECEIVABLES

- How much money is owed by the business and to whom: its suppliers or TRADE PAYABLES

- How much money the business holds in hand (CASH and PETTY CASH) and in its bank account (BANK)

There is an important distinction to be made at this point between cash and credit transactions.

CASH TRANSACTIONS occur when cash changes hands at the time of the transaction: payment is made or received immediately. These include payments and receipts made:

- In notes and coins (actual cash)
- By cheque, credit card or debit card

The important factor is the timing of the payment. No trade receivables or trade payables are involved in a cash transaction. The primary documentation created for this type of transaction is a TILL RECEIPT.

CREDIT TRANSACTIONS occur when the goods or services are given or received now but it is agreed that payment will be made or received at a future date after a period of credit. Credit transactions involve the issue or receipt of an INVOICE and the creation of a trade receivable or a trade payable for the amount outstanding. When the amount is finally paid over, this may be in the form of cash or a cheque, card or automated payment.

Task 1

Tara sells goods to Cathy for £100 and they agree Cathy will pay Tara in cash in two weeks' time. This is (tick ONE):

A cash transaction	
A credit transaction	

THE PURPOSE OF ACCOUNTING

The basic purpose of ACCOUNTING is to record and classify accurately the business's transactions.

It is the business's documentation that contains details of its transactions, so the information on these documents must be complete, accurate and properly checked.

We shall cover these processes in this Text, but first we need to get more of an insight into what businesses actually do, and how this is reflected in the types of information found on business documents. We shall therefore look initially at four key pieces of business documentation, each of which is designed to allow accurate recording. These are:

- Invoices
- Credit notes
- Remittance advice notes
- Petty cash vouchers
- Statements of account

3

INVOICES

The primary business document that relates to credit transactions is the invoice. This is given by the seller to the buyer. For the seller it is a sales invoice and for the buyer the same document is a purchase invoice.

An invoice is a request for payment for the goods or services that have been sold and it details precisely how much is due and when.

HOW IT WORKS

Here is an example, for a credit transaction in which a buyer or customer (Whitehill Superstores) purchases six dishwashers from a seller or supplier (Southfield Electrical). The supplier has agreed that the buyer only has to pay 30 days after taking the goods. This 30 days is the period of credit which distinguishes the sale as a credit sale rather than a cash sale. The period is called '30 days credit'.

INVOICE	Invoice number 56314		
Southfield Electrical **Industrial Estate** **Benham DR6 2FF** **Tel: 01239 345639**			
VAT registration:	0264 2274 49		
Date/tax point:	7 September 20XX		
Order number:	32011		
Customer:	Whitehill Superstores 28 Whitehill Park Benham DR6 5LM		
Account number (customer code)	SL 44		
Description/product code	**Quantity**	**Unit amount £**	**Total £**
Zanpoint dishwashers /4425	6	200.00	1,200.00
Net total			1,200.00
VAT at 20%			240.00
Invoice total			1,440.00
Terms 30 days net			

BPP
LEARNING MEDIA

Let's look at the details of the invoice from the supplier (Southfield Electrical) to the buyer (Whitehill Superstores):

- It shows the supplier's name, address and VAT registration number (VAT will be considered in more detail in Chapter 2).

- It has its own unique, sequential document number or code (56314), which allows it to be identified easily (it is much more accurate to refer to 'Invoice 56314' rather than 'the invoice we sent the other day').

- The date of the invoice (also known as the tax point) is important information for Whitehill. It allows Whitehill to see when the invoice is due for payment – in this case 30 days after the invoice date.

- The account number or customer account code is another example of coding in accounting. Eventually Southfield will have to enter this invoice into its accounting records and this shows exactly which account relates to Whitehill.

- The details of the goods are included both in words and by using its product code.

- The price of the dishwashers, excluding VAT, as quoted to Whitehill is shown per unit. To find the total price the quantity is multiplied by the unit price to arrive at the net total of the invoice. To this must be added VAT charged at 20%. The resulting invoice total (also known as the 'gross' total since it includes VAT) is the amount that Whitehill must pay.

- The term '30 days net' shows that payment of the invoice total is due 30 days after the invoice date.

Task 2

Tara agrees to sell goods to Cathy for £100 and they agree Cathy will pay Tara in two weeks' time. The business document that Tara should send to Cathy to record this agreement is (tick ONE):

An invoice	
A receipt	

CREDIT NOTES

Another key document is the CREDIT NOTE, which is used to show that the buyer owes less money to the supplier than was originally agreed. Credit notes can be used:

- In credit transactions to reduce an amount that has already been invoiced, so the buyer pays the net amount (the invoice less the credit note)

- In cash transactions when the supplier does not want to refund cash to the buyer but is willing to acknowledge that it owes the buyer some money

HOW IT WORKS

Suppose that one of the dishwashers supplied by Southfield is damaged. When the damaged dishwasher is returned to Southfield, it should issue a CREDIT NOTE to Whitehill which reverses the part of the sales invoice that relates to the damaged dishwasher.

CREDIT NOTE	Credit note number 08641
Southfield Electrical **Industrial Estate** **Benham DR6 2FF** **Tel: 01239 345639**	
VAT registration:	0264 2274 49
Date/tax point:	12 September 20XX
Order number:	32011
Customer:	Whitehill Superstores 28 Whitehill Park Benham DR6 5LM
Account number (customer code)	SL 44

Description/product code	Quantity	Unit amount £	Total £
Zanpoint dishwasher /4425 Reason for credit note: Delivered damaged	1	200.00	200.00
Net total			200.00
VAT at 20%			40.00
Credit note total			240.00
Terms 30 days net			

The credit note is almost identical to an invoice. The only differences are:

- It is described as a credit note.
- It has a unique, sequential credit note number rather than an invoice number.
- A reason for the credit is noted at the bottom of the credit note.

To make sure that buyers do not get invoices and credit notes mixed up, credit notes are often printed in red.

Task 3

Cathy is not happy with her goods when she receives them and Tara agrees that they are not quite of the required standard, so she will only expect payment of £80 rather than £100 at the due time. The business document that Tara should send to Cathy to record this is (tick ONE):

An invoice	
A credit note	

REMITTANCE ADVICE NOTES

When the buyer pays the supplier in a credit transaction, a variety of payment methods may be used, such as a cheque, a debit card or an automated payment from the buyer's bank account to the supplier's. To let the supplier know which invoices are being paid, and which credit notes are being deducted (or netted off), the buyer usually sends the supplier a REMITTANCE ADVICE NOTE which contains that information.

HOW IT WORKS

Suppose that on 20 September Whitehill Superstores has decided to pay Southfield Electrical by cheque what it owed to the company at the beginning of September, which was for invoice 56019 for £316.40 received on 21 August less credit note number 08613 for £47.46 received on 28 August. Along with the cheque it sends the supplier the following remittance advice note.

REMITTANCE ADVICE NOTE Whitehill Superstores 28 Whitehill Park Benham DR6 5LM	Remittance advice note number 0937498	
Supplier:	**Southfield Electrical** **Industrial Estate** **Benham DR6 2FF**	
Account number (supplier code)	**PL 526**	

Date	Transaction reference	Amount £
21/08/XX	Invoice 56019	316.40
28/08/XX	Credit note 08613	(47.46)
20/09/XX	Payment made – cheque enclosed	268.94

Note that this remittance advice note:

- Is described as a remittance advice note

- Has a unique, sequential remittance advice note number

- Is going from the buyer to the supplier so instead of a customer code it contains a supplier code

- Deducts the amount of the credit note from the amount of the invoice to arrive at the amount of the payment made – though it could contain other invoices or credit notes, and other reductions in the amount owed (especially discounts, which we shall see in Chapter 2)

Task 4

Cathy sends a cheque to Tara for £80 and wishes to make it clear that both the invoice and the credit note are being settled by means of this payment. To clarify this matter for Tara, Cathy should send her (tick ONE):

An invoice	
A credit note	
A remittance advice note	

PETTY CASH VOUCHERS

We noted above that businesses will often have to pay expenses from small amounts of cash held on the premises in a box, known as PETTY CASH. The key document for the proper functioning of a petty cash system is the PETTY CASH VOUCHER, which must be completed and authorised before any cash can be paid out of the petty cash box.

HOW IT WORKS

Suppose that Lara Moschetta, an employee in Southfield Electrical, is sent out by her boss, Trish Epstein, one day to Riseworth Stationers to buy some stationery for use in the administrative office. Lara pays the shop £48 with her own cash (this includes £8 VAT) and understandably wants Southfield Electrical to pay her back. She should therefore get Trish to authorise the Riseworth till receipt, give the authorised receipt to the accountant and then receive her £48 in cash. The accountant will prepare the following petty cash voucher for the expenditure to place in the petty cash box once the £48 has been paid out:

Petty Cash Voucher	Number 067
Date prepared:	12/09/XX
Expenditure	**Amount** £
Stationery (till receipt attached)	40.00
VAT at 20%	8.00
Total	48.00
Supporting documentation:	
Till receipt dated 12/09/XX	
Cash paid to Lara Moschetta	
Receipt authorised by Trish Epstein	

There are a number of important points to note about this petty cash voucher:

- It has a sequential number, which ensures that all petty cash vouchers are accounted for.

- The details of the expense are clear and an authorised receipt is attached.

- The amount of the expense is shown (£48 – £8 = £40) plus the VAT of £8.

- The voucher is signed by the person claiming the petty cash (Lara Moschetta).

- The voucher shows that the receipt was authorised by an appropriate member of staff.

We shall see much more about petty cash vouchers in a later chapter.

Task 5

The document that is used to record payments out of petty cash is (tick ONE):

A petty cash voucher	
An invoice	
A till receipt	

STATEMENTS OF ACCOUNT

When a customer has many transactions it is very useful for the supplier to be able to let them know exactly how much they owe, and the transactions that together make up that amount. For this reason a business with credit customers will aim to produce a STATEMENT OF ACCOUNT for each customer, usually at least once a month. This is sent to the customer as a useful reminder to the customer that it still owes money. The statement also gives the customer the opportunity to raise any queries about the amount owed. It is not unknown for invoices, credit notes and even payments to go astray in transit between organisations. Often the first time either party knows that there is a disagreement is when the supplier sends the customer a statement of account, and the customer cannot agree it.

Often a remittance advice is included at the bottom of a statement of account. Completing the remittance advice with the amount of a payment being made by the customer in response to the statement helps both customer and supplier in maintaining accurate records.

HOW IT WORKS

Southfield Electrical prepares a STATEMENT OF ACCOUNT for each of its credit customers at the end of each month. On Whitehill's statement at the end of September Southfield lists out all the invoices and credit notes sent to the customer in August and September, and the payment received from the customer in September. At the bottom of the statement is the final amount owed by Whitehill to Southfield Electrical at the end of September. This is arrived at by adding up all the invoices and deducting all the credit notes and payments received.

STATEMENT OF ACCOUNT	
Southfield Electrical **Industrial Estate** **Benham DR6 2FF** **Tel: 01239 345639**	
VAT registration:	0264 2274 49
Date:	30 September 20XX
Customer:	Whitehill Superstores 28 Whitehill Park Benham DR6 5LM
Account number (customer code)	SL 44

Date	Details	Increase amount owed £	Decrease amount owed £	Amount owed £
21.08.XX	Inv56019	+316.40		+316.40
28.08.XX	CN08613		-47.46	+268.94
07.09.XX	Inv56314	+1,440.00		+1,708.94
12.09.XX	CN08641		-240.00	+1,468.94
20.09.XX	Payment received – thank you		-268.94	+1,200.00
Amount now due				+1,200.00

Note that the September statement includes the August invoice less the August credit note (net amount £268.94) that are settled or cleared by the net payment of £268.94 in September. As the invoice, credit note and payment cancel each other out, none of them will appear on the October statement when Southfield prepares it. The October statement will however include the unpaid September items, plus October transactions (which will hopefully include a payment of £1,200, the net amount owed at the end of September).

We shall look at how statements of account are prepared in a later chapter.

CODING SYSTEMS

We noted above that sales invoices generally have a CUSTOMER CODE on them to denote the particular customer in question, and similarly communications from buyers have a SUPPLIER CODE on them. Invoices and credit notes also routinely include PRODUCT CODES for the items sold. The use of CODING SYSTEMS in an organisation is designed to ensure that:

- Information can be recorded accurately and in a timely manner
- Documents can be filed and retrieved efficiently

Each organisation will have its own coding system, designed to help it run its processes in the most efficient manner. The system may be:

- Numeric, so that all documents are given a sequential code number or DOCUMENT NUMBER, with the most recent document being given the document number that immediately follows the one before. Different types of document, for example sales invoices and purchase orders, are part of different numbering systems

- Alpha-numeric, so that there is an initial run of letters that tells us something about the items being coded, and then a sequential numeric system as well. The numeric run follows the same principles as for document numbers, and the alpha run may denote:

  - The part of the accounting system in which the document will be recorded

  - The first few letters of a product, supplier, customer or employee name

  - The first few letters of some other classification

HOW IT WORKS

In the case of Southfield Electrical, we saw that the customer code on its invoice was 'SL 44'. An alpha-numeric coding system has been used to create a customer code for its sales invoices:

- The 'alpha' part is SL, which stands for 'Sales Ledger', part of the accounting system for credit customers which we shall come back to in later chapters. All customer codes for credit customers of Southfield Electrical will have this prefix.

- The 'numeric' part is 44, which is the unique part of the code. This will have been allocated because at the time when Whitehill Superstores became a customer, Southfield had allocated 43 customer codes and so Whitehill was given the 44th.

The invoice document number however was 56314, a simple numeric code (the next invoice issued will be 56315), and the credit note document number was 08641 (so the next one issued will be 08642).

In the case of Whitehill Superstores, it used a numeric system for coding its remittance advice note (0937498) and an alpha-numeric system for its supplier code (PL 526, in which 'PL' stands for 'purchases ledger', a record we shall come back to in a later chapter).

Using coding systems

A coding system has two main purposes:

- It allows information to be included in documents in an abbreviated manner, saving time and making the document more user-friendly.

- It facilitates filing of documents: sequentially numbered invoices, for instance, can be filed in number order so they are easier to find, and a copy can also be filed in customer code order so it is easy to find all invoices sent to a particular customer. This makes it much easier to deal with enquiries related to that document.

As with anything to do with accounting in particular and business transactions in general, it is very important that coding systems are applied carefully and consistently in practice. Most computerised accounting systems, for instance, rely on the accurate use of coding systems.

Task 6

An organisation codes all invoices received from suppliers with a supplier code. A selection of the codes used is given below:

Supplier	Supplier code
Benson Ltd	BEN41
Immer plc	IMM56
Presley Co	PRE62

The organisation has received an invoice from Presley Co. What supplier code should it use for the invoice?

✓	Supplier code
	BEN41
	IMM56
	PRE62

CHAPTER OVERVIEW

- A business's transactions can be categorised as either cash or credit transactions

- An invoice is used in credit transactions to record how much is owed and when it should be paid

- A credit note is used in credit transactions to record that less is owed than was originally invoiced, and in cash transactions to record that the business still owes some money back to a customer

- A remittance advice note is used in credit transactions to help the business receiving the advice note identify which invoices etc are being paid

- A petty cash voucher is used to record payments of petty cash

- A statement of account is prepared by the supplier and sent to the customer, so the latter knows exactly how much they owe and how that amount is made up

- Coding systems are used to ensure accuracy of recording and filing

Keywords

Profit – the excess of income over expenses made by a business

Owner – the person who has invested money in the business

Income – what the business earns when it makes sales of goods or services to other parties

Expenses – what the business spends to purchase goods or services for the company

Assets – something that a business owns

Liabilities – something that a business owes

Sole trader – a business that is owned and run by an individual

Capital – the amount of money invested by the owner in the business

Loan – the amount of money invested in a business by a person who is not its owner

Drawings – amounts taken out of the business by the owner

Trade receivable – someone who owes money to the business

Trade payable – someone to whom the business owes money

Cash – amounts of cash held physically by the business as notes and coin, usually as a result of making cash sales, pending banking

Petty cash – small amounts of cash held physically within the business and used to make small payments

Bank – amounts of money held for the business by its bank

Cash transactions – transactions whereby payment happens at the same time as goods/services are exchanged

Till receipt – the primary documentation for a sale or purchase in cash

Credit transactions – transactions whereby payment is to be made at some future date

Invoice – a document that clearly sets out what money is owed by a named trade receivable to a named trade payable in respect of particular goods or services

Accounting – the process by which a business's transactions are recorded and classified

Credit note – a document that clearly sets out reductions in the amount owed by a trade receivable to a trade payable

Remittance advice note – a document setting out exactly how a payment is made up (ie the invoices/credit notes that it is paying/netting off)

Petty cash voucher – a document that records payments out of petty cash

Statement of account – a document prepared by a supplier and sent to the customer so the customer knows how much they owe

Coding systems – are used to ensure accuracy of filing and recording

Customer code – a unique code given to a customer by a supplier when recording transactions that relate to that customer

Supplier code – a unique code given to a supplier by a customer when recording transactions that relate to that supplier

Product code – a unique code given to a product by a supplier or customer to help in recording transactions involving that product

Document number – the unique number allocated from a sequence to a particular document as part of the organisation's coding system

TEST YOUR LEARNING

Test 1

For each of the following transactions determine whether it should be classified as a cash or credit transaction.

	Cash ✓	Credit ✓
Purchase of a van with an agreed payment date in one month's time		
Sale of goods by credit card in a shop		
Purchase of computer disks by cheque		
Purchase of computer disks which are accompanied by an invoice		
Sale of goods which are paid for by cheque		

Test 2

For each of the following transactions, indicate the primary business document that will be created by drawing an arrow from each of the four boxes on the left to one of the boxes on the right.

Sale of goods for cash	Credit note
Return of goods purchased on credit	Remittance advice note
Reminder to customer of how much it owes and why	Invoice
Reimbursement of employee for expense by cash	Till receipt
Indication of which amounts that are owed are being paid	Cheque
	Petty cash voucher
	Statement of account

BPP
LEARNING MEDIA

Test 3

Complete the following sentences by deleting one option in each case:

- Where income is more than expenses, a business makes a profit/loss.

- Where expenses are more than income, a business makes a profit/loss.

- Bank loans and overdrafts are examples of assets/liabilities.

- Cash and trade receivables are example of assets/liabilities.

- When a business owner contributes money to the business, this is known as capital/drawings.

- When a business owner takes out money from the business, this is known as capital/drawings.

chapter 2:
DISCOUNTS AND VAT

chapter coverage 📖

This chapter considers two very important aspects of the transactions that businesses make: discounts and VAT. The topics covered are:

✍ VAT

✍ Rates of VAT

✍ VAT calculations

✍ Discounts

VAT

We saw on the invoice, credit note and petty cash voucher in Chapter 1 that VALUE ADDED TAX (or VAT) is an issue for businesses that buy and sell. But what is VAT?

VAT is due to HM Revenue and Customs (HMRC) on many goods and services that are sold. It is a tax that is paid by the final consumer but is collected along the way by each seller in the supply chain.

VAT registration

If the sales of a business exceed a certain amount for a year, then a business must register for VAT with HMRC. This means that they have a VAT registration number which, as we saw in Chapter 1, must be included on invoices, credit notes and other business documents.

It also means that the business must charge VAT on all of its sales (known as 'taxable supplies'). This is usually at the STANDARD RATE of 20%. VAT charged on sales is known as OUTPUT TAX.

There is however a benefit, in that the VAT that the business pays when buying from suppliers or paying expenses can be recovered back from HMRC. This is known as INPUT TAX.

Usually every three months the business must complete a VAT return showing the output and input tax. The excess of output tax over input tax must be paid to HMRC. However, if the input tax exceeds the output tax then a refund is due from HMRC.

Task 1

Complete the following statement:

Output tax is VAT on	purchases
	sales
Input tax is VAT on	purchases
	sales

RATES OF VAT

The standard VAT rate of 20% applies to most items that are bought and sold but some items (such as food and children's clothing) are ZERO-RATED for VAT purposes. This means that the seller of these items charges VAT at 0% (ie no VAT) on his sales. However, if he is charged VAT by his suppliers on his expenses and purchases he can reclaim the input VAT from HMRC.

Other items (such as postal services and rail travel) are EXEMPT from VAT ie no VAT is charged. A seller who makes exempt supplies also does not charge VAT on his sales. The difference is that he is unable to reclaim any input VAT charged on his expenses and purchases.

VAT CALCULATIONS

VAT must be calculated accurately. The rule is that, if the VAT calculation comes up with a figure of more than two decimal places, you always round VAT down to the nearest penny.

The two main calculations that you might be required to make are:

- Calculating VAT on the NET TOTAL

- Calculating VAT from the GROSS TOTAL (note that sometimes this may be referred to as the invoice total, or just 'total', or just 'gross')

We shall look at these in turn.

HOW IT WORKS

On the invoice from Southfield Electrical to Whitehill Superstores in Chapter 1, we saw the sale of six dishwashers with a total sales price of £1,200 by a business that had a VAT registration number and that therefore had to charge output VAT.

The net total of the invoice was £1,200.00, so the VAT was calculated as 20% of £1,200.00. This means that the fraction 20/100 is to be applied to £1,200.00.

VAT to be charged = £1,200.00 × 20/100 = £240.00

There is no need to round the amount.

Note the fraction of 20/100 can also be expressed as 1/5 – so all you have to do is divide the net total by 5 to get the VAT:

VAT = £1,200.00/5 = £240.00

Task 2

If the net amount of an invoice is £230.00 then the output VAT is:

£ [   ]

HOW IT WORKS

Suppose, however, that you are only told the gross invoice total (or VAT-inclusive amount) – a situation that arises quite often in the case of a small purchase from a shop.

If the total of the price of goods plus the VAT is £70.50, how much VAT is included in this amount and what is the net total for the goods?

This time the £70.50 includes 20% VAT and therefore to find the VAT part of that, the fraction 20/120 must be applied to the gross amount.

VAT = £70.50 × 20/120 = £11.75

Therefore the net total for the goods is £70.50 – £11.75 = £58.75.

Note the fraction of 20/120 can also be expressed as 1/6 – so all you have to do is divide the gross total by 6 to get the VAT:

VAT = £70.50/6 = £11.75

Task 3

If the gross total is £246.00 then the output tax is:

£ [   ]

DISCOUNTS

When selling goods or services a business usually has a standard or LIST PRICE that it charges to all its customers. However, the business may not always charge all customers the full list price of the goods or services – the business may choose to offer a DISCOUNT. There are three types of discount that we must consider:

- Trade discount
- Bulk discount
- Settlement discount

BPP
LEARNING MEDIA

Trade discount

A TRADE DISCOUNT is a percentage reduction from the list price of goods or services. This reduced price may be offered because:

- The customer is regular and valued; or
- As an incentive to a new customer to buy; or
- The customer is in the same trade as the supplier and the supplier wants to develop good relations.

The amount of the trade discount will be shown on the face of the invoice as a deduction from the list price before arriving at the net total.

HOW IT WORKS

Continuing with Southfield Electrical and Whitehill Superstores, suppose now that the initial price quotation from Southfield was the list price of £200 per dishwasher but Whitehill were to be allowed a trade discount of 10%.

The invoice would now appear as follows:

INVOICE	Invoice number 56314		
Southfield Electrical **Industrial Estate** **Benham DR6 2FF** **Tel: 01239 345639**			
VAT registration:	0264 2274 49		
Date/tax point:	7 September 20XX		
Order number:	32011		
Customer:	Whitehill Superstores 28 Whitehill Park Benham DR6 5LM		
Account number (customer code)	SL 44		
Description/product code	**Quantity**	**Unit amount** **£**	**Total** **£**
Zanpoint dishwashers /4425 Less trade discount 10%	6	200.00	1,200.00 (120.00)
Net total			1,080.00
VAT at 20%			216.00
Gross total			1,296.00
Terms 30 days net			

This is how the calculations were made:

Step 1   Calculate the total price before the discount by multiplying the quantity by the list price:

$$6 \times £200 = £1,200.00$$

Step 2   Calculate the trade discount as 10% of this total list price:

$$£1,200.00 \times 10\% \ (10/100) = £120.00$$

Step 3   Deduct the trade discount from the total list price to reach the invoice net total:

£1,200.00 – £120.00 = £1,080.00

Step 4   Calculate the VAT at 20% of the net total:

£1,080.00 × 20% (20/100) = £216.00

Step 5   Calculate the gross total by adding the VAT to the net total:

£1,080.00 + £216.00 = £1,296.00

Task 4

Goods with a list price of £2,400.00 are to be sent to a customer. The customer is allowed a trade discount of 15% and VAT is to be charged at 20%. What is the gross total?

£ [   ]

Bulk discount

A BULK DISCOUNT is also a percentage reduction from the list price of goods or services, offered because the customer's order is large. The business will offer this to encourage customers to place large orders so costs of administration and delivery are reduced.

Like the trade discount, the amount of the bulk discount will be shown on the face of the invoice as a deduction from the list price before arriving at the net total. It may be offered as well as or instead of a trade discount.

If a bulk discount is offered in addition to a trade discount, it is normal practice to calculate the bulk discount on the amount **after** trade discount has been deducted.

HOW IT WORKS

Suppose now that as well as a trade discount of 10% Southfield Electrical were also to offer Whitehill Superstores a 5% discount on orders over £1,000 net of trade discount.

The invoice would now appear as follows.

INVOICE	Invoice number 56314
Southfield Electrical **Industrial Estate** **Benham DR6 2FF** **Tel: 01239 345639**	
VAT registration:	0264 2274 49
Date/tax point:	7 September 20XX
Order number:	32011
Customer:	Whitehill Superstores 28 Whitehill Park Benham DR6 5LM
Account number (customer code)	SL 44

Description/product code	Quantity	Unit amount £	Total £
Zanpoint dishwashers /4425 Less trade discount 10% Less bulk discount 5%	6	200.00	1,200.00 (120.00) 1,080.00 (54.00)

Net total		1,026.00
VAT at 20%		205.20
Gross total		1,231.20
Terms 30 days net		

This is how the calculations were made:

> Step 1   Calculate the total price less trade discount as before:
>
> £1,200.00 − £120.00 = £1,080.00

Step 2   As this is over the £1,000.00 limit we calculate and deduct the bulk discount at 5% to arrive at the net total:

$$£1,080.00 - £(1,080.00 \times 5/100) = £1,026.00$$

Step 3   Calculate the VAT at 20% of the net total:

$$£1,026.00 \times 20\% (20/100) = £205.20$$

Step 4   Calculate the gross total by adding the VAT to the net total:

$$£1,026.00 + £205.20 = £1,231.20$$

Task 5

Goods with a list price of £2,400.00 are to be sent to a customer. The customer is allowed a trade discount of 10% and a bulk discount of 12% for orders of £2,000 and over after trade discount has been deducted. VAT is to be charged at 20%. What is the gross total?

£	

Settlement discount

A SETTLEMENT DISCOUNT is a percentage discount of the net total that is offered to a customer to encourage that customer to pay or settle the invoice earlier. For example, if it is normal policy to request that payment is made by customers 30 days after the invoice date, a settlement discount of 4% might be offered for payment within ten days of the invoice date.

A settlement discount differs from a trade or bulk discount in that although the seller offers the discount to the customer it is up to the customer to decide whether or not to accept the offer of the discount. Therefore the discount does not appear on the face of the invoice. Instead it is noted at the bottom of the invoice in the 'Terms' section.

We also need to consider how to calculate the VAT on an invoice where a settlement discount is offered. If a settlement discount is offered the rule is that:

- The VAT is always calculated on the assumption that the settlement discount is taken up by the customer, and therefore

- The VAT calculation is based on the net total **after deducting** the settlement discount

- The VAT calculated in this way is then added to the net total to arrive at the gross total

- The VAT figure in relation to this sale is not adjusted even if the customer does not take the settlement discount in the end

HOW IT WORKS

Continuing with Southfield and Whitehill, suppose now that Southfield not only offers the 10% trade discount and 5% bulk discount but also a 4% settlement discount for settlement within ten days of the invoice date.

This is what the invoice would look like:

INVOICE	Invoice number 56314		
Southfield Electrical **Industrial Estate** **Benham DR6 2FF** **Tel: 01239 345639**			
VAT registration:	0264 2274 49		
Date/tax point:	7 September 20XX		
Order number:	32011		
Customer:	Whitehill Superstores 28 Whitehill Park Benham DR6 5LM		
Account number (customer code)	SL 44		
Description/product code	**Quantity**	**Unit amount £**	**Total £**
Zanpoint dishwashers /4425 Less trade discount 10% Less bulk discount 5%	6	200.00	1,200.00 (120.00) 1,080.00 (54.00)
Net total			1,026.00
VAT at 20%			196.99
Gross total			1,222.99
Terms 4% settlement discount for payment within 10 days, otherwise 30 days net			

Now let's look at the calculations involved here. The figures are exactly the same as on the previous invoice until the VAT section is reached. So we will now look at how to calculate the VAT.

Step 1 Calculate the amount of the settlement discount offered by finding 4% of the net total:

£1,026.00 × 4% (4/100) = £41.04

Step 2 In a working, deduct the settlement discount from the net total:

£1,026.00 – £41.04 = £984.96

Step 3 Calculate the VAT at 20% on the net total minus the settlement discount:

£984.96 × 20% (20/100) = £196.99 (remember to round down to the nearest penny)

Step 4 Add this VAT amount to the net total to arrive at the gross total:

£1,026.00 + £196.99 = £1,222.99

Step 5 State the terms of the settlement discount at the bottom of the invoice.

Task 6

Goods with a net total of £368.00 are to be sold to a customer and the customer is offered a 3% settlement discount for payment received within 14 days of the invoice date. What is the gross total?

£ [   ]

CHAPTER OVERVIEW

- Most businesses will be registered for VAT and must therefore add VAT at 20%, the standard rate, to the list price of the goods or services charged to the customer on the invoice

- From a net total, calculate standard rate VAT at 20/100 or 1/5 of the net amount

- From a gross total, calculate standard rate VAT at 20/120 or 1/6 of the gross amount

- The seller may offer the customer a trade discount, a bulk discount and/or a settlement discount

- Trade and bulk discounts are reductions of list price and are shown on the face of the invoice before arriving at the net total

- A settlement discount is offered to the customer who may or may not take up the offer, and is shown at the bottom of the invoice as part of the terms

- The amount of the settlement discount must be deducted from the net total of the invoice when calculating VAT, but VAT is then added to the unadjusted net total to arrive at the gross total

Keywords

VAT – a tax levied by HM Revenue and Customs (HMRC) which must be added to the selling price of goods and services at all stages in the production process, paid over to HMRC at each stage of the process and borne by the final consumer

Standard rate of VAT – is 20%

Output tax – VAT on sales

Input tax – VAT on purchases and expenses

Zero–rated for VAT – sellers of zero-rated items charge 0% on their sales

Exempt from VAT – no VAT is charged (but unlike zero-rated supplies the seller is unable to reclaim input tax)

Net total – the total of the invoice after settlement and trade discount is deducted and before VAT is added

Gross total – the total of the invoice after VAT is added to the net total

Trade discount – a percentage discount deducted from the list price of goods and services to arrive at the net total. Offered to some long-standing customers or participants in the same trade, or as an incentive to new customers

Bulk discount – a percentage discount from the list price of goods and services less trade discount to arrive at the net total once an order over a certain size has been placed. Designed to encourage large orders

Settlement discount – a percentage discount from the net total offered in order to provide an incentive to pay the invoice amount early. Appears only in a terms note on the face of the invoice, not as a deduction from the net or gross total. Deducted from net total in order to perform the VAT calculation

TEST YOUR LEARNING

Test 1

A business sells 400 items to its customer for £30 per item. Trade discount of 5% is offered, plus a bulk discount of 10% for orders after trade discount of £1,000 or more. No settlement discount is offered.

What is the net total on the invoice?

£ [   ]

Test 2

(a) A sale is made for £378.00 plus VAT. How much VAT should be charged?

£ [   ]

(b) A sale is made for £378.00 including VAT. How much VAT has been charged and what is the net amount of the sale?

VAT	£	
Net amount	£	

Test 3

For each of the following gross amounts, calculate the VAT and the net amount.

Gross amount	VAT		Net amount	
(a) £3,154.80	£		£	
(b) £446.40	£		£	
(c) £169.20	£		£	

Test 4

(a) A customer is purchasing 23 items each with a list price of £56.00. A trade discount of 15% is given to this customer.

Calculate:

(i)	Total cost before discount	£	
(ii)	Trade discount	£	
(iii)	Net total	£	
(iv)	VAT	£	
(v)	Gross total	£	

(b) Suppose that a settlement discount of 3% is also offered. Calculate the same figures on this basis.

(i)	Total cost before discount	£	
(ii)	Trade discount	£	
(iii)	Net total	£	
(iv)	VAT	£	
(v)	Gross total	£	

chapter 3:
THE BOOKS OF PRIME ENTRY

chapter coverage 📖

In this chapter we will consider the basics of recording business transactions in the accounting records. The topics covered are:

- ✍ Books of prime entry
- ✍ Invoices and the Sales Day Book
- ✍ The sales ledger
- ✍ Credit notes and the Sales Returns Day Book
- ✍ Analysed Sales Day Book
- ✍ Invoices and the analysed Purchases Day Book
- ✍ The purchases ledger
- ✍ Credit notes and the Purchases Returns Day Book
- ✍ The Cash Book for receipts
- ✍ The Cash Book for payments

BOOKS OF PRIME ENTRY

In the previous two chapters we looked at some of the basic transactions of a business. We are now ready to start recording some of these transactions in the business's accounting system.

The first stage of the accounting process is to enter details of transaction documents into BOOKS OF PRIME ENTRY. These books of prime entry are often known as DAY BOOKS as, in theory at least, they would be written up every day.

TRANSACTION   BOOKS OF
DOCUMENTS   PRIME ENTRY

We are concerned first with invoices and credit notes, which we shall record in the records of the business making the sale.

INVOICES AND THE SALES DAY BOOK

All of the business's sales invoices sent to credit customers for a period are initially recorded in its book of prime entry which is known as the SALES DAY BOOK.

HOW IT WORKS

A typical Sales Day Book looks like this:

Date 20XX	Customer	Invoice number	Customer code	Gross £	VAT £	Net £
1 May	Grigsons Ltd	10356	SL21	199.20	33.20	166.00
1 May	Hall & Co	10357	SL05	103.60	15.60*	88.00
1 May	Harris & Sons	10358	SL17	120.00	20.00	100.00
2 May	Jaytry Ltd	10359	SL22	309.60	51.60	258.00

* Note that Hall & Co has been offered a £10 settlement discount, so VAT is calculated as £((88 – 10) × 20%) = £15.60, and the gross is £88.00 + £15.60 = £103.60.

You may also see the Gross column headed up as 'Total' or 'Invoice total'.

The writing-up of the Sales Day Book for these four transactions has the following steps:

Step 1 Gather the invoices that have been sent out to the customers since the day book was last written up and check that there are no invoices missing (the invoice numbers should be in sequence). All the information needed to enter into the Sales Day Book is on the face of each invoice.

Step 2 Enter the dates of the invoices, the names of the customers and the invoice numbers in the appropriate columns of the day book.

Step 3 The customer code column is also sometimes headed up 'reference' or 'folio'. This is the column where the account numbers for the customers are entered from the face of the invoices. As we saw in Chapter 1, the customer code is the account number given to the customers in the sales ledger (which we will come back to shortly) and therefore is often given the prefix 'SL'. Accuracy and consistency in using this code is important as it helps with the eventual entry of the figures into the accounts.

Step 4 Only three figures are entered from the invoices:

- The gross column contains the gross total including VAT shown on the face of the invoice.

- The VAT is the amount shown on the face of the invoice.

- The net column is the net total (before VAT) on the face of the invoice.

Task 1

An invoice shows the following amounts. Which columns in the Sales Day Book would each amount appear in? Tick ONE box for each amount.

	£	Gross	VAT	Net
Goods total	1,236.00			
VAT	247.20			
Total	1,483.20			

THE SALES LEDGER

For each individual credit customer the business needs to keep a record of how much that customer owes to the business at any one time. The way this is done is to record each invoice total in the customer's LEDGER ACCOUNT in the SALES LEDGER. The sales ledger is a record that contains ledger accounts for every credit customer. As we saw in Chapter 1, credit customers which owe money to the business are also known as TRADE RECEIVABLES.

Each credit customer's ledger account contains two sides:

- On the **left-hand side** we record invoices, which **increase** the amount owed by the customer.

- On the **right-hand side** we record credit notes, settlement discounts taken by and payments received from the customer, all of which **decrease** the amount owed by the customer.

HOW IT WORKS

Step 1   Find the individual customer's account in the sales ledger using the customer code.

Step 2   Enter the **gross** amount, which is the amount the customer actually owes, on the left-hand side of this account.

Step 3   In the 'details' section next to the amount, enter '**SDB**' followed by the **invoice number**. If there is space denoted by 'Date' you should also write in the date.

Looking back at the four invoices entered in the Sales Day Book, they would be entered in the sales ledger as follows.

Sales ledger

Grigsons Ltd			**SL 21**
Details	£	Details	£
SDB – 10356	199.20		

Hall & Co			**SL 05**
Details	£	Details	£
SDB – 10357	103.60		

Harris & Sons			SL 17
Details	£	Details	£
SDB – 10358	120.00		

Jaytry Ltd			SL 22
Details	£	Details	£
SDB – 10359	309.60		

We enter the invoice number for each entry as this will be useful when dealing with customer enquiries.

CREDIT NOTES AND THE SALES RETURNS DAY BOOK

Just as invoices are initially entered in their own book of prime entry, so too are credit notes – in the SALES RETURNS DAY BOOK. This looks very similar to the Sales Day Book with the same details being entered.

HOW IT WORKS

A typical Sales Returns Day Book would look like this:

Date 20XX	Customer	Credit note number	Customer code	Gross £	VAT £	Net £
4 May	Grigsons Ltd	CN668	SL21	72.00	12.00	60.00
5 May	Harris & Sons	CN669	SL17	96.00	16.00	80.00

You may also see the Gross column headed up as 'Total' or 'Credit note total'.

The only difference here is that the credit note number is entered rather than an invoice number. Again, all of the details required can be found on the face of the credit note that is used to write up the day book.

Now we must enter each individual credit note in the customer's account in the sales ledger. The amount to be used is the credit note total and this must be entered in the **right-hand side** of the ledger account as it **decreases** how much the customer owes us.

Step 1   Find the individual customer's account in the sales ledger using the customer code.

Step 2   Enter the **gross** total, which is the amount of the reduction in what the customer actually owes, on the right-hand side of this account.

Step 3   In the 'details' section next to the amount, enter '**SRDB**' followed by the **credit note number** (and the date if required).

Sales ledger

Grigsons Ltd			SL 21
Details	£	Details	£
SDB – 10356	199.20	SRDB – CN668	72.00

We can now see that Grigsons Ltd owes the business £(199.20 – 72.00) = £127.20.

Task 2

(a) Complete the following sentences:

An invoice is entered on the	left right	side of the customer's account
An credit note is entered on the	left right	side of the customer's account

(b)   The ledger account for Harris & Sons is shown here:

Harris & Sons			SL 17
Details	£	Details	£
SDB – 10358	120	SRDB – CN669	96

How much does Harris & Sons owe the business?

£ _____

ANALYSED SALES DAY BOOK

Most organisations include a more detailed analysis of the net amount of sales into different categories in their sales day books, by using analytical columns in an ANALYSED SALES DAY BOOK.

HOW IT WORKS

A business that makes sales of its products around the country may wish to analyse its sales by geographical area. Its analysed Sales Day Book might look something like this:

< Basic Sales Day Book columns >							< Extra analysis columns for net amount >			
Date	Customer	Invoice number	Ref	Gross £	VAT £	Net £	North £	South £	East £	West £
1 June	AB Ltd	936	SL23	120.00	20.00	100.00		100.00		
1 June	CD & Co	937	SL03	240.00	40.00	200.00			200.00	
2 June	EF Ltd	938	SL45	64.80	10.80	54.00	54.00			
3 June	GH Ltd	939	SL18	144.00	24.00	120.00				120.00
4 June	IJ Bros	940	SL25	72.00	12.00	60.00		60.00		
				640.80	106.80	534.00	54.00	160.00	200.00	120.00

This type of Sales Day Book contains the same seven columns as an unanalysed Sales Day Book, and then adds on extra columns to the right that break down each net amount into the separate geographical areas. Shading is often used to denote the analysis columns.

A business may also wish to analyse its sales by type of product. For example, a computer manufacturer may wish to analyse net sales between computers, printers and scanners. In this case there would be a column for each in the Sales Day Book. The Sales Returns Day Book should be analysed in the same manner.

Task 3

An extract from an invoice for a computer manufacturer that analyses its sales into those for computers, printers and scanners is given below:

Quantity	Description	£
1	GH3 Computer	800.00
1	Z3 Colour printer	300.00
1	S4 Scanner	200.00
		1,300.00
VAT		260.00
		1,560.00

Show how this invoice would be entered into the analysed Sales Day Book.

Gross £	VAT £	Net £	Computers £	Printers £	Scanners £

We shall return to writing up the day books relating to the sales ledger in a later chapter.

INVOICES AND THE ANALYSED PURCHASES DAY BOOK

Of course, a business that makes sales will also make purchases of goods and services. All of the invoices the business receives from its credit suppliers for a period are initially recorded by the business in a book of prime entry which is known as the PURCHASES DAY BOOK. (These invoices are, of course, recorded in the Sales Day Book of the supplier which is making the sale.) The Purchases Day Book is nearly always analysed into different types of purchases or expenses.

HOW IT WORKS

A typical analysed Purchases Day Book would look like this:

	< Basic Purchases Day Book columns >					< Extra analysis columns for net amount >		
Supplier	Supplier's invoice number	Supplier code	Gross £	VAT £	Net £	Purchases £	Telephone £	Stationery £
Haley Ltd	33728	PL 25	60.00	10.00	50.00			50.00
JJ Bros	242G	PL 14	1,440.00	240.00	1,200.00	1,200.00		
B Tel	530624	PL 06	154.00	24.00*	130.00		130.00	

*Note that the B Tel invoice offers a £10 discount if it is paid early, so VAT is calculated as £(130.00 − 10.00) × 20% = £24.00, and the gross is £130 + £24 = £154.

You may also see the Gross column headed up as 'Total' or 'Invoice total'.

The writing up of the Purchases Day Book for a period has the following steps:

Step 1   Gather the invoices that have been received from suppliers since the day book was last written up. All the information needed to enter into the Purchases Day Book is on the face of each invoice.

Step 2   Enter the date of the invoice, the name of the supplier and the supplier's invoice number in the appropriate columns – note that as all suppliers are likely to have different ways of numbering their invoices, the invoice numbers in the Purchases Day Book will not be sequential.

Step 3   The supplier code column is entered with the account number for the supplier. The supplier code is the account number given to the supplier in the purchases ledger (which we will come back to shortly) and therefore is often given the prefix 'PL'. This code is important as it helps with the eventual entry of these figures into the accounts.

Step 4   Enter the figures from the invoice.

- The gross column contains the gross total including VAT shown on the face of the invoice.

- The VAT is the amount shown on the face of the invoice.

- The net total on the invoice (ie the gross amount less the VAT) is then entered into the net column and into appropriate analysis columns, which are often shaded in practice to denote their separation from the net amount. This is where

the Purchases Day Book differs from the Sales Day Book in that there are likely to be different types of invoice being received and therefore an analysed Purchases Day Book is nearly always used.

THE PURCHASES LEDGER

For each individual credit supplier the business needs to keep a record of how much it owes to that supplier at any one time. The way this is done is to record each invoice total in the supplier's ledger account in the PURCHASES LEDGER, a record that contains ledger accounts for every credit supplier. As we saw in Chapter 1, suppliers which the business owes money to are also known as TRADE PAYABLES.

Each credit supplier's ledger account contains two sides:

- On the **right-hand side** we record invoices, which **increase** the amount owed to the supplier.

- On the **left-hand side** we record credit notes, settlement discounts taken and payments to the supplier, all of which **decrease** the amount owed to the supplier.

HOW IT WORKS

Step 1   Find the individual supplier's account in the purchases ledger using the supplier code.

Step 2   Enter the **gross** total of the invoice, which is the amount the business actually owes to the supplier, on the right-hand side of this account.

Step 3   In the 'details' section next to the amount, enter 'PDB' followed by the invoice number (and the date if required).

Looking back at the three invoices entered in the Purchases Day Book, they would be entered in the purchases ledger as follows:

Purchases ledger

Haley Ltd			PL 25
Details	£	Details	£
		PDB – 33728	60.00

	JJ Bros		**PL 14**
Details	£	Details	£
		PDB – 242G	1,440.00

	B Tel		**PL 06**
Details	£	Details	£
		PDB – 530624	154.00

The details for each entry is the supplier's invoice number recorded in the Purchases Day Book (PDB). The invoice number is entered as this will be useful when dealing with supplier enquiries.

CREDIT NOTES AND THE PURCHASES RETURNS DAY BOOK

Just as invoices received from suppliers are initially entered in their own book of prime entry, so too are credit notes – in the PURCHASES RETURNS DAY BOOK. This looks very similar to the Purchases Day Book with the same analysis columns and the same details needing to be entered.

HOW IT WORKS

A typical analysed Purchases Returns Day Book would look like this:

Date 20XX	Supplier	Supplier's credit note number	Supplier code	Gross £	VAT £	Net £	Purchases £	Telephone £	Stationery £
4 May	Haley Ltd	CN783	PL25	24.00	4.00	20.00			20.00
5 May	JJ Bros	C52246	PL14	69.60	11.60	58.00	58.00		

You may also see the Gross column headed up as 'Total' or 'Credit note total'.

The only difference here is that the credit note number is entered rather than an invoice number – and again these will not be sequentially numbered, as they are the suppliers' numbers. All of the details required can be found on the face of the credit note that is used to write up the Day Book.

Now we must enter each individual credit note in the supplier's account in the purchases ledger. The amount to be used is the gross amount and this must be entered in the **left-hand side** of the ledger account as it is a decrease in how much we owe the supplier.

Step 1   Find the individual supplier's account in the purchases ledger using the supplier code.

Step 2   Enter the **gross** total, which is the amount of the reduction in what the business actually owes, on the left-hand side of this account.

Step 3   In the 'details' section next to the amount, enter '**PRDB**' followed by the **credit note number** (and the date if required).

Purchases ledger

Haley Ltd			PL 25
Details	£	Details	£
PRDB – CN783	24.00	PDB – 33728	60.00

JJ Bros			PL 14
Details	£	Details	£
PRDB – C52246	69.60	PDB – 242G	1,440.00

Task 4

(a)   Complete the following sentences:

An invoice is entered on the	left	side of the supplier's account
	right	
A credit note is entered on the	left	side of the supplier's account
	right	

(b)   With reference to the ledger account above, the business owes Haley Ltd

£ _____

Task 5

An extract from an invoice from a supplier of dishwashers is given below:

Quantity	Description	£
1	RDX dishwasher	650.00
1	KJG dishwasher	480.00
1	XXX dishwasher	520.00
		1,650.00
VAT		330.00
		1,980.00

Show how this invoice would be entered into the analysed Purchases Day Book for a business that retails dishwashers and other electrical goods to consumers.

Gross £	VAT £	Net £	Purchases £	Expenses £

We shall return to writing up the day books relating to the purchases ledger in a later chapter.

THE CASH BOOK FOR RECEIPTS

For receipt of money into the business and for payments of money by the business, the book of prime entry is known as the CASH BOOK. We shall look first at the cash book in relation to receipts.

All notes and coin received by the business are recorded in the Cash Book. All money being paid into the bank account is also recorded in the Cash Book, whether it is banking of notes and coin, or payments received by cheque, credit card, debit card or directly through the banking system by automated payment.

The types of receipt that an organisation has depends entirely on the nature of its business. However for most businesses the following types are typical:

Notes and coin:

- Cash sales
- Cash received from trade receivables in respect of past credit sales
- Cash paid into the business by the owner

Other forms of receipt (cheques, credit and debit card payments, automated payments):

- Cheques etc paid by trade receivables for credit sales

- Cheques etc paid into the business by the owner

- Bank interest paid by the bank by automated payment

- Automated payments made by credit customers direct into the bank account

- Cheques etc for miscellaneous income such as rent, commission income and proceeds of sales of assets held for a long time, such as a car

Most businesses will have an ANALYSED CASH BOOK which reflects the most common types of receipt.

HOW IT WORKS

A typical analysed Cash Book for receipts is shown below, though you should note that in practice a variety of formats is possible:

		< Basic Cash Book columns >				< Extra analysis columns for Cash or Bank amount >			
Date	Details	Ref	Discount allowed £	Cash £	Bank £	VAT £	Cash sales £	Trade receivables £	Sundry income £
9 May	Cash sale			90.00		15.00	75.00		
10 May	Grigsons Ltd	SL21			127.20			127.20	
10 May	Hall & Co	SL05	10.00	93.60				93.60	

Date – the date recorded will be the date the payment was received or written up in the Cash Book, depending upon the organisation's policy.

Details – the details should be sufficient to describe the transaction so that it can easily be analysed and checked at a later date, eg if it is a receipt from a trade receivable, the name of that trade receivable.

Ref – the reference will depend upon the type of receipt. If it is a receipt from a trade receivable then the reference will normally be the customer code from the sales ledger for that trade receivable.

Cash – the figure in the 'Cash' column is the total amount of the receipt of notes and coin or cheques.

Bank – the figure in the 'Bank' column is the total amount of the receipt into the business's bank account.

Discount allowed – the DISCOUNT ALLOWED column is known as a 'memorandum column', which is why it is shaded here. What is recorded here is the amount of any settlement discount that has been deducted by a credit customer before making payment. When a settlement discount offered by the business is taken by a credit customer, the amount recorded in the Cash or Bank column is the amount actually received, and this is also the amount recorded in the VAT/Cash sales or Trade receivables columns (as we shall see shortly). The amount of discount allowed to and taken by the customer is recorded completely separately, in the shaded Discounts allowed column. This column will be used when the receipt is recorded in the sales ledger.

VAT – when money is received from a trade receivable no VAT is recorded, as the VAT was recorded when the original sales invoice was entered into the Sales Day Book. However, when cash sales which include VAT are made, the VAT element must be entered in the VAT column, and the net amount must be entered into the Cash sales column, so that the total of the Cash sales and VAT amounts is the figure in the Cash or Bank column. Notice that unlike the other day books we have looked at, **the Cash Book for receipts does not have a Net column**. This would only be needed in the case of cash sales by a VAT-registered business, so it is not standard. Instead the Cash sales analysis column (see below) acts as the Net column for cash sales that include VAT. All other amounts in the Cash or Bank columns are just analysed in the analysis columns.

Cash sales – the **net** amount of the cash sale, that is the total received minus the VAT, is recorded in this column. Remember that when we refer to a cash sale we mean a sale that is not on credit – the actual receipt could be in the form of notes and coin, cheque, credit or debit card, or automated payment online by the customer.

- When it is in the form of notes and coin or a cheque the gross amount is recorded in the Cash column.

- When it is by debit or credit card, or automated payment online, the gross amount is recorded in the Bank column, since the money is transferred directly into the business's bank account by the customer's bank (in the case of debit card or automated payment) or by the credit card company.

Trade receivables – this column is used to record the amount of the actual receipts from credit customers. The details of VAT, net and gross were recorded in the Sales Day Book when the sales invoice was sent out to the customer. When the customer pays the invoice only the total of the actual payment needs to be recorded here. The amount is the actual value of the payment received, that is after deduction of any settlement discount that was offered. It is the same amount as is recorded in the Cash or Bank column.

Sundry income – the sundry income (or miscellaneous income, or other income) column is used for other miscellaneous receipts that do not occur on a regular basis, such as payments into the business by its owner, interest paid by the bank,

rental income and income received on commission. It is important that their 'details' and reference coding are detailed enough for the receipt to be identified.

Task 6

Identify whether the following statement is True or False.

VAT can only be recorded in the Cash Book for receipts that have not come from credit customers.

True	
False	

Finally, we enter each receipt in respect of credit sales into the customer's account in the sales ledger. The amount to be used is the amount in the 'Trade receivables' column and this must be entered in the **right-hand side** of the customer's ledger account as it is a **decrease** in how much the customer owes the business. If settlement discount has been taken by the customer, the amount in the Discounts allowed column is also recorded, separately, in the sales ledger.

Step 1   Find the individual customer's account in the sales ledger using the customer code.

Step 2   Enter the amount from the Trade receivables column, and from the Discount allowed column, which are the amounts of the reduction in what the customer actually owes, on the right-hand side of this account.

Step 3   In the 'details' section next to the amount(s), enter '**CB – receipt**' for the actual receipt (this can be followed by another code number such as the number of the customer's remittance advice if this is available) and '**CB – discount allowed**' if the customer has taken a settlement discount. Enter the date(s) if this is required.

Sales ledger

		Grigsons Ltd		SL 21
Details	£	Details		£
SDB – 10356	199.20	SRDB – CN668		72.00
		CB – receipt		127.20

		Hall & Co		SL 05
Details	£	Details		£
SDB – 10357	103.60	CB – receipt		93.60
		CB – discount allowed		10.00

BPP LEARNING MEDIA

Task 7

With reference to the ledger accounts above:

Grigsons Ltd owes the business:

£ [   ]

Hall & Co owes the business:

£ [   ]

The Cash Book format that we have looked at is known as a THREE COLUMN CASH BOOK, since it has three columns which require entries in ledger accounts: the Cash column, the Bank column and the Discounts allowed column. (If you see references to a two column Cash Book, this will not have a Cash column; instead all entries are made in the Bank column.)

THE CASH BOOK FOR PAYMENTS

When payments are made by the business for any purpose, like receipts they are initially recorded in the CASH BOOK. The cash book for payments is the mirror image of the cash book for receipts.

All notes and coin (except petty cash, to which we shall come back in a later chapter) paid by the business are recorded in the Cash Book. All money being paid out of the bank account is also recorded in the Cash Book whether it is payment by cheque, banker's draft (a type of cheque which cannot be cancelled), debit card or directly through the banking system by automated payment.

Automated payments are usually authorised by the business, such as to pay employees or suppliers by BACS (Bankers Automated Clearing Service) or CHAPS (Clearing House Automated Payments System), or to pay regular bills by standing order or direct debit. Sometimes it is the bank itself that authorises the payment, as when it deducts interest that the business owes to the bank.

There is nearly always an ANALYSED CASH BOOK for payments as there will be different reasons for making the payment.

HOW IT WORKS

The layout of a typical analysed Cash Book for payments is shown below, though you should note that in practice a variety of formats is possible:

	< Basic Cash Book columns >					< Extra analysis columns for Cash or Bank amount >				
Date	Details	Ref	Discount received £	Cash £	Bank £	VAT £	Cash purchases £	Trade payables £	Petty cash £	Expens £
9 May	Cash purchase – books			72.00		6.00	66.00			
10 May	Haley Ltd	PL 25			36.00			36.00		
10 May	B Tel	PL 06	10.00		144.00			144.00		

Date – the date will be the date on which the transaction was authorised (such as when the cheque was written or the BACS payment was notified to the bank) or the date on which the Cash Book is written up, depending upon the organisation's policy.

Details – the details should be sufficient to describe the payment so that it can be easily analysed and checked at a later date – the usual detail to enter is the name of the person being paid.

Ref – the reference will depend upon the type of payment that is being made. If the payment is to a credit supplier (Trade payable) then the reference will be the supplier code (the purchases ledger account number for the supplier). If it is a BACS salary transfer, 'BACS' will be entered. If the payment is by cheque, the cheque number should also be added.

Cash – the figure in the 'Cash' column is the total amount of the payment of notes and coin

Bank – the figure in the 'Bank' column is the total value of the payment leaving the bank account by cheque, debit card or automated payment. (Note payment by credit card by the business will not affect the Cash Book since this payment will be reflected in the business's credit card account, which is separate from its bank account.)

Discount received – like the discount allowed column in relation to receipts, the DISCOUNT RECEIVED column is known as a 'memorandum' column, which is why it is shaded here. What is recorded is the amount of any settlement discount that was deducted by the business before the payment was made to the supplier. When a settlement discount offered by a credit supplier is taken by the business, the amount recorded in the Cash or Bank column is the amount actually paid, and this is also the amount recorded in the VAT/Cash purchases or Trade

payables columns. The amount of discount received by the business is recorded completely separately, in the shaded Discount received column. This column will be used when the payment is recorded in the purchases ledger.

VAT – when a payment is made to a trade payable no VAT is recorded, as the VAT was recorded when the original purchase invoice was entered into the Purchases Day Book. However, when cash purchases are made on which VAT is charged the VAT element is recorded in the VAT column, and the net amount is recorded in the 'Cash purchases' column, so that the total of the Cash purchases and VAT amounts is the figure in the Cash or Bank column.

Like the Cash Book for receipts, **the Cash Book for payments does not have a Net column**. This would only be needed in the case of cash purchases that include VAT, so is not standard. Instead the Cash purchases analysis column (see below) acts as the Net column for cash purchases that include VAT. All other amounts in the Cash or Bank columns are just analysed in the analysis columns.

Cash purchases – if the payment is for purchases of goods that are not bought on credit, the **net** amount of the purchase (the total paid minus the VAT) is entered in this column. Remember that a cash purchase is one that does not involve a period of credit – the actual purchase can be by:

- Cheque, debit card or automated transfer online (when the Bank column would be used)

- Notes and coin (when the Cash column would be used).

Trade payables – this column is used to record the payments made to credit suppliers. The details of VAT, net and gross were recorded in the Purchases Day Book when the invoice was received from the supplier. When the business pays the supplier, only the total amount of the actual payment needs be recorded here. The amount is the actual value of the payment made, after the deduction of any settlement discount that is taken. It is the same amount as is recorded in the Cash or Bank column.

Petty cash – this column is used to record any amounts that are taken out of the bank account in the form of notes and coins to be placed in the petty cash box. We shall come back to this in a later chapter.

Expenses – this column is used for the amount of any other payments that are made from the bank account, such as by BACS for salaries or interest paid to the bank. The heading may relate directly to such expenditure, for instance instead of Expenses the heading may be Salaries or Interest paid etc.

Task 8

When should VAT be recorded in the Cash Book in relation to payments? Tick one.

On all payments

On any payments that are not payments to credit suppliers (trade payables)

Finally, we enter each payment in respect of credit purchases in the supplier's account in the purchases ledger. The amount to be used is the amount in the 'Trade payables' column and this must be entered in the **left-hand side** of the supplier's ledger account as it is a **decrease** in how much the business owes the supplier. If settlement discount has been taken from the supplier, the amount in the Discounts received column is also recorded, separately, in the purchases ledger.

Step 1   Find the individual supplier's account in the purchases ledger using the supplier code.

Step 2   Enter the amount from the Trade payables column, and from the Discount received column, which are the amounts of the reduction in the amount owed to the supplier, on the left-hand side of this account.

Step 3   In the 'details' section next to the amount(s), enter '**CB – payment**' (this can be followed by another code number such as the number of the cheque if this is appropriate) and '**CB – discount received**' if the business has taken a settlement discount. Enter the date(s) if this is required.

Purchases ledger

Haley Ltd				**PL 25**
Details	£	Details		£
PRDB – CN783	24.00	PDB – 33728		60.00
CB – payment	36.00			

B Tel				**PL 06**
Details	£	Details		£
CB – payment	144.00	PDB – 530624		154.00
CB – discount received	10.00			

Task 9

With reference to the ledger accounts above:

the business owes Haley Ltd:

£ [   ]

the business owes B Tel:

£ [   ]

We shall return to writing up both sides of the Cash Book in Chapter 7.

CHAPTER OVERVIEW

- In order to reduce the number of entries necessary in the ledger accounts, documents of the same type are initially recorded in the books of prime entry

- Sales invoices are all recorded initially in the Sales Day Book (SDB), which shows the net amount, VAT and gross totals from each invoice; the net amount may also be analysed to show the different types of sale

- The gross total from each individual sales invoice must also be entered into the individual trade receivable's account in the sales ledger

- Sales credit notes are initially recorded in the Sales Returns Day Book (SRDB). It shows the net amount, VAT and gross total from each credit note, and may be analysed. The gross total is also entered in the individual trade receivable's account in the sales ledger

- Purchases invoices are all recorded initially in the Purchases Day Book (PDB). It shows the net amount, VAT and gross totals from each invoice, and the net amount is nearly always analysed to show the different types of purchase or expense

- The gross total from each individual purchase invoice must also be entered into the individual trade payable's account in the purchases ledger

- Purchases credit notes from suppliers are initially recorded in the Purchases Returns Day Book (PRDB). It shows the net amount, VAT and gross total from each credit note, and may be analysed. The gross total is also entered in the individual trade payable's account in the purchases ledger

- Receipts of money into the business are recorded in the Cash Book (CB) on the receipts side

- Receipts from credit customers are entered from the Cash Book into the customer's account in the sales ledger

- Payments of money by the business are recorded in the Cash Book on the payments side

- Payments to credit suppliers are entered from the Cash Book into the supplier's account in the purchases ledger

58

Keywords

Books of prime entry – the books in which the details of the organisation's transactions are initially recorded prior to entry into the ledger accounts

Day books – another name for books of prime entry

Sales Day Book (SDB) – primary record for recording sales invoices in credit sales

Ledger account – a record of all transactions of the same type made by the business

Sales ledger – record that contains ledger accounts for every credit customer

Trade receivables – credit customers who owe money to the business

Sales Returns Day Book (SRDB) – the primary record for recording credit notes sent to credit customers

Analysed Sales Day Book – a Sales Day Book where the net amount is analysed into the different types of sale for each invoice

Purchases Day Book (PDB) – primary record for recording purchases invoices in credit purchases

Purchases ledger – record that contains ledger accounts for every credit supplier

Trade payables – credit suppliers to whom the business owes money

Purchases Returns Day Book (PRDB) – the primary record for recording credit notes received from credit suppliers

Cash Book (CB) – the book of prime entry in which all **receipts** and **payments** by the business are recorded

Analysed Cash Book – a cash book which reflects the most common types of receipt or payment

Discount allowed – column of the Cash Book which records settlement discounts deducted by credit customers

BACS – Bankers Automated Clearing Service – automated payment method

CHAPS – Clearing House Automated Payment System – automated payment method

Discount received – column of the Cash Book which records the amount of any settlement discount deducted by the business before the payment was made to the supplier

TEST YOUR LEARNING

Test 1

Write up the Sales Day Book and the Sales Returns Day Book from the invoices and credit notes given below.

Sales Day Book

Date	Customer	Invoice number	Customer code	Gross £	VAT £	Net £
Total						

Sales Returns Day Book

Date	Customer	Credit note number	Customer code	Gross £	VAT £	Net £
Total						

Invoice no. 44263	1 June	J Jepson	SL34	£118.00 + VAT
Invoice no. 44264	2 June	S Beck & Sons	SL01	£320.00 + VAT
Credit note 3813	2 June	Scroll Ltd	SL16	£18.00 + VAT
Invoice no. 44265	3 June	Penfold Ltd	SL23	£164.00 + VAT
Invoice no. 44266	4 June	S Beck & Sons	SL01	£256.00 + VAT
Invoice no. 44267	4 June	J Jepson	SL34	£144.00 + VAT
Credit note 3814	5 June	Penfold Ltd	SL23	£16.80 + VAT

Test 2

Today's date is 6 June and you are required to write up the Purchases Day Book and the Purchases Returns Day Book from the invoices and credit notes given below. It is organisational policy to use the date column to record the date of entry rather than the date of invoice.

Purchases Day Book

Date	Supplier	Invoice number	Supplier code	Gross £	VAT £	Net £
Total						

Purchases Returns Day Book

Date	Supplier	Credit note number	Supplier code	Gross £	VAT £	Net £
Total						

1 June	Invoice 224363 from Y H Hill (PL16)	£158.40 + VAT
1 June	Credit note CN92 from Letra Ltd (PL24)	£100.00 + VAT
2 June	Invoice PT445 from Letra Ltd (PL24)	£228.00 + VAT
2 June	Invoice 77352 from Coldstores Ltd (PL03)	£158.00 + VAT
5 June	Credit note C7325 from Y H Hill (PL16)	£26.00 + VAT

Test 3

Write up the Cash Book from the details of receipts and payments given below.

Cash Book – receipts

Date	Details	Ref	Disc allowed £	Cash £	Bank £	VAT £	Cash sales £	Trade receivables £	Sundry income £

Cash Book – payments

Date	Details	Ref	Disc received £	Cash £	Bank £	VAT £	Cash purchases £	Trade payables £	Petty cash £	Expenses £

Receipt	1 June	J Jepson	SL34	£220.00, discount £10
Payment	2 June	Letra Ltd	PL24	£500.00, discount £20
Payment	2 June	Cash purchase		£48.00 including VAT
Receipt	3 June	Cash sale		£72.00 including VAT

chapter 4:
RECORDING CREDIT SALES

chapter coverage 📖

This chapter considers in more detail all of the documents involved in making credit sales, and the checks that must be made on those documents. We recap the recording of invoices and credit notes in the books of prime entry and we cover the preparation of statements of account for customers, before going on to the checking of payments received from credit customers. The topics covered are:

- ✎ Documents involved in credit sales

- ✎ Preparing and checking sales invoices

- ✎ Preparing credit notes

- ✎ Coding invoices and credit notes

- ✎ Payments from credit customers

- ✎ Procedure for checking payments from customers

DOCUMENTS INVOLVED IN CREDIT SALES

The diagram below gives an overview of the main documents potentially involved in a credit sale from initial customer enquiry to final settlement of the invoice. We have already looked at some of these documents when we recorded them in the day books, but in this chapter our aim is to examine in more detail the sequence of processes involved in accounting for credit sales.

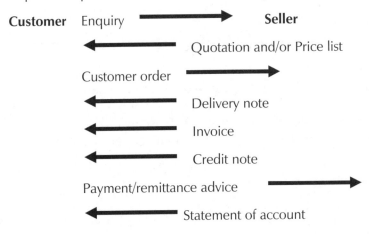

Customer Enquiry → **Seller**

← Quotation and/or Price list

Customer order →

← Delivery note

← Invoice

← Credit note

Payment/remittance advice →

← Statement of account

Quotation and price list

The credit sale process will normally be initiated by the customer making an enquiry about the purchase of goods. The seller replies to the customer's enquiry confirming that the requested goods can be supplied, on what date and at what price. This may be done verbally, or by sending a PRICE LIST and/or a QUOTATION.

HOW IT WORKS

Earlier today, Southfield Electrical's sales department received a phone call from the purchasing manager of Whitehill Superstores enquiring whether Southfield could supply six Zanpoint dishwashers as soon as possible. Southfield is able to supply these so the sales department sends out the following quotation and extract from its price list.

QUOTATION

Southfield Electrical
Industrial Estate
Benham DR6 2FF
Tel 0303379 Fax 0303152
VAT Reg 0264 2274 49

To:

Whitehill Superstores
28, Whitehill Park
Benham DR6 5LM

Date: 3 Sept 20XX

Number: 04217

Thank you for your enquiry of earlier today. We are pleased to confirm that we can deliver the following goods on the day after receiving your purchase order.

6 Zanpoint dishwashers (Code 4425) at a price of £200 each, excluding VAT.

Authorised: *J Hampton*

Sales Manager

SOUTHFIELD ELECTRICAL

PRICE LIST (extract)

Product code	Product description	Unit price (excl VAT) £
Zanpoint 4425	Dishwasher	200.00

Customer order

The purchasing manager at Whitehill has received this quotation and price list and finds the price and terms acceptable. The purchasing department will produce the order shown next, which as far as Southfield is concerned is a CUSTOMER ORDER.

ORDER

WHITEHILL SUPERSTORES
28 Whitehill Park
Benham DR6 5LM
Tel 0303446 Fax 0303447

To: Southfield Electrical
Industrial Estate
Benham
DR6 2FF

Number: 32011

Date: 5 Sept 20XX

Delivery address: Whitehill Superstores
28, Whitehill Park
Benham DR6 5LM

Product code	Quantity	Description	Unit list price £
4425	6	Zanpoint Dishwasher	200 (excluding VAT)

Authorised by: *P. Winterbottom* **Date:** *5 Sept 20XX*

Let's consider the details of this order:

- Using a coding system it has its own unique, sequential document number which will be quoted on subsequent documentation such as the delivery note and invoice.

- The address to which the goods are to be delivered is given, as this may be different from the address of the purchasing department if there is, for example, a separate warehouse.

- The product is described in words but is also given a product code – coding is useful in all areas of the accounting process to identify goods and transactions. If a code is used as well as words it helps to reduce the chances of an error being made in the sale, but it is very important that the code is used accurately in every detail.

- The price has been confirmed in order to avoid any misunderstanding at a later date.

- The order must be signed by an appropriate person within Whitehill Superstores.

Task 1

Who issues an order?

The buyer of goods

The seller of goods

Delivery note

Once the order is received by the sales department of Southfield Electrical it will be checked against the quotation number 04217 to ensure that this was the quantity and price that had been quoted to Whitehill. The delivery of the goods must then be organised. The sales department will draw up the DELIVERY NOTE, shown next, to accompany the dishwashers.

DELIVERY NOTE

Southfield Electrical
Industrial Estate
Benham DR6 2FF
Tel 0303379 Fax 0303152

Delivery address:

Whitehill Superstores
28, Whitehill Park
Benham DR6 5LM

Number: 34619

Date: 6 Sept 20XX

Order number: 32011

Product code	Quantity	Description
4425	6	Zanpoint Dishwasher

Received by: [Signature] .... **Print name:** ....

Date: ....

On the delivery note:

- The address of the delivery is included so that the carrier knows where to take the goods.

- The delivery note has its own unique, sequential number which can be used on other documentation and in any dispute.

- The order number relating to this delivery is also included so the delivery note can be matched to the order easily.

- A precise description of the goods is given both by including the description in words and including the product code. Again, this is important as the goods despatched must be exactly what the customer has ordered.

- When the delivery note leaves Southfield it is unsigned. The signature that is required is that of the person receiving the dishwashers at Whitehill. The stores department at Whitehill must check that the goods that have been delivered were the ones ordered and stated on the delivery note. If there is any discrepancy then this must be recorded on the delivery note.

- There will normally be more than one copy of the delivery note. Once it has been signed to confirm that the correct goods have been delivered, the carrier and the customer will keep one copy each as proof of delivery and a further copy will be returned to Southfield as proof of delivery and acceptance by Whitehill.

- No price information is included on the delivery note as this is not relevant at this stage.

Invoice

The next stage in the process is for Southfield Electrical to produce a sales INVOICE. This is the request for payment for the dishwashers from Whitehill Superstores and details precisely how much is due and when.

INVOICE	Invoice number 56314
Southfield Electrical **Industrial Estate** **Benham DR6 2FF** **Tel: 01239 345639**	
VAT registration:	0264 2274 49
Date/tax point:	7 September 20XX
Order number:	32011
Customer:	Whitehill Superstores 28 Whitehill Park Benham DR6 5LM
Account number (customer code)	SL 44

Description/product code	Quantity	Unit amount £	Total £
Zanpoint dishwashers /4425	6	200.00	1,200.00
Net total			1,200.00
VAT at 20%			240.00
Gross total			1,440.00
Terms 30 days net			

The invoice is prepared by the sales department with reference to the information on the customer order (its number is included on the invoice to help the customer trace the details), quotation/price list and delivery note. We shall see more about preparing invoices later in this chapter.

Writing up the Sales Day Book and sales ledger

As we saw in Chapter 3, this invoice must be entered by Southfield into its Sales Day Book and from there into the sales ledger account for Whitehill (note that in this sales ledger account, some other entries have already been made, and we have used dates here as we shall shortly be preparing a statement of account, but note that in your assessment you may not need to insert dates).

Sales Day Book

Date 20XX	Customer	Invoice number	Customer code	Gross £	VAT £	Net £
7 Sept	Whitehill	56314	SL44	1,440.00	240.00	1,200.00

Sales ledger

Whitehill Superstores   **SL 44**

Date	Details	£	Date	Details	£
21/8	SDB – 56019	316.40	28/8	SRDB – 08613	47.46
7/9	SDB – 56314	1,440.00			

Credit note

If a damaged dishwasher is returned to Southfield then notification is needed. A RETURNS NOTE may be sent by Whitehill to Southfield with details, or alternatively, Southfield may raise its own returns note when the goods are received back. Southfield's stores department must ensure that the dishwasher is in fact returned damaged, then Southfield will issue a CREDIT NOTE to Whitehill which reverses the part of the sales invoice that relates to the damaged dishwasher.

CREDIT NOTE	Credit note number 08641		
Southfield Electrical **Industrial Estate** **Benham DR6 2FF** **Tel: 01239 345639**			
VAT registration:	0264 2274 49		
Date/tax point:	12 September 20XX		
Order number:	32011		
Customer:	Whitehill Superstores 28 Whitehill Park Benham DR6 5LM		
Account number (customer code)	SL 44		
Description/product code	Quantity	Unit amount £	Total £
Zanpoint dishwasher/4425 Reason for credit note: Delivered damaged	1	200.00	200.00
Net total			200.00
VAT at 20%			40.00
Gross total			240.00
Terms 30 days net			

The credit note is prepared by Southfield with reference to the information on the customer order (its number is included on the credit note to help the customer trace the details), quotation/price list and returns note. The calculations are done by the sales department.

The credit note is entered by Southfield into its Sales Returns Day Book and from there into the sales ledger account for Whitehill.

Sales Returns Day Book

Date 20XX	Customer	Credit note number	Customer code	Gross £	VAT £	Net £
12 Sept	Whitehill	08641	SL44	240.00	40.00	200.00

Sales ledger

Whitehill Superstores		SL 44	
Date Details	£	Date Details	£
21/8 SDB – 56019	316.40	28/8 SRDB – 08613	47.46
7/9 SDB – 56314	1,440.00	12/9 SRDB – 08641	240.00

Receipt from a customer

At some stage the credit customer will pay the supplier for goods that have been supplied. This may be by cheque, debit or credit card payment or by automated payment from the customer's bank account to the supplier's.

HOW IT WORKS

Suppose that on 20 September Whitehill Superstores paid Southfield Electrical by cheque the amount that it owed to the company at the beginning of September, which was for invoice 56019 received on 21 August for £316.40 less credit note number 08613 for £47.46 received on 28 August. Along with the cheque it sends the supplier the following remittance advice note, which we saw first in Chapter 1.

REMITTANCE ADVICE NOTE	Remittance advice note number
Whitehill Superstores	0937498
28 Whitehill Park	
Benham DR6 5LM	
Supplier:	**Southfield Electrical**
	Industrial Estate
	Benham DR6 2FF
Account number (supplier code)	**PL 526**

Date	Transaction reference	Amount £
21/08/XX	Invoice 56019	316.40
28/08/XX	Credit note 08613	(47.46)
20/09/XX	Payment made – cheque enclosed	268.94

The receipt is entered by Southfield into its Cash Book and from there into the sales ledger account for Whitehill.

Cash Book

Date	Details	Ref	Discount allowed £	Cash £	Bank £	VAT £	Cash sales £	Trade receivables £	Sundry income £
20 Sept	Whitehill Superstores	SL44			268.94			268.94	

Sales ledger

	Whitehill Superstores			SL 44
Date Details	£	Date Details		£
21/8 SDB – 56019	316.40	28/8 SRDB – 08613		47.46
07/9 SDB – 56314	1,440.00	12/9 SRDB – 08641		240.00
		20/9 CB – receipt		268.94

Statements of account for credit customers

There is one final document in the document cycle for credit sales and that is the STATEMENT OF ACCOUNT, which we saw briefly in Chapter 1. A customer's statement of account shows all the invoices and credit notes that have been sent to the customer that month together with any amounts outstanding from previous months, along with any payments received from the customer and discounts

taken by the customer in the month. It is common practice to send out statements to customers on a regular basis, usually monthly. The customer can use the statement to check that its records are complete. Often it is following receipt of a statement that discrepancies between the records of customers and suppliers come to light.

As we saw in Chapter 1, Southfield Electrical's statement of account to Whitehill Superstores might look like this:

STATEMENT OF ACCOUNT				
Southfield Electrical				
Industrial Estate				
Benham DR6 2FF				
Tel: 01239 345639				
VAT registration:	0264 2274 49			
Date:	30 September 20XX			
Customer:	Whitehill Superstores 28 Whitehill Park Benham DR6 5LM			
Account number (customer code)	SL 44			
Date	**Details**	**Increase amount owed £**	**Decrease amount owed £**	**Amount owed £**
21.08.XX	Inv56019	316.40		316.40
28.08.XX	CN08613		47.46	268.94
07.09.XX	Inv56314	1,440.00		1,708.94
12.09.XX	CN08641		240.00	1,468.94
20.09.XX	Payment received – thank you		268.94	1,200.00
Amount now due				1,200.00

You should now be able to see that for the most part the information in the statement of account exactly replicates the information in the customer's sales ledger account.

HOW IT WORKS

Let's now consider how to prepare this statement from Whitehill Superstores' sales ledger account:

- Address it to Whitehill Superstores and again, in order to ease finding the relevant information, include the customer code.

- Prepare it in date order, so the transactions in the sales ledger account are entered in chronological order, starting with the 21 August invoice.

- The credit note of 28 August is shown along with the invoice on 7 September and the credit note sent out on 12 September.

- The payment received on 20 September in respect of the invoice on 21 August and the credit note on 28 August is shown last, by convention with the narrative 'Payment received – thank you'.

- After each entry the amount currently owing by Whitehill – the amount owed or 'BALANCE' – is shown.

- By the end of September the amount due is the September invoice less the September credit note, £1,440.00 – £240.00 = £1,200.00.

The next time a statement is prepared the August invoice and credit note and the September payment will not be shown, as the latter is allocated to and 'clears' the former.

Often customers will return payments with a copy of their statement on which the items that are being paid are ticked off. Alternatively, the statement sent out by the seller may include a tear-off REMITTANCE ADVICE NOTE at the bottom which allows the customer to show which invoices from the statement are being paid. The customer will then return the remittance advice note to the supplier together with the payment.

A typical combined statement and remittance advice is shown on the next page.

STATEMENT OF ACCOUNT	

Southfield Electrical

Industrial Estate

Benham DR6 2FF

Tel: 01239 345639

VAT registration:	0264 2274 49
Date:	31 October 20XX
Customer:	Whitehill Superstores 28 Whitehill Park Benham DR6 5LM
Account number (customer code)	SL 44

Date	Details	Increase amount owed £	Decrease amount owed £	Amount owed £
01.10.XX	Balance from Sept	1,200.00		1,200.00
		2,448.45		3,648.45
02.10.XX	Inv56389	1,118.23		4,766.68
15.10.XX	Inv56436		123.80	4,642.88
18.19.XX	CN08662		1,200.00	3,442.88
28.10.XX	Payment received – thank you			
Amount now due				3,442.88

REMITTANCE ADVICE	
To: Southfield Electrical **Industrial Estate** **Benham DR6 2FF**	From: Whitehill Superstores 28 Whitehill Park Benham DR6 5LM
Account number (customer code)	SL 44

Please indicate the items you are paying ✓ and return with your payment

Details	Increase amount owed £	Decrease amount owed £	✓
Inv56389	2,448.45		
Inv56436	1,118.23		
CN08662		123.80	
Payment enclosed £			

PREPARING AND CHECKING SALES INVOICES

There are a lot of details and calculations involved in preparing an invoice and it is extremely important that these details and calculations are done properly and thoroughly checked.

We will now work through the whole process of preparing a sales invoice in order to illustrate all of the checks that must be made.

HOW IT WORKS

You work for Southfield Electrical and are responsible for preparing sales invoices. Today is 8 October 20XX and you have on your desk the following customer order from Whitehill Superstores for which an invoice must be prepared.

ORDER

WHITEHILL SUPERSTORES
28 Whitehill Park
Benham DR6 5LM
Tel 0303446 Fax 0303447

To: Southfield Electrical
Industrial Estate
Benham
DR6 2FF

Number: 32174

Date: 2 Oct 20XX

Delivery address: Whitehill Superstores
28, Whitehill Park
Benham DR6 5LM

Product code	Quantity	Description	Unit list price £
6160	4	Hosch Washing Machine	300.00
3172	10	Temax Mixer	40.00

Authorised by: *P. Winterbottom*   **Date:** *2 Oct 20XX*

Step 1 You must first check that the goods were in fact sent to Whitehill, so you find the delivery note that relates to order 32174. This is given on the following page.

DELIVERY NOTE

Southfield Electrical
Industrial Estate
Benham DR6 2FF
Tel 0303379 Fax 0303152

Delivery address:

Whitehill Superstores
28, Whitehill Park
Benham DR6 5LM

Number: 34772

Date: 5 Oct 20XX

Order number: 32174

Product code	Quantity	Description
6160	4	Hosch Washing Machine
3172	9	Temax Mixer

Received by: [Signature] *J. Jones*   **Print name:** *J. JONES*

Date: *5 Oct 20XX*

Step 2   You should note that only nine mixers were delivered and accepted (the delivery note is signed by J Jones at Whitehill) and therefore only nine mixers must be invoiced, not the ten that were ordered. You might also make a note to follow up why only nine and not ten were delivered, or to inform the appropriate person in your organisation.

Step 3   The prices quoted on the order are the unit list prices. You must now check that these list prices are correct. An extract from Southfield's price list is given on the following page.

BPP
LEARNING MEDIA

SOUTHFIELD ELECTRICAL

PRICE LIST (extract)

Product code	Product description	Unit price (excl VAT) £
HOSCH		
6040	Tumble dryer	250.00
6050	Tumble dryer	280.00
6060	Tumble dryer	300.00
6140	Washing machine	220.00
6150	Washing machine	260.00
6160	Washing machine	300.00
6170	Washing machine	340.00
TEMAX		
3160	Food processor	100.00
3162	Food processor	120.00
3164	Food processor	140.00
3170	Mixer	35.00
3172	Mixer	40.00
3174	Mixer	46.00

The prices included on the order agree with the list prices and therefore can be used on the invoice.

Step 4   You must now find the customer file for Whitehill Superstores which will show details of addresses, the customer code and DISCOUNT POLICY in respect of the customer (ie what trade, bulk and settlement discounts should be applied to sales to the customer).

The customer file for Whitehill Superstores shows the following:

- Customer code – SL44

- Discount policy effective 1 Oct 20XX:

    – 10% trade discount is allowed on all sales

    – 5% bulk discount on orders where list price net of trade discount exceeds £1,000

    – 4% settlement discount for payment within 10 days, otherwise net 30 days

Step 5   You now have all of the information required to start preparing the invoice. The final invoice is now shown and we will then work through the remaining steps in completing it.

INVOICE	Invoice number 56483		
Southfield Electrical			
Industrial Estate			
Benham DR6 2FF			
Tel: 01239 345639			
VAT registration:	0264 2274 49		
Date/tax point:	8 October 20XX		
Order number:	32174		
Customer:	Whitehill Superstores 28 Whitehill Park Benham DR6 5LM		
Account number (customer code)	SL 44		
Description/product code	**Quantity**	**Unit amount** **£**	**Total** **£**
Hosch washing machine /6160	4	300.00	1,200.00
Temax Mixer /3172	9	40.00	360.00
List price			1,560.00
Less trade discount 10%			(156.00)
List price net of trade discount			1,404.00
Less bulk discount 5%			(70.20)
Net total			1,333.80
VAT at 20%			256.09
Gross total			1,589.89
Terms			
4% discount for settlement within 10 days of invoice date, otherwise 30 days net			

Step 6   Enter the customer's name and address and customer code from the customer file. The invoice number is the next number in sequence after the previous invoice. Enter today's date.

Step 7 Enter the quantities, codes and descriptions from the delivery note – remember that only nine mixers were delivered.

Step 8 Enter the unit prices from the price list. Calculate the total list price by multiplying the quantity by the list price:

$$4 \times £300 \quad = \quad £1,200.00$$

$$9 \times £40 \quad = \quad £360.00$$

Step 9 Calculate the total list price by adding together the totals for each product:

$$£1,200.00 + £360.00 = £1,560.00$$

Step 10 Calculate the trade discount as 10% of the total list price:

$$£1,560.00 \times 10\% \, (10/100) = £156.00$$

Deduct the trade discount from the total list price:

$$£1,560.00 - £156.00 = £1,404.00$$

Step 11 As the list price net of trade discount is more than £1,000, calculate the bulk discount as 5% of the list price net of trade discount:

$$£1,404.00 \times 5\% \, (5/100) = £70.20$$

Deduct the bulk discount from the list price net of trade discount to arrive at the net total:

$$£1,404.00 - £70.20 = £1,333.80$$

Step 12 To calculate the VAT, first of all determine the amount of settlement discount (round it down to the nearest penny):

$$£1,333.80 \times 4\% \, (4/100) = £53.35$$

In a working deduct this from the net total:

$$£1,333.80 - £53.35 = £1,280.45$$

Calculate the VAT at 20% based on the net amount after the discount has been deducted:

$$£1,280.45 \times 20\% \, (20/100) = £256.09$$

Step 13 Add the VAT calculated to the net total to arrive at the gross total for the invoice:

$$£1,333.80 + £256.09 = £1,589.89$$

Step 14 Enter the settlement discount terms at the bottom of the invoice.

PREPARING CREDIT NOTES

When preparing a credit note the same types of procedure need to be followed as those for an invoice. The approach as listed below should be followed:

- Check that the goods were actually returned by reference to the returns note.

- Ensure that the credit note is being issued to the correct customer.

- Check that the goods returned are the ones on the credit note by checking the product code.

- Check the price of the returned goods on the price list and/or quotation.

- Check the calculations on the credit note, eg quantity × unit price = total price.

- Check that any trade and bulk discounts that applied to the invoice have been allowed for in relation to the goods returned.

- Check that the VAT has been correctly calculated, remembering to adjust for a settlement discount if this adjustment had been made on the original invoice.

CODING INVOICES AND CREDIT NOTES

Coding invoices and credit notes

Invoices and credit notes must be coded for their eventual inclusion in the accounting records using the business's coding system. The invoice or credit note should always include the customer code; with Whitehill Superstores this was SL 44. There may also be a coding to indicate what type of sale was made, or the geographical region of the sale. If this is the policy of the organisation then each invoice must be correctly coded to show the type of product or where the sale was made.

HOW IT WORKS

Southfield Electrical is considering a coding system which allows it to code sales according to the type of sale made. It has revised its price list to show sales codes as follows:

SOUTHFIELD ELECTRICAL

PRICE LIST (extract)

Product code	Sales code	Product description	Unit price (excl VAT) £
HOSCH			
6040	H6	Tumble dryer	250.00
6050	H6	Tumble dryer	280.00
6060	H6	Tumble dryer	300.00
6140	H6	Washing machine	220.00
6150	H6	Washing machine	260.00
6160	H6	Washing machine	300.00
6170	H6	Washing machine	340.00
TEMAX			
3160	T3	Food processor	100.00
3162	T3	Food processor	120.00
3164	T3	Food processor	140.00
3170	T3	Mixer	35.00
3172	T3	Mixer	40.00
3174	T3	Mixer	46.00

A sales invoice using the sales codes would look like this:

INVOICE	Invoice number 56484			
Southfield Electrical **Industrial Estate** **Benham DR6 2FF** **Tel: 01239 345639**				
VAT registration:	0264 2274 49			
Date/tax point:	8 October 20XX			
Order number:	56237			
Customer:	Rampton Ltd 45 Janes Trading Estate Benham DR6 8DF			
Account number (customer code)	SL 62			
Description/product code	**Quantity**	**Unit amount £**	**Total £**	**Sales code**
Hosch tumble dryer /6040	2	250.00	500.00	H6
Temax food processor /3162	4	120.00	480.00	T3
Net total			980.00	
VAT at 20%			196.00	
Gross total			1,176.00	
Terms 30 days net				

In the analysed Sales Day Book the sale can now be analysed using the sales codes.

Sales Day Book

Date 20XX	Customer	Invoice number	Customer code	Gross £	VAT £	Net £	H6 £	T3 £
8 Oct	Rampton	56484	SL62	1,176.00	196.00	980.00	500.00	480.00

PAYMENTS FROM CREDIT CUSTOMERS

The next stage of the credit sale process is for the customer to pay the business. This may be by:

- Cheque through the post
- Automated payment from the customer's bank account to the supplier's
- Debit or credit card payment over the phone or on the internet
- Cash (occasionally – we shall not consider this method further here)

In each case the business must check to ensure that the amount of the receipt:

- Is accurately calculated

- Is valid, ie it ties in with supporting documentation (the remittance advice note, statement of account, invoice and sales ledger account)

Once these checks have been completed the receipt will be recorded in the Cash Book.

Remittance advice note

When a payment is received the first check that must be carried out is that it is for the correct amount. In order to do this you will need to know what invoices are being paid. In many situations a REMITTANCE ADVICE NOTE will be received from the customer with the payment detailing precisely what the payment relates to.

The remittance advice may have been prepared by the customer or it may be a blank remittance advice sent out by your organisation either with the regular statements that are sent to customers or with the invoice itself.

Here is a typical remittance advice:

REMITTANCE ADVICE

To: Southfield Electrical
Industrial Estate
Benham
DR6 2FF
Tel 0303379 Fax 0303152

From: Dagwell Enterprises
Number: 012561
Account no: PL 813
Date: 22 September 20XX

Reference	Amount	Paid (✓)
30112	723.80	✓
30126	811.59	✓
CN2351	218.65	✓
30164	928.83	
CN2377	239.70	

CHEQUE ENCLOSED	£1,316.74

You must check that the total of the invoices and credit note indicated as being paid does agree to the payment amount (£723.80 + £811.59 – £218.65 = £1,316.74).

If the customer has prepared the remittance advice by completing the invoice and credit note amounts then you should also check that correct amounts have been included. This can be done by examining the sales ledger account for that customer in the sales ledger.

Valid cheques

When payment is received in the form of a cheque then you must ensure that the cheque itself is valid. We shall come back to this in the Control Accounts, Journals and the Banking System unit.

Correct settlement discount

If the customer has taken advantage of a settlement discount then very careful checks must be made to ensure that this discount is both valid and correctly calculated.

- Has this customer been offered a settlement discount? This can be checked either by examining the copy of the invoice or finding the discount policy in relation to this customer which will include details of the settlement discount that is routinely offered to this customer.

- Has the invoice been paid within the timescale set for the settlement discount? For this the copy of the invoice should be examined to determine the invoice date and the terms of the settlement discount. For example if an invoice was dated 10 September and a settlement discount was offered for payment received within ten days, if the payment was received before or on 20 September it would be valid, but if payment arrived after this date then the claiming of the discount would not be valid.

- Has the discount been correctly calculated? Again, the invoice will need to be checked for this as, due to the VAT complication with settlement discounts, the discount has to be calculated as a percentage of the VAT exclusive amount and the VAT then added on.

HOW IT WORKS

An extract from a sales invoice shows the following:

	£
Net	600.00
VAT	115.20
Gross	715.20
Terms 4% settlement discount for payment received within 10 days of invoice, otherwise net 30 days	

The discount that can be deducted is 4% of the **net** total £600.00

£600.00 × 4/100 = £24.00

Therefore the payment should be for £715.20 – £24.00 = £691.20.

Payment received without a remittance advice note

If a customer sends a payment without a remittance advice note and it is in settlement of more than one invoice, you must examine the customer's account in the sales ledger to determine which invoices are being paid by this payment.

HOW IT WORKS

Southfield Electrical has received this cheque through the post with no accompanying documentation.

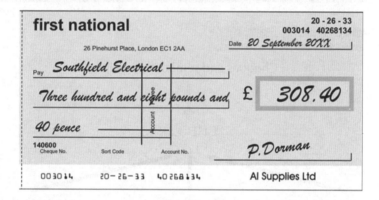

Clearly, this cheque is from A1 Supplies Ltd and therefore the account for this customer should be found in the sales ledger. The customer's account shows the following:

A1 Supplies Ltd					SL 41
Date	Details	£	Date	Details	£
3 Sept	SDB – 30118	115.68	12 Sept	SDB – CN2355	35.97
8 Sept	SDB – 30131	228.69			
15 Sept	SDB – 30144	147.25			
19 Sept	SDB – 30159	279.46			

By trial and error you find that the following invoices less the credit note add up to the cheque total:

	£
30118	115.68
30131	228.69
CN 2355	(35.97)
	308.40

When the receipt is recorded in the sales ledger these invoices and credit note can be marked as paid. This is called 'allocating' the receipt.

PROCEDURE FOR CHECKING PAYMENTS FROM CUSTOMERS

Cheques and remittance advices

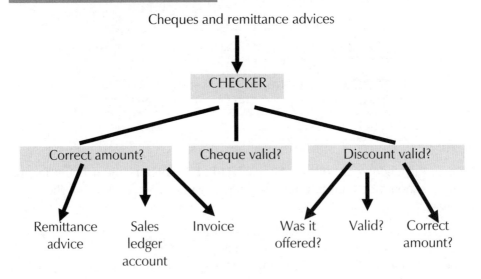

Task 2

Goods with a net total of £400.00 were sold to a customer and VAT of £76.00 was added to the net total to give a gross invoice total of £476.00. The invoice was dated 20 November and a cheque for £456.00 was received today, 28 November. The invoice terms stated that a 5% settlement discount was offered for payment received within 14 days of the invoice date.

Is the receipt for the correct amount?

Yes

No

Automated payments

Many customers pay amounts due by automated payment, such as by Bankers Automated Clearing System (BACS) or online transfer, from their bank accounts into the supplier's. This means that your organisation's bank account will be increased directly by the amount of the payment. Normally the customer will send your organisation notification that the payment is being made in the form of a remittance advice note showing precisely which invoices are being paid.

The same checks should be carried out as for a receipt of a cheque:

- Has the correct amount been transferred?
- If a settlement discount has been taken, is this valid and correct?

If no remittance advice or other notification is sent by the customer, the increase in your organisation's bank account will be noticed when the Cash Book and the bank statement sent by the bank itself or downloaded from the internet are compared, as they should be on a regular basis. When the receipt is spotted, it will be necessary to work out which invoices have been paid by this automated payment, as we saw above with any other payment not accompanied by a remittance advice note.

Errors in payments

In this chapter we have considered a number of checks that must be made on payments received (or receipts):

- Is the payment for the correct amount, or has the customer overpaid or underpaid?

- Is the payment valid?

- Has the settlement discount been correctly calculated and should it have been taken?

Any discrepancy in the amount is usually caused by:

- The customer underpaying an invoice by mistake, for instance by making a payment of £210.36 when the invoice was for £210.63, so the customer still owes 27p

- The customer overpaying the invoice by mistake, for instance by making a payment of £54.00 when the invoice was for £45.00, so the business owes the customer £9.00

- The customer deducting the wrong amount of settlement discount, for instance by calculating it on the gross amount rather than the net amount

- The customer deducting settlement discount even though the deadline for taking advantage of this is past

Where there is a discrepancy the following actions must be taken:

- Record the payment as received in the Cash Book.

- Report the discrepancy to the appropriate person within the organisation. In most cases the customer will need to be informed of the problem and may possibly be asked to issue a replacement cheque or make an additional automated payment.

We shall see more about the actual process of recording receipts in the Cash Book in a later chapter.

CHAPTER OVERVIEW

- When credit sales are made there are potentially many documents involved

- The process is started by an initial enquiry from the prospective customer

- The seller then answers the enquiry with a quotation and/or a price list

- The customer confirms with an order

- The goods are despatched to the customer with a delivery note that must be signed by the customer upon receipt of the goods and a copy returned to the seller

- The seller sends out an invoice requesting payment from the customer

- Upon return of any goods from the customer, the seller sends out a credit note effectively cancelling all or part of the invoice

- A statement of account is sent out to the customer on a regular basis, normally monthly, showing invoices and credit notes issued during the month, payments received (if any) and the final amount outstanding from the customer at the end of the month

- Many checks are necessary when preparing an invoice to ensure that it is for the correct goods, to the correct customer and for the correct amount

- Similar checks are also required for credit notes, in particular details of the goods that have been returned

- Each organisation will have its own procedures that should be followed for coding of sales invoices and credit notes

- Organisations that make credit sales will receive most payments from customers in the form of automated transfers into their bank account or cheques through the post

- The receipt must be thoroughly checked – is it for the correct amount? – is the payment valid? – is any settlement discount deducted valid and correctly calculated?

- If no remittance advice is received with the payment then the customer's sales ledger account must be examined to determine which invoices (less credit notes) are being paid

- If any discrepancies arise with a payment from a customer the payment should still be recorded, but the discrepancy should be reported to the appropriate person within the organisation

Keywords

Price list – written confirmation from a supplier as to the price of goods

Quotation – a written statement sent from supplier to customer advising them of the price of a specific good or service (or combination of the two)

Customer order – sent from the customer to the supplier confirming the required purchase

Delivery note – document sent to the customer with the items being despatched which must be signed by the customer confirming receipt of the items

Invoice – a document that clearly sets out what money is owed by a named customer to a named supplier in respect of particular goods or services

Returns note – the document sent by the customer to the supplier detailing the goods returned and the reason for their return

Credit note – a document stating that the amount owed by the buyer has decreased by a certain amount

Statement of account – a statement sent out to credit customers on a regular basis showing the amount outstanding and due from the customer at the end of the period

Remittance advice note – a document setting out exactly how a payment is made up (ie the invoices/credit notes that it is paying/netting off)

Discount policy – a company's system for giving the different types of discount to customers in order to encourage certain buying behaviours

TEST YOUR LEARNING

Test 1

Using the picklist below, identify which type of document would be used for the following purposes.

To inform the customer of the amount due for a sale	
To inform the supplier of the quantities required	
To inform the supplier that some of the delivery was not of the standard or type required	
To inform the customer of the quantity delivered	
To inform the customer that the invoiced amount was overstated	

Picklist:

Delivery note
Returns note
Quotation
Invoice
Credit note
Customer order

Test 2

(a) A customer is purchasing 23 items each with a list price of £56.00. A trade discount of 15% is given to this customer.

Calculate the total price before the discount, the discount, the net of discount price, the VAT and the gross amount.

	£
Price before discount	
Trade discount	
Net	
VAT	
Gross	

(b) Suppose that a settlement discount of 3% is also offered. Calculate the same figures on this basis.

	£
Price before discount	
Trade discount	
Net	
VAT	
Gross	

Test 3

Given below is a sales invoice. Check it carefully, state what is wrong with it and calculate the correct figures.

INVOICE

Southfield Electrical
Industrial Estate
Benham DR6 2FF
Tel 0303379 Fax 0303152
VAT Reg 0264 2274 49

To: G. Bender & Sons
14, High St.
Wentford
DR10 6LT

Invoice number: 56503

Date/tax point:

Order number: 32216

Account number:

Quantity	Description	Stock code	Unit amount £	Total £
21	Zanpoint Tumble Dryer	4610	180.00	3,870.00
10	Temax Mixer	3172	40.00	400.00
				4,270.00
Less:	15% discount			683.20

Net total	3,586.80
VAT	717.36
Invoice total	4,304.16

Terms
5% cash discount for payment within 10 days, otherwise 30 days net
E & OE

BPP
LEARNING MEDIA

Errors:

Corrected figures

	£
Tumble dryers	
Mixers	
Goods total	
Trade discount	
Net total	
VAT	
Invoice total	

Test 4

Given below are four sales invoices for Southfield Electrical:

(a) Write up the Sales Day Book using these invoices

(b) Total the columns of the Sales Day Book

Date	Customer	Invoice number	Customer code	Gross £	VAT £	Net £
	Totals					

INVOICE

Southfield Electrical
Industrial Estate
Benham DR6 2FF
Tel 0303379 Fax 0303152
VAT Reg 0264 2274 49

To: Dagwell Enterprises
Dagwell House
Hopchurch Rd
Winnish
DR2 6LT

Invoice number: 56401

Date/tax point: 21 Sept 20XX

Order number: 6123

Account number: SL 15

Quantity	Description	Product code	Unit amount £	Total £
3	Milo Dishwasher	8641	310.00	930.00
Less:	15% discount			139.50

Net total	790.50
VAT	158.10
Invoice total	948.60

Terms
Net 30 days
E & OE

INVOICE

Southfield Electrical
Industrial Estate
Benham DR6 2FF
Tel 0303379 Fax 0303152
VAT Reg 0264 2274 49

To: G. Thomas & Co
48, High Street
Cabland
DR3 8QT

Invoice number: 56402

Date/tax point: 21 Sept 20XX

Order number: 6124

Account number: SL 30

Quantity	Description	Product code	Unit amount £	Total £
16	Zanpoint Tumble Dryer	3462	220.00	3,520.00
11	Temax Kettle	6180	15.00	165.00
				3,685.00
Less:	20% discount			737.00

Net total	2,948.00
VAT	566.01
Invoice total	3,514.01

Terms
4% discount for settlement within 10 days of invoice date, otherwise net 30 days
E & OE

INVOICE

Southfield Electrical
Industrial Estate
Benham DR6 2FF
Tel 0303379 Fax 0303152
VAT Reg 0264 2274 49

To:
Polygon Stores
Grobler Street
Parrish
DR7 4TT

Invoice number: 56403

Date/tax point: 22 Sept 20XX

Order number: 6127

Account number: SL 03

Quantity	Description	Product code	Unit amount £	Total £
4	Milo Dishwasher	8641	310.00	1,240.00
2	Milo Washing Machine	8649	290.00	580.00
				1,820.00
Less:	10% discount			182.00

Net total		1,638.00
VAT		327.60
Invoice total		1,965.60

Terms
Net 30 days
E & OE

INVOICE

Southfield Electrical
Industrial Estate
Benham DR6 2FF
Tel 0303379 Fax 0303152
VAT Reg 0264 2274 49

To:

Weller Enterprises
Booker House
Industrial Estate
Benham
DR6 2FM

Invoice number: 56404

Date/tax point: 23 Sept 20XX

Order number: 6128

Account number: SL 18

Quantity	Description	Product code	Unit amount £	Total £
2	Habark cooker	1264	480.00	960.00

Net total		960.00
VAT		184.32
Invoice total		1,144.32

Terms
4% discount for settlement within 10 days of invoice date, otherwise net 30 days
E & OE

Test 5

Here are two cheques received by Southfield Electrical in the post this morning and the accompanying remittance advices. Check that the correct amount has been sent in each case. Today's date is 22 October 20XX.

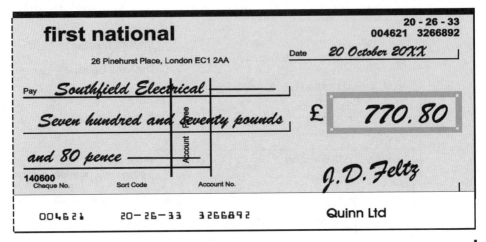

first national		20 - 26 - 33
		004621 3266892

26 Pinehurst Place, London EC1 2AA

Date   *20 October 20XX*

Pay   *Southfield Electrical*

Seven hundred and seventy pounds   £   *770.80*

and 80 pence

140600
Cheque No.   Sort Code   Account No.

J.D. Feltz

    004621   20—26—33   3266892   **Quinn Ltd**

REMITTANCE ADVICE

To: Southfield Electrical
          Industrial Estate
          Benham
          DR6 2FF
          Tel 0303379 Fax 0303152

From: Quinn Ltd

Date: 20 October 20XX

Reference	Amount	Paid (✓)
30128	325.61	✓
CN2269	18.80	✓
30201	463.27	✓

CHEQUE ENCLOSED	£770.08

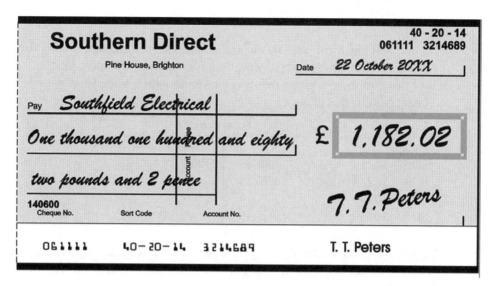

REMITTANCE ADVICE

To: Southfield Electrical
Industrial Estate
Benham
DR6 2FF
Tel 0303379 Fax 0303152

From: T.T. Peters

Date: 22 October 20XX

Reference	Amount	Paid (✓)
30196	556.28	✓
30217	180.53	✓
30223	267.03	
30237	454.21	✓

CHEQUE ENCLOSED	£1,182.02

Test 6

Southfield Electrical have received a cheque from a customer, Long Bros, for £226.79 with no accompanying documentation. The sales ledger account for this customer is given below. Determine which invoices/credit notes are being paid by this cheque.

Long Bros			SL 42
Details	£	Details	£
SDB – 30219	88.37	SRDB – CN2381	15.80
SDB – 30234	157.35		
SDB – 30239	85.24		
SDB – 30250	265.49		

Invoice/credit note number	£
Total	

Test 7

The following transactions all took place on 30 November and have been entered into the Sales Day Book as shown below. No entries have yet been made into the ledger system.

Sales Day Book

Date 20XX	Details	Invoice number	Gross £	VAT £	Net £
30 Nov	Fries & Co	23907	2,136	356	1,780
30 Nov	Hussey Enterprises	23908	3,108	518	2,590
30 Nov	Todd Trading	23909	3,720	620	3,100
30 Nov	Milford Ltd	23910	2,592	432	2,160
	Totals		11,556	1,926	9,630

What will be the entries in the sales ledger?

Sales ledger

Account name	Amount £	Left side of account ✓	Right side of account ✓	Details in account

Test 8

Sales invoices have been prepared and partially entered in the analysed Sales Day Book, as shown below.

(a) Complete the entries in the Sales Day Book by inserting the appropriate figures for each invoice.

(b) Total the last five columns of the Sales Day Book.

Sales Day Book

Date 20XX	Details	Invoice number	Gross £	VAT £	Net £	Sales type 1 £	Sales type 2 £
30 Nov	Wright & Co	5627		2,000		10,000	
30 Nov	H Topping	5628	1,560				1,300
30 Nov	Sage Ltd	5629	600			500	
	Totals						

Test 9

On 1 December Wendlehurst Trading delivered the following goods to a credit customer, Stroll In Stores.

Wendlehurst Trading
Delivery note No. 8973 01 Dec 20XX Stroll In Stores Customer account code: ST725   600 1 litre bottles Tiger pop, product code TIG300.

The list price of the goods was £10 per case of 12 bottles plus VAT. Stroll In Stores are to be given a 15% trade discount and a 4% early settlement discount.

Complete the invoice below.

Wendlehurst Trading
VAT Registration No. 876983479

Stroll In Stores

Customer account code:
Delivery note number:
Date: 1 Dec 20XX

Invoice No: 624

Quantity of cases	Product code	Total list price £	Net amount after discount £	VAT £	Gross £

Test 10

The following is a summary of transactions between Wendlehurst Trading and Holroyda, a new credit customer.

£4,390 re invoice 5607 of 18 November
£1,400 re invoice 5612 of 21 November
£160 re credit note 524 of 22 November
£980 re invoice 5616 of 29 November
Payment of £4,000 received 30 November

Complete the statement of account below.

Wendlehurst Trading
VAT Registration No. 876983479

To: Holroyda   Date: 30 Nov 20XX

Date 20XX	Details	Transaction amount £	Outstanding amount £

chapter 5:
RECORDING CREDIT PURCHASES

---

chapter coverage 📖

In this chapter we look at credit purchases and all of the documents that accompany a purchase on credit. The topics covered are:

- ✍ Ordering goods
- ✍ Receiving goods
- ✍ Returning goods
- ✍ Checking the invoice and credit note
- ✍ Authorisation of purchase invoices
- ✍ Writing up the Purchases Day Book and ledger
- ✍ Reconciling suppliers' statements
- ✍ When to pay supplier invoices
- ✍ Amount of the payment
- ✍ The remittance advice note

ORDERING GOODS

We have seen how the business document cycle works when looking at it from the viewpoint of the supplier of goods. Now we will look at it in more detail from the customer's or purchaser's side.

The initial stage is that of ordering the goods. This can be done in a variety of ways:

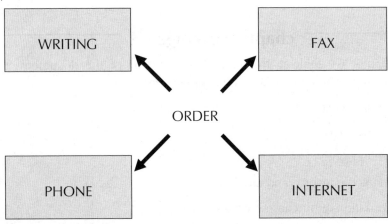

In writing or by fax

A common way of ordering goods is in writing. This could be in the form of a letter but if many orders are placed with suppliers then it is more likely that the organisation will have pre-printed and sequentially numbered purchase order forms.

The order seen in Chapter 4 that was a customer order from the point of view of the supplier (Southfield Electrical) is a PURCHASE ORDER from the point of view of the customer (Whitehill Superstores).

PURCHASE ORDER

WHITEHILL SUPERSTORES
28 Whitehill Park
Benham DR6 5LM
Tel 0303446 Fax 0303447

To: Southfield Electrical
Industrial Estate
Benham
DR6 2FF

Number: 32011

Date: 5 Sept 20XX

Delivery address: Whitehill Superstores
28, Whitehill Park
Benham DR6 5LM

Product code	Quantity	Description	Unit list price £
4425	6	Zanpoint Dishwasher	200 (excluding VAT)

Authorised by: _P. Winterbottom_   **Date:** _5 Sept 20XX_

The purchase order is from Whitehill Superstores to Southfield Electrical and details the quantity, the specific item and the agreed price. The important issue from Whitehill's side is that it is properly authorised. Obviously, it is necessary for any business to ensure that only goods that are absolutely necessary are purchased, and therefore there should be strict controls over who can authorise purchase orders.

Over the phone

Goods are often ordered by phone, particularly where either the customer and supplier are well known to each other or the purchases are of small quantities. If an order is placed over the phone the most important issue is that a record is kept of what has been agreed in case of future dispute. The customer may ask the supplier for a confirmation of the order that has been placed or, at the very least, make a file note of the price and any other terms agreed over the phone.

On the internet

Goods can be ordered over the internet (on a website or by email) if it is an allowed method of ordering items according to the organisation's policy manual, and if it has been authorised by an appropriate member of senior staff. Many internet orders are actually cash purchases using the business debit card, but in this chapter we shall assume that they are all credit transactions.

When placing an order, ensure that a copy is printed out to be placed on file.

Order details

Whatever method of ordering is used, a copy of the order details must be kept in the filing system in the accounts department. This will be compared with the supplier's delivery note and invoice to ensure that only goods that have been properly authorised for ordering are received and paid for.

RECEIVING GOODS

Once the goods have been ordered, the next stage in the process is that they will be received. This will usually take place in the stores department or warehouse and an important part of the process takes place here.

When the goods arrive they will normally be accompanied by a delivery note. The DELIVERY NOTE used in Chapter 4 for the delivery from Southfield to Whitehill is reproduced on the following page:

DELIVERY NOTE

Southfield Electrical
Industrial Estate
Benham DR6 2FF
Tel 0303379 Fax 0303152

Delivery address:

Whitehill Superstores
28, Whitehill Park
Benham DR6 5LM

Number: 34619
Date: 6 Sept 20XX
Order number: 32011

Product code	Quantity	Description
4425	6	Zanpoint Dishwasher

Received by: [Signature] *R. Stansted*   **Print name:** *R. STANSTED*

Date: *6 Sept 20XX*

- The delivery note details the quantity and precise description of the goods using both the description in words and the product code.

- There is no price as this is not relevant in the stores department.

- The delivery note includes the related order number.

- The delivery note must be signed to evidence the fact that these goods have been delivered.

The signature of the stores personnel is extremely important. It proves that the carrier of the goods did indeed deliver these goods and that the purchaser actually received them.

The most important point for the stores personnel to check is that the quantity actually delivered is what is stated on the delivery note. In some cases, it may be possible to check that none of the goods has any defects at the time of delivery but normally this will take place later. The initial signature from the stores manager on this delivery note is simply evidence that this number of these precise goods were delivered on this date.

Goods received note

In many organisations, in addition to signing the delivery note, an internal document will also be filled out by the customer's stores department known as the GOODS RECEIVED NOTE. This is completed once there has been an opportunity to examine the goods in more detail. A goods received note for the delivery to Whitehill from Southfield is shown below:

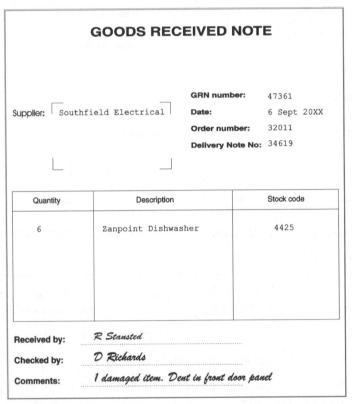

GOODS RECEIVED NOTE

GRN number:	47361
Date:	6 Sept 20XX
Order number:	32011
Delivery Note No:	34619

Supplier: Southfield Electrical

Quantity	Description	Stock code
6	Zanpoint Dishwasher	4425

Received by: R Stansted

Checked by: D Richards

Comments: 1 damaged item. Dent in front door panel

Note the main points:

- The goods received note (GRN) has its own sequential number.

- It is referenced to the order number and delivery note number, both taken from the copy of the supplier's delivery note kept by the stores department.

- The quantity and precise detail of the goods received are noted.

- In order to ensure the security of the goods being received, the GRN is not only signed by the person who received delivery of the goods but also by a second person who checked them.

- Once there has been a chance to examine the goods in detail, any comments on their condition can then be added to the GRN. Note that in this case one of the machines is damaged and this has been noted.

Documentation for the accounts department

Once the stores department has dealt with checking the goods, all the documentation is then passed over to the accounts department. At this stage the accounts department potentially has a price list and quotation from the supplier, its own purchase order, a delivery note from the supplier and its own goods received note.

The accounts department must check that the delivery note agrees with the purchase order to ensure that what was ordered has actually arrived. The details should then be compared with the goods received note to ensure that the goods that were actually delivered were of the correct quality and condition.

RETURNING GOODS

If the goods supplied are the wrong ones or are not of the quality or in the condition expected they will be returned to the supplier. Often the return of the goods will be accompanied by a RETURNS NOTE detailing the goods returned and the reason for their return. The contents of this are very similar to the goods received note.

Whitehill Superstores	**RETURNS NOTE**	
Supplier	Southfield Electrical	
Goods received note number		47361
Returns note number		8909
Date		7 Sept 20XX
Order number		32011
Delivery note number		34619
Quantity	**Description**	**Product code**
1	Zanpoint dishwasher	4425
Returned by	D Richards	
Comment	Dent to front door panel	

CHECKING THE INVOICE AND CREDIT NOTE

The next item in the purchase cycle is the receipt of the INVOICE from the supplier. This is the document that will eventually form the authorisation for payment of the amount due to the supplier. Many checks must be carried out on this invoice before it is authorised for payment.

Step 1   Have the goods been received? Agree the details to the purchase order, the delivery note and the goods received note. Do they all agree in terms of quantity, quality and price? In the scenario of Whitehill and Southfield the following invoice is received from Southfield:

INVOICE	Invoice number 56314		
Southfield Electrical **Industrial Estate** **Benham DR6 2FF** **Tel: 01239 345639**			
VAT registration:	0264 2274 49		
Date/tax point:	7 September 20XX		
Order number:	32011		
Customer:	Whitehill Superstores 28 Whitehill Park Benham DR6 5LM		
Account number (customer code)	SL 44		
Description/product code	**Quantity**	**Unit amount £**	**Total £**
Zanpoint dishwashers /4425	6	200.00	1,200.00
Net total			1,200.00
VAT at 20%			240.00
Gross total			1,440.00
Terms 30 days net			

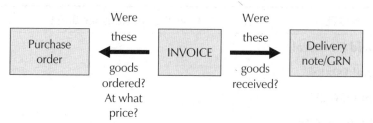

This invoice is for the six dishwashers delivered although the delivery note shows that though six dishwashers were delivered the goods received note indicates that one was not of acceptable quality.

Whitehill's accounts department will check that a returns note was sent when the damaged dishwasher was returned and will not pay the invoice until the related credit note is received.

When the CREDIT NOTE arrives it is again checked to the file of documentation on this purchase which now consists of (potentially):

- Quotation and price list
- Purchase order
- Delivery note
- Goods received note
- Returns note
- Invoice

CREDIT NOTE	Credit note number 08641
Southfield Electrical **Industrial Estate** **Benham DR6 2FF** **Tel: 01239 345639**	
VAT registration:	0264 2274 49
Date/tax point:	12 September 20XX
Order number:	32011
Customer:	Whitehill Superstores 28 Whitehill Park Benham DR6 5LM
Account number (customer code)	SL 44

Description/product code	Quantity	Unit amount £	Total £
Zanpoint dishwasher /4425 Reason for credit note: Delivered damaged	1	200.00	200.00
Net total			200.00
VAT at 20%			40.00
Gross total			240.00
Terms 30 days net			

Step 2   Are the calculations on the documents correct?

HOW IT WORKS

The invoice and credit note considered so far have been very uncomplicated. However, when trade, bulk and settlement discounts are introduced the checks that have to be made become more involved.

Given below is the more complex invoice that Whitehill Superstores received from Southfield Electrical in Chapter 4:

INVOICE	Invoice number 56483		
Southfield Electricals Industrial Estate Benham DR6 2FF Tel: 01239 345639			
VAT registration:	0264 2274 49		
Date/tax point:	8 October 20XX		
Order number:	32174		
Customer:	Whitehill Superstores 28 Whitehill Park Benham DR6 5LM		
Account number (customer code)	SL 44		
Description/product code	Quantity	Unit amount £	Total £
Hosch washing machine /6160	4	300.00	1,200.00
Temax Mixer /3172	9	40.00	360.00
List price			1,560.00
Less trade discount 10%			(156.00)
List price net of trade discount			1,404.00
Less bulk discount 5%			(70.20)
Net total			1,333.80
VAT at 20%			256.09
Gross total			1,589.89
Terms 4% discount for settlement within 10 days of invoice date, otherwise 30 days net			

Task 1

The net total of goods purchased from a supplier is £1,600 and the supplier has offered a settlement discount of 5%. What is the correct amount of VAT to be charged on the invoice?

£ |

The checks that should be made on this invoice are as follows (the same sorts of check will apply to credit notes):

- Compare the purchase order, delivery note and goods received note to the invoice to ensure that the correct quantity has been invoiced.

- Check the percentage discounts agree to the discount policy agreed with this supplier: 10% trade discount, 5% bulk discount for orders over £1,000, 4% settlement discount for payment within ten days.

- Check that the unit prices are correct – this may be noted from the supplier's quotation or price list.

- Check that the total price for each item has been correctly calculated by multiplying the unit price by the quantity, eg 4 × £300 = £1,200.

- Check that the total list price has been correctly added up, eg £1,200 + £360.00 = £1,560.00.

- Check that the trade discount has been correctly calculated, eg £1,560 × 10/100 = £156, and that it has been deducted correctly, eg £1,560.00 – £156.00 = £1,404.00.

- Check that the bulk discount has been deducted as due (since the total after trade discount exceeds £1,000) and that it has been calculated correctly, eg £1,404.00 × 5/100 = £70.20; net total is therefore £1,404.00 – £70.20 = £1,333.80.

- Check that the VAT is correct – remember that when a settlement discount is offered the VAT is calculated on the basis that the discount is actually taken:

	£
Net total	1,333.80
Less settlement discount (£1,333.80 × 4/100)	(53.35)
	1,280.45
VAT £1,280.45 × 20/100.00	256.09

- Check that the VAT has been correctly added to the net total, eg £1,333.80 + £256.09 = £1,589.89.

Services received

One of the initial checks on goods is that they are actually received, evidenced by a delivery note or goods received note. With services there will not be any physical goods.

It is still important to check that the services that have been invoiced have been received. Typical invoices for services might include utilities such as electricity, gas and phone bills. Such bills can usually be checked to meter readings and for reasonableness, for example each organisation should have an idea of the normal value of the phone bill and therefore if a very different amount is billed then this should be investigated.

Other services that may be invoiced are items such as cleaning services carried out by contractors. There should be evidence of the hours that have been worked and billed, such as clock cards or time sheets. Alternatively, service providers such as the cleaning contractors or annual auditors may have already agreed a fee, so the documentation for that agreement should be checked upon receipt of the invoice.

AUTHORISATION OF PURCHASE INVOICES

When the accuracy of an invoice has been thoroughly checked it is ready for payment at the appropriate time and is passed to the person in the accounts department who is responsible for making payments.

There must be some evidence to show that the invoice has been checked and is therefore correct and authorised for payment. Each organisation will have different methods of indicating that an invoice has been checked and authorised as illustrated below.

- The simplest method is for the invoice to be stamped or marked 'pay' and signed by the checker.

- A more detailed method might be to stamp the invoice with a standard checklist or attach such a checklist to the invoice to be marked off as each check is carried out, an example of which follows.

INVOICE AUTHORISATION		
	Initials	**Date**
Checked to order		
Checked to delivery note/GRN		
Unit price checked		
Trade/bulk discounts checked		
Total price checked		
VAT checked		
Authorised by:	**Date:**	

Settlement discounts

Some authorisation stamps may also include space for the amount of any settlement discount that can be deducted when making the payment. This should be calculated when checking the invoice and entered in this space.

The discount that can be deducted is the relevant percentage of the net total of goods, as the VAT calculation should have already taken the settlement discount into account.

An extract from an invoice where a 3% settlement discount has been offered is given:

	£
Net total	2,000.00
VAT	388.00
Gross total	2,388.00

The amount of settlement discount that could be deducted from the invoice total is 3% of the net total calculated as follows:

$£2,000 \times 3/100 = £60.00$

This amount can be entered onto the authorisation stamp and the payer can decide whether or not to pay the invoice in time to claim the settlement discount. Alternatively, it may be the policy of the organisation that the discount is not calculated until the person responsible for paying the invoice deals with it.

Task 2

An invoice for goods shows the net total of the goods as £800.00 and the VAT as £155.20 giving a gross total of £955.20. A settlement discount of 3% is offered. How much discount can be deducted?

£ [   ]

Coding of purchase invoices/credit notes

The authorisation stamp may also have space for entries to be made to code the purchase invoice and/or credit note. The document will eventually have to be entered into the accounting records and the codes that may be included on the authorisation stamp would be:

- The supplier code, probably the purchase ledger account number

- A product code for the type of goods or service that is being invoiced in order to aid recording in the accounting records, especially in the analysed Purchases Day Book where, as we saw in relation to the Sales Day Book, analysis may be based on the prefixes of the product codes

WRITING UP THE PURCHASES DAY BOOK AND LEDGER

The invoice is entered by Whitehill Superstores into its Purchases Day Book and from there into the purchases ledger account for Southfield Electricals (the supplier code and purchases ledger account code are both PL 73).

Purchases Day Book

Date 20XX	Supplier	Invoice number	Supplier code	Gross £	VAT £	Net £
8 Oct	Southfield Electricals	56483	PL 73	1,589.89	256.09	1,333.80

Purchases ledger

		Southfield Electricals	**PL 73**
Details	£	Details	£
		PDB – 56483	1,589.89

Where a credit note from a supplier has been received, the Purchases Returns Day Book and purchases ledger are written up.

RECONCILING SUPPLIERS' STATEMENTS

The final document that may be received by a purchaser of goods from the supplier is a statement of account. As we have already seen from the supplier's side, this is produced by the supplier on a regular basis and sent out to the purchaser.

A supplier's statement of account is a very important double check on the accuracy of the purchasing organisation's accounting records. The statement is checked for accuracy to the individual supplier's account in the purchaser's purchases ledger, with any differences carefully explained. This process is called RECONCILING supplier statements.

HOW IT WORKS

At the end of February 20XX Whitehill Superstores has the following transactions recorded in its purchases ledger account for Southfield Electricals:

Purchases Ledger

Southfield Electricals			PL 73
Details	£	Details	£
PRDB – CN09543	734.25	PDB – 58256	2,089.76
CB – payment	1,301.31	PDB – 58311	1,240.00
CB – discount received	54.20	PDB – 58325	3,287.09

Whitehill Superstores knows that the history of the account in February is as follows:

- Three invoices from Southfield were recorded towards the end of the month.

- In respect of the first invoice (total £2,089.76) a credit note for £734.25 was received.

- Whitehill wished to settle the remaining amount of the first invoice (£2,089.76 – £734.25 = £1,355.51), after deducting a settlement discount of £54.20, so it sent a payment of £1,355.51 – £54.20 = £1,301.31.

- Whitehill has decided to leave paying the second two invoices until March, so at the end of February it owed Southfield £1,240.00 + £3,287.09 = £4,527.09.

Right at the beginning of March Whitehill receives the following statement of account from Southfield:

STATEMENT OF ACCOUNT	
Southfield Electricals **Industrial Estate** **Benham DR6 2FF** **Tel: 01239 345639**	
VAT registration:	0264 2274 49
Date:	28 February 20XX
Customer:	Whitehill Superstores 28 Whitehill Park Benham DR6 5LM
Account number (customer code)	SL 44

Date	Details	Amount £	Balance £
23 Feb	Invoice 58256	2,089.76	2,089.76
27 Feb	Credit note 09543	(734.25)	1,355.51
27 Feb	Invoice 58311	1,240.00	2,595.51
28 Feb	Invoice 58325	3,287.09	5,882.60

Amount now due	5,882.60

Terms

4% discount for settlement within 10 days of invoice date, otherwise 30 days net

Evidently the customer and the supplier do not agree how much is outstanding. The difference between them is:

	£
Amount per supplier statement	5,882.60
Amount per purchases ledger	4,527.09
Difference	1,355.51

The supplier, Southfield Electricals, is saying that the customer, Whitehill Superstores, owes £1,355.51 more than Whitehill thinks it does.

By looking at the amount of the difference it is clear that Southfield Electricals thinks that Whitehill still owes the net amount of the first invoice and the credit note, while Whitehill shows in the purchases ledger account that it has settled this amount. This is confirmed when we note that the supplier's statement does not contain details of the automated payment made and settlement discount taken. Clearly, the automated payment had not yet reached Southfield Electricals by the time it prepared the statement.

We can therefore explain the difference between the parties as a TIMING DIFFERENCE, and produce a RECONCILIATION which shows how the difference is made up:

Reconciliation statement

As at 28 February 20XX	£
Amount per Southfield statement	5,882.60
Amount per Whitehill purchases ledger	4,527.09
Difference	1,355.51

Explained by: timing differences

Automated payment made, not received as at 28 Feb	1,301.31
Settlement discount taken with payment, not recorded as at 28 Feb	54.20
	1,355.51

WHEN TO PAY SUPPLIER INVOICES

When all the checks have been carried out and it has been determined that the invoice is correct then it must be passed for payment. Organisations use different methods to determine when invoices should be paid.

Paying by supplier statement

Once the supplier statement has been reconciled to the purchases ledger, in many organisations the statement is used as the means of identifying what amounts should be paid. In other words, payment is only made upon receipt and reconciliation of a supplier's statement of account. Such statements are normally received just after the end of the month and will have been prepared as at the end of the month. Payment will then be made according to the supplier's terms. This means that all invoices, less credit notes, that are more than, say, 30 days old will be paid.

HOW IT WORKS

The following statement is received by Dagwell Enterprises from their supplier Southfield Electricals on 4 December 20XX.

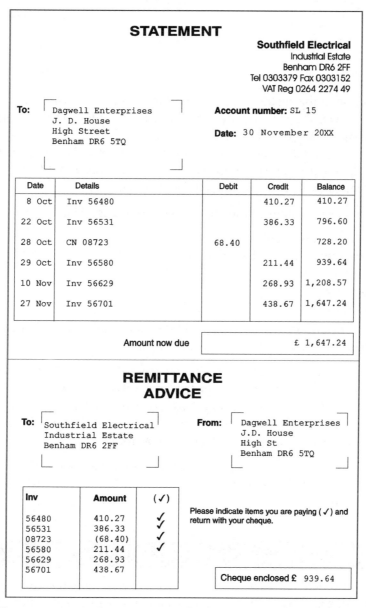

STATEMENT

Southfield Electrical
Industrial Estate
Benham DR6 2FF
Tel 0303379 Fax 0303152
VAT Reg 0264 2274 49

To: Dagwell Enterprises
J. D. House
High Street
Benham DR6 5TQ

Account number: SL 15

Date: 30 November 20XX

Date	Details	Debit	Credit	Balance
8 Oct	Inv 56480		410.27	410.27
22 Oct	Inv 56531		386.33	796.60
28 Oct	CN 08723	68.40		728.20
29 Oct	Inv 56580		211.44	939.64
10 Nov	Inv 56629		268.93	1,208.57
27 Nov	Inv 56701		438.67	1,647.24

Amount now due	£ 1,647.24

REMITTANCE ADVICE

To: Southfield Electrical
Industrial Estate
Benham DR6 2FF

From: Dagwell Enterprises
J.D. House
High St
Benham DR6 5TQ

Inv	Amount	(✓)
56480	410.27	✓
56531	386.33	✓
08723	(68.40)	✓
56580	211.44	✓
56629	268.93	
56701	438.67	

Please indicate items you are paying (✓) and return with your cheque.

Cheque enclosed £	939.64

If Dagwell Enterprises' policy is to pay all of the invoices dated up to a month before the statement date, it would pay off the following invoices with one payment:

	£
Invoice 56480	410.27
Invoice 56531	386.33
CN 08723	(68.40)
Invoice 56580	211.44
	939.64

The advantage of this method of payment is that only one payment is made each month. However, the main disadvantage is that any settlement discounts offered would be lost, as any payment made would be too late to take advantage of the discount. It also means that a longer period of credit is being taken than the stated 30 days. For example the invoice dated 8 October is not being paid until early December, which is closer to 60 days of credit.

Rather than pay by statement therefore some businesses will make:

- Payment by invoice; or
- Payment on a regular timescale.

Paying by invoice

This system means that a precise payment date for each invoice is set when it has been checked and authorised as ready for payment.

The payment date will depend upon the payment terms of the invoice and whether or not any settlement discount is to be taken. If there is no settlement discount offered then most organisations are likely to take as much credit as possible in order to keep money in their own bank account for as long as possible, thereby earning interest or reducing overdraft interest.

Therefore when the invoice is passed for payment, the invoice date and terms should be checked in order to determine the latest date on which payment should be made.

HOW IT WORKS

If an invoice dated 23 May is received on 26 May and the terms state that payment is due in 30 days then the payment date would be calculated as 22 June (as there are 31 days in May). The payment should reach the supplier on this date so the day for writing the cheque or authorising the automated payment is 20 June. This payment date must then be recorded in a diary system which will show the precise invoices that are due to be paid each day.

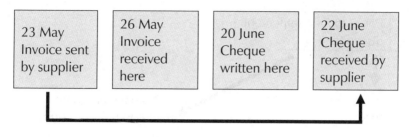

30 days

Task 3

An invoice is received on 14 July. The invoice is dated 9 July and the terms are stated as 'net 30 days'. Payment is to be made by cheque and posted and this takes three days from writing out the cheque to receipt by the supplier. When should the cheque be written?

Settlement discounts

If a settlement discount is offered on an invoice then there are further considerations in deciding when to make payment.

- Is it the organisation's policy to take settlement discounts? If a settlement discount is taken then obviously a smaller amount is paid to the supplier, but it is paid earlier, meaning that money leaves the organisation's bank account earlier. This reduces any interest receivable on the account or increases any overdraft interest.

- If the policy of the organisation is only to take settlement discounts from some suppliers, depending upon the terms that they offer, is this supplier one of those for which a settlement discount should be taken?

- If the settlement discount is to be taken, how much should the payment be and when should it be made?

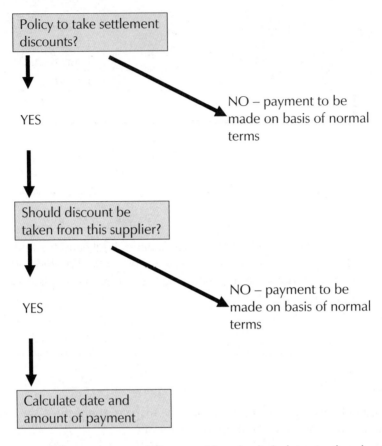

The amount of the payment will be considered a little later in the chapter. Here we will consider the timing of the payment.

HOW IT WORKS

An invoice is received on 10 December and is dated 8 December. The terms show that a settlement discount of 3.5% is offered for payment received within 14 days of the invoice date. Payment is to be made by cheque and posted, which takes two days. When should the cheque be written in order to take advantage of the discount?

The invoice is dated 8 December, so to take advantage of the settlement discount the payment must reach the supplier no later than 22 December. Therefore the cheque should be written on 20 December at the very latest.

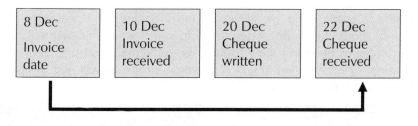

14 days

Task 4

An invoice dated 23 November is received on 25 November. The settlement discount of 4% for payment within ten days of the invoice date is to be taken and the payment will be received by the supplier two days after the cheque is written. What is the latest date that the cheque should be written?

Payment on a regular timescale

In practice, many organisations may make payments on a weekly basis rather than a daily or monthly basis. So, for example, payments may be made every Friday instead of every day. In this case, when an invoice is passed for payment it must be determined which Friday the payment must be paid in order not to exceed the credit period.

HOW IT WORKS

An invoice dated Monday 7 August is received from the supplier on Thursday 10 August. The stated credit terms are 30 days from the invoice date. With 30 days credit the payment should reach the supplier by Wednesday 6 September, so the cheque needs to be written on the previous Friday, 1 September.

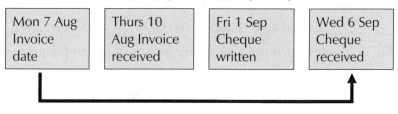

30 days

If payment is made on a weekly basis and a settlement discount is offered, calculations should be made to determine in which week the payment must be made in order to be able validly to take the settlement discount. This must be done promptly or the period in which the discount is valid will pass, no payment will be made and the discount will be lost.

AMOUNT OF THE PAYMENT

As well as making sure that payments are made according to the organisational timescales that are set, the correct amount must be paid.

Settlement discounts

Calculation of the settlement discount to be deducted may be made when the invoice is checked for accuracy as we saw earlier or it may be made at this later stage.

Remember that the settlement discount to be deducted from the invoice total is the discount percentage of the net total on the invoice. The VAT has already been calculated on the basis that the discount will be taken.

HOW IT WORKS

Given below is an extract from one of Whitehill Superstores' invoices:

	£
Net total	3,000.00
VAT	588.00
Gross total	3,588.00

Terms 2% settlement discount for payment received within 14 days of the invoice date

The payment that will be made if the discount is taken is calculated as follows:

Step 1   Calculate the discount to be deducted:

£3,000.00 × 2/100 = £60.00

Step 2   Deduct the discount from the gross total to find the amount to be paid:

£3,588.00 – £60.00 = £3,528.00

Task 5

An invoice is received by your organisation on which a settlement discount of 2.5% is offered. The totals are given below:

	£
Net total	2,000.00
VAT	390.00
Gross total	2,390.00

Calculate the amount of the payment required if the discount is taken.

£ _____

THE REMITTANCE ADVICE NOTE

We saw earlier that when a supplier sends a statement of account to a customer a tear-off REMITTANCE ADVICE NOTE is often added to the bottom, for the customer to fill in showing the details and amounts of the invoices being paid, less credit notes and settlement discounts. When filling in a remittance advice note – on a statement or generated within the business – and totalling it to find the total payment, care should be taken to ensure that the total is correctly added up.

HOW IT WORKS

The statement of account received by Dagwell Enterprises earlier is shown again.

STATEMENT

Southfield Electrical
Industrial Estate
Benham DR6 2FF
Tel 0303379 Fax 0303152
VAT Reg 0264 2274 49

To: Dagwell Enterprises
J. D. House
High Street
Benham DR6 5TQ

Account number: SL 15

Date: 30 November 20XX

Date	Details	Debit	Credit	Balance
8 Oct	Inv 56480		410.27	410.27
22 Oct	Inv 56531		386.33	796.60
28 Oct	CN 08723	68.40		728.20
29 Oct	Inv 56580		211.44	939.64
10 Nov	Inv 56629		268.93	1,208.57
27 Nov	Inv 56701		438.67	1,647.24

Amount now due £ 1,647.24

REMITTANCE ADVICE

To: Southfield Electrical
Industrial Estate
Benham DR6 2FF

From: Dagwell Enterprises
J.D. House
High St
Benham DR6 5TQ

Inv	Amount	(✓)
56480	410.27	✓
56531	386.33	✓
08723	(68.40)	✓
56580	211.44	✓
56629	268.93	
56701	438.67	

Please indicate items you are paying (✓) and return with your cheque.

Cheque enclosed £ 939.64

The invoices and credit notes that are being settled by this payment are ticked and then added up and the total entered in the 'cheque enclosed' section. If the addition is incorrect then the amount paid will also be incorrect.

CHAPTER OVERVIEW

- The main methods of ordering goods are in writing, by fax, over the telephone and over the Internet

- Whatever method of ordering is used, there must be some form of evidence of the goods ordered as this will be needed later when the goods and then the invoice are received

- When the goods are received they will normally be accompanied by a delivery note which must be checked and signed as evidence that the stated quantity of goods was delivered

- On receipt of goods many organisations complete an internal document, the goods received note, detailing the quantity and condition of the goods received

- The accounts department opens a file for each purchase which will include the purchase quotation, the purchase order, the delivery note and the goods received note

- If goods have to be returned to the supplier a returns note may be issued, formally requesting a credit note from the supplier for the returned goods

- When the invoice is received it must first be checked to the purchase order to ensure that the goods were ordered and to the delivery note and GRN to ensure that they were received

- When any related credit note is received this should be filed with the invoice awaiting payment

- All of the calculations on a supplier's invoice should be checked including the deduction of trade discount, any bulk discount, the calculation of total price from quantity and unit price, the additions and the VAT calculation

- Credit notes received should be checked in exactly the same manner

- When invoices for services are received there will be no delivery note or GRN but evidence must be sought that the service has been provided and that the amount charged is reasonable or the agreed amount

- When all of the checks have been carried out and it has been determined that the invoice is correct then it must be passed for payment

- At this point it may be the organisation's policy for the amount of any settlement discount offered to be calculated – this is the given percentage of the net total of the invoice

- The invoice will probably be coded at this stage to indicate the supplier and the type of goods or services using the supplier code and some element of the product code

- At regular intervals it is likely that the organisation may receive statements from suppliers showing the amount currently due – this may include a tear-off remittance advice which should be returned with the payment indicating which invoices have been paid

Keywords

Purchase order – the written document sent from the buyer to the supplier detailing the goods that are being ordered and the agreed price

Delivery note – the document sent by the supplier with the goods detailing which goods, and in what quantities, are being sent

Goods received note – an internal document completed by the buyer on receipt of the goods showing the quantity and condition of the goods received

Returns note – the document sent by the customer to the supplier detailing the goods returned and the reason for their return

Credit note – a document stating that the amount owed by the buyer has decreased by a certain amount

Invoice – a document that clearly sets out what money is owed by a named customer to a named supplier in respect of particular goods or services

Reconciliation – a statement showing how any difference owing between parties is made up

Remittance advice note – a document setting out exactly how a payment is made up (ie the invoices/credit notes that it is paying/netting off)

Reconciling – process of checking a suppliers statement of account with organisational records and finding reasons for any discrepancies

Timing difference – reason for a variance in a reconciliation – for example, a payment has been made but has not yet reached the supplier's account when the statement is prepared

TEST YOUR LEARNING

Test 1

Using the picklist below, identify which type of document would be used for the following purposes.

To accompany goods being returned to a supplier	
To record for internal purposes the quantity of goods received	
To request payment from a purchaser of goods	
To order goods from a supplier	
To accompany payment to a supplier	

Picklist:

Delivery note
Returns note
Quotation
Remittance advice note
Invoice
Credit note
Goods received note
Purchase order

Test 2

Given below are an invoice and credit note received by A J Hammond and the related purchase order, delivery note and goods received note. Check the invoice and credit note thoroughly and note any problems that there might be.

INVOICE

P T Cards
Foram Road
Winnesh DR3 4TP
Tel 0611223 Fax 0611458
VAT Reg 0661 3247 98

To:

A.J. Hammond
Brockham Park Estate
Winnesh DR3 2XJ

Invoice number: 46298

Date/tax point: 5 Oct 20XX

Order number: 304051

Account number: H03

Quantity	Description	Product code	Unit amount £	Total £
200	Birthday Cards	TN451	0.89	178.00
600	Christmas Cards	SJ106	0.45	270.00
100	Get Well Cards	GW444	0.33	33.00

Net total	481.00
VAT	96.20
Invoice total	577.20

Terms
E & OE

CREDIT NOTE

P T Cards
Foram Road
Winnesh DR3 4TP
Tel 0611223 Fax 0611458
VAT Reg 0661 3247 98

Credit note to:

A.J. Hammond
Brockham Park Estate
Winnesh DR3 2XJ

Credit note number: 31313
Date/tax point: 10 Oct 20XX
Order number: 304051
Account number: H03

Quantity	Description	Product code	Unit amount £	Total £
30	Get Well Cards	GW444	0.25	7.50

Net total		7.50
VAT		1.50
Gross total		9.00

Reason for credit note:

Not ordered

PURCHASE ORDER

A J HAMMOND
Brockham Park Estate
Winnesh DR3 2XJ

To: P.T.Cards
Foram Road
Winnesh DR3 4TP

Number: 304051

Date: 13 Sept 20XX

Delivery address: As above

Product code	Quantity	Description	Price (£)
SJ106	600	Christmas Cards	0.45
GW444	70	Get well Cards	0.33
TN451	200	Birthday Cards	0.89

Authorised by: *P T Thomas*   **Date:** *13 Sept 20XX*

DELIVERY NOTE

P T Cards
Foram Road
Winnesh DR3 4TP
Tel 0611223 Fax 0611458

Delivery address:

A.J.Hammond
Brockham Park Estate
Winnesh DR3 2XJ

Number: 21690

Date: 20 Sept 20XX

Order number: 304051

Product code	Quantity	Description
SJ106	600	Christmas Cards
GW444	100	Get Well Cards
TN451	200	Birthday Cards

Received by: [Signature] *J T Turner*   **Print name:** *J T TURNER*

Date: *20 Sept 20XX*

GOODS RECEIVED NOTE

A J Hammond
Brockham Park Estate
Winnesh DR3 2XJ

Supplier:

GRN number: 27420

Date: 21 Sept 20XX

Order number: 304051

Delivery Note No: 21690

Quantity	Description	Product code
200	Birthday Cards	TN 451
100	Get Well Cards	GW 444
600	Christmas Cards	SJ 106

Received by: *P Darren*

Checked by: *D Gough*

Comments: *All in good condition*

Test 3

Given below are three invoices received from suppliers by Whitehill Superstores.

An extract from the supplier code listing is given:

Bass Engineers   PL 13

Southfield Electrical   PL 20

Herne Industries   PL 15

Today's date is 20 October. You are required to record the invoice details in the Purchases Day Book and also total the Purchases Day Book.

Purchases Day Book

Date	Supplier	Invoice number	Supplier code	Gross £	VAT £	Net £
		Total				

INVOICE

Herne Industries
Fuller House
Bean Park
Benham DR6 3PQ
Tel 0303226 Fax 0303582
VAT Reg 0624 3361 29

To:
Whitehill Superstores
28, Whitehill Park
Benham DR6 5LM

Invoice number: 46121

Date/tax point: 16 Oct 20XX

Order number: 32216

Account number: SL 23

Quantity	Description	Product code	Unit amount £	Total £
3	Komax Camcorder	KC410	240.00	720.00

Net total	720.00
VAT	144.00
Invoice total	864.00

Terms
Net 30 days
E & OE

INVOICE

Bass Engineers
Bass House
Parrish DR3 2FL
Tel 0462333 Fax 0462334
VAT Reg 2016 2131 87

To: Whitehill Superstores
28, Whitehill Park
Benham DR6 5LM

Invoice number: 663211

Date/tax point: 15 Oct 20XX

Order number: 32213

Account number: W15

Quantity	Description	Product code	Unit amount £	Total £
16	Standard lamps	33116	24.00	384.00

Net total	384.00
VAT	76.80
Invoice total	460.80

Terms
Net 30 days
E & OE

INVOICE

Southfield Electrical
Industrial Estate
Benham DR6 2FF
Tel 0303379 Fax 0303152
VAT Reg 0264 2274 49

To: ⌐ Whitehill Superstores ⌐
28, Whitehill Park
Benham DR6 5LM

Invoice number: 56521

Date/tax point: 12 Oct 20XX

Order number: 3226

Account number: SL 44

Quantity	Description	Product code	Unit amount £	Total £
6	Zanpoint Freezer	6540	310.00	1,860.00
Less:	10% discount			186.00

Net total		1,674.00
VAT		321.40
Invoice total		1,995.40

Terms
4% discount for settlement within 10 days, otherwise 30 days net
E & OE

Test 4

Today's date is 20 October. Given below are two credit notes received by Whitehill Superstores. Enter the details of these credit notes into the Purchases Returns Day Book and then total the Day Book – use the account references from the previous question.

Purchases Returns Day Book

Date	Supplier	Credit note number	Supplier code	Gross £	VAT £	Net £
		Total				

CREDIT NOTE

SOUTHFIELD ELECTRICAL
INDUSTRIAL ESTATE
Benham DR6 2FF
Tel 0303379 Fax 0303152
VAT Reg 0264 2274 49

Invoice to:

Whitehill Superstores
28 Whitehill Park
Benham DR6 5LM

Credit note number: 08702

Date/tax point: 16 Oct 20XX

Order number   32217

Account number: SL 44

Quantity	Description	Product code	Unit amount	Total
			£	£
2	Temax Coffee maker	9130	50.00	100.00

Net total	100.00
VAT	20.00
Gross total	120.00

Reason for credit note:

Not ordered by customer

....

CREDIT NOTE

HERNE INDUSTRIES
Fuller House
Bean Park
Benham DR6 3PQ
Tel 0303226 Fax 0303582
VAT Reg 0624 3361 29

Invoice to:

Whitehill Superstores
28 Whitehill Park
Benham DR6 5LM

Credit note number: CN 4502

Date/tax point: 17 Oct 20XX

Order number 32221

Account number: SL 23

Quantity	Description	Product code	Unit amount	Total
			£	£
1	Kemax Camera	KC450	110.00	110.00
		Net total		110.00
		VAT		22.00
		Gross total		132.00

Reason for credit note:

Wrong items

148

Test 5

The following transactions all took place on 30 November and have been entered into the Purchases Day Book as shown below. No entries have yet been made into the ledger system.

Purchases Day Book

Date 20XX	Details	Invoice number	Gross £	VAT £	Net £
30 Nov	Lindell Co	24577	2,136	356	1,780
30 Nov	Harris Rugs	829	5,256	876	4,380
30 Nov	Kinshasa Music	10/235	2,796	466	2,330
30 Nov	Calnan Ltd	9836524	2,292	382	1,910
	Totals		12,480	2,080	10,400

What will be the entries in the purchases ledger?

Purchases ledger

Account name	Amount £	Left side of account ✓	Right side of account ✓	Details in account

Test 6

Purchase invoices have been received and partially entered in the analysed Purchases Day Book, as shown below.

(a) Complete the entries in the Purchases Day Book by inserting the appropriate figures for each invoice.

(b) Total the last five columns of the Purchases Day Book.

Purchases Day Book

Date 20XX	Details	Invoice number	Gross £	VAT £	Net £	Purchases £	Expenses £
30 Nov	Papford & Co	29000	3,180				2,650
30 Nov	Havelock Beauty	120/22		196		980	
30 Nov	Hareston Ltd	7638		1,564		7,820	
	Totals						

Test 7

A supply of printer paper has been delivered to Wendlehurst Trading by Patel Stationery. The purchase order sent from Wendlehurst Trading, and the invoice from Patel Stationery, are shown below.

Wendlehurst Trading
Purchase Order No. PO89346

To: Patel Stationery

Date: 7 Dec 20XX

Please supply 100 reams printer paper product code PAP6735
Purchase price: £80 per box of 20 reams, plus VAT
Discount: less 12.5% trade discount, as agreed.

Patel Stationery
Invoice No. 109273

Wendlehurst Trading
10 Dec 20XX

100 reams printer paper product code PAP6735 @ £4 each	£400.00
Trade discount	(£40.00)
Net amount	£360.00
VAT @ 20%	£ 72.00
Total	£432.00

Terms: 30 days net

Check the invoice against the purchase order and answer the following questions.

	Yes ✓	No ✓
Has the correct purchase price of the printer paper been charged?		
Has the correct trade discount been applied?		
What would be the VAT amount charged if the invoice was correct?	£	
What would be the total amount charged if the invoice was correct?	£	

chapter 6:
DOUBLE ENTRY BOOKKEEPING

chapter coverage 📖

Now that we have considered the preparation of invoices and credit notes, and their entry into the books of prime entry and sales/purchases ledgers, in this chapter we turn to the basics of double entry bookkeeping.

The topics covered are:

- ✍ Double entry bookkeeping
- ✍ Principles of double entry bookkeeping
- ✍ The accounting equation
- ✍ Ledger accounts
- ✍ General rules for double entry bookkeeping
- ✍ Balancing the ledger accounts
- ✍ Double entry and the accounting equation
- ✍ Capital and revenue expenditure
- ✍ Capital and revenue income
- ✍ Double entry for credit sales in general ledger
- ✍ Double entry for credit purchases in general ledger
- ✍ Types of ledger

DOUBLE ENTRY BOOKKEEPING

Accounting is based upon a system of DOUBLE ENTRY BOOKKEEPING, the fundamental principle of which is:

Each and every transaction has two effects

This principle actually incorporates three related principles, two of which we encountered very briefly in Chapter 1 of this Text and which we shall look at further now.

PRINCIPLES OF DOUBLE ENTRY BOOKKEEPING

The three main principles that underlie the practice of recording transactions in a double entry bookkeeping system are:

(a)   The SEPARATE ENTITY CONCEPT – the owner of a business is a completely separate entity to the business itself

(b)   There is an ACCOUNTING EQUATION which always holds true:

ASSETS minus LIABILITIES equals CAPITAL or, re-arranging slightly,

ASSETS equal CAPITAL plus LIABILITIES

(c)   The DUAL EFFECT of transactions – each and every transaction that a business undertakes has two effects on the business

THE ACCOUNTING EQUATION

To understand the accounting equation a little better you need to know more about its different elements:

- ASSETS are items that the business owns, such as cash and machinery and amounts owed to the business by trade receivables.

- LIABILITIES are amounts that are owed to other parties, such as loans, overdrafts and amounts owed to trade payables.

- CAPITAL is the amount that is owed by the business to its owner as a separate entity. Capital at any point in time is made up of:

  - Initial capital introduced; plus
  - The business's INCOME; less
  - The business's EXPENSES; less
  - The owner's DRAWINGS of cash or goods for their own use.

- The main sources of INCOME for a business will be from sales of goods and services, but may also include interest paid to the business by its bank and other sundry income such as rent received from tenants, and commission received from acting as an agent.

- The main EXPENSES of the business will be the goods that it purchases for resale as well as the other ongoing costs of running the business such as wages to employees (**not** the owner), rent paid for its premises, utilities and stationery.

HOW IT WORKS

We will look at the initial transactions of a small business to illustrate the dual effect, and eventually the accounting equation. For the moment we shall assume that all transactions related to cash are passed through the business's bank account.

- Ben Charles sets up in business on 1 May by paying £10,000 into a business bank account from his redundancy money as the business's initial capital.

    Effect 1

    Cash into the business of £10,000

    Effect 2

    The business 'owes' Ben his £10,000 capital

- Ben buys some goods for resale for £1,000 in cash.

    Effect 1

    Purchases of £1,000 have been made

    Effect 2

    Cash of £1,000 is paid out

- Ben buys some goods for resale for £2,000 on credit.

    Effect 1

    Purchases of £2,000 have been made

    Effect 2

    A trade payable for £2,000 exists

- Ben pays rent for premises of £600 in cash.

    Effect 1

    A rent expense of £600 has been incurred

    Effect 2

    Cash of £600 is paid out

- Sales of £1,500 for cash are made by selling some of the goods.

  Effect 1   **Effect 2**

  Cash has increased by   Sales of £1,500 have been
  £1,500   made

- Sales of £1,800 are made on credit.

  Effect 1   **Effect 2**

  A trade receivable for   Sales of £1,800 have been
  £1,800 exists   made

- Ben purchases a computer to help with the accounting process at a cost of £1,000 and pays for this by cheque.

  Effect 1   **Effect 2**

  The business now has a   Cash has decreased by
  computer worth £1,000 that   £1,000
  it will keep

- Ben buys computer disks and other stationery for £200 by cheque.

  Effect 1   **Effect 2**

  An expense of £200 is   Cash is decreased by £200
  incurred

- Ben takes out £500 from the business for his own living expenses.

  Effect 1   **Effect 2**

  Drawings of £500 have been   Cash is decreased by £500
  made

- Ben pays his trade payable £1,500.

  Effect 1   **Effect 2**

  The amount of the trade   Cash is reduced by £1,500
  payable is reduced by
  £1,500

- Ben's credit customer pays £1,750 by cheque.

  Effect 1   **Effect 2**

  Cash is increased by £1,750   The amount of the trade
                                  receivable is reduced by
                                  £1,750

- Ben agrees with his credit customer that, as it paid so quickly, Ben would deduct £50 from the amount owed as settlement discount.

Effect 1

Ben has suffered an expense (discount allowed) of £50

Effect 2

The amount of the trade receivable is reduced by £50

Task 1

What are the two effects of the following transactions?

(a) Purchase of goods on credit

Increase expense	
Increase sales	
Increase trade payable	
Increase trade receivable	

(b) Sale of goods on credit

Increase expense	
Increase sales	
Increase trade payable	
Increase trade receivable	

(c) Receipt of money for sale of goods on credit

Increase cash	
Decrease cash	
Decrease trade receivable	
Increase trade receivable	

(d) Payment to a trade payable for purchase of goods on credit

Increase cash	
Decrease cash	
Decrease trade payable	
Increase trade payable	

LEDGER ACCOUNTS

Both sides of each transaction need to be recorded in the organisation's accounting records.

The traditional method of recording these transactions is in a LEDGER ACCOUNT in the organisation's GENERAL LEDGER.

- 'Ledger' simply means 'book'.

- The general ledger is the accounting record which forms the complete set of ledger accounts for the organisation.

Each type of transaction has a ledger account in the general ledger. An illustration of a ledger account follows below (they are often called T accounts because of how they look):

		Title				GL 000	
Date	Ref	Details	£	Date	Ref	Details	£

You have already seen ledger accounts like this in relation to the sales and purchases ledger in Chapters 3 to 5. It is now time to make the structure of a ledger account explicit. Each one has:

- Two sides, because each transaction has two effects

  - The left-hand side is the DEBIT side
  - The right-hand side is the CREDIT side

- A title, which explains which transaction it is recording eg sales, purchases

The fundamental principle of double entry bookkeeping is that:

Each and every transaction has two effects

So for every transaction that a business makes there must be:

- A debit entry in one ledger account
- An equal and opposite credit entry in another ledger account

The skill that you must acquire is to know which accounts to put the debit and credit entries into.

Note that as well as a title, general ledger accounts also have a general ledger code – in this case GL 000. As with customer and supplier codes in the sales and purchases ledgers, a general ledger code makes it much easier to identify which account should be written up, and allows for easy cross-referencing to where the other side of the entry has been made.

GENERAL RULES FOR DOUBLE ENTRY BOOKKEEPING

There are some general rules for double entry bookkeeping which can help you to decide where debit and credit entries should be made:

- If cash, which is an asset, comes into the business, then the Cash or Bank account is always debited – therefore some other account must be credited:

  INCREASE IN ASSET = DEBIT ENTRY

- If cash is paid out of the business (an asset has decreased), then the Cash or Bank account is always credited – therefore some other account must be debited:

  DECREASE IN ASSET = CREDIT ENTRY

- An increase in liabilities – eg a bank loan – is always recorded on the credit side of the liability account:

  INCREASE IN LIABILITY = CREDIT ENTRY
  DECREASE IN LIABILITY = DEBIT ENTRY

- An increase in capital is always recorded on the credit side of the capital account:

  INCREASE IN CAPITAL = CREDIT ENTRY
  DECREASE IN CAPITAL = DEBIT ENTRY

- An increase in expenses is always a debit entry in the expenses account:

  INCREASE IN EXPENSE = DEBIT ENTRY
  DECREASE IN EXPENSE = CREDIT ENTRY

- An increase in income is always a credit entry in the income account:

  INCREASE IN INCOME = CREDIT ENTRY
  DECREASE IN INCOME = DEBIT ENTRY

Asset account eg Bank

	£		£
Debit entry	+	Credit entry	–

Liability account eg Bank loan

	£		£
Debit entry	–	Credit entry	+

Capital account

	£		£
Debit entry	–	Credit entry	+

Expense account

Details	£	Details	£
Debit entry	+	Credit entry	–

Income account

Details	£	Details	£
Debit entry	–	Credit entry	+

HOW IT WORKS

We will now return to Ben Charles's business and enter each of his initial transactions into general ledger accounts. For this example we will simplify the ledger accounts slightly, not worrying about the date or any reference, just concentrating on the debit and the credit entry, and entering the details for each transaction, which is the name of the account to which the other side of the entry is made.

Ben sets up in business on 1 May by paying £10,000 into a business bank account

Cash has come into the business therefore the Bank account must be debited. The money paid in is from the owner of the business. It is therefore capital of the business so the credit entry is to the Capital account.

Bank account

Details	£	Details	£
Capital	10,000		

Capital account

Details	£	Details	£
		Bank	10,000

Note how the details for each entry shows where the other side of the entry is.

In terms of the accounting equation, we see at this point that:

ASSETS (£10,000) – LIABILITIES (£0) = CAPITAL (£10,000)

Ben buys some goods for resale for £1,000 in cash

Cash is going out of the business so the Bank account must be credited.

The payment was for goods for resale which are known as Purchases, an expense account, so this is the account that must be debited.

Bank account

Details	£	Details	£
Capital	10,000	Purchases	1,000

Purchases account

Details	£	Details	£
Bank	1,000		

Ben buys some goods for resale for £2,000 on credit

Again, these goods are purchases so the purchases account must be debited.

The transaction is not for cash this time so there is no entry into the Bank account, instead the credit entry is to a Trade payables account (a trade payable is another form of liability, so an increase is always a credit entry as with the bank loan account that we saw above).

Purchases account

Details	£	Details	£
Bank	1,000		
Trade payables	2,000		

Trade payables account

Details	£	Details	£
		Purchases	2,000

Ben pays rent for premises of £600 in cash

Cash out of the business; therefore credit the Bank account.

The rent is an expense of the business so the Rent account must be debited – an increase in expenses is always a debit entry in the expense ledger accounts.

Bank account

Details	£	Details	£
Capital	10,000	Purchases	1,000
		Rent	600

Rent account

Details	£	Details	£
Bank	600		

Sales of £1,500 for a cheque are made by selling some of the goods

Cash is coming into the business from these sales therefore debit the Bank account.

The credit is to the Sales account – remember that an increase in income is always a credit entry.

Bank account

Details	£	Details	£
Capital	10,000	Purchases	1,000
Sales	1,500	Rent	600

Sales account

Details	£	Details	£
		Bank	1,500

Sales of £1,800 are made on credit

Again, we have a sale so the Sales account must be credited.

This time however there is no cash coming in so it is not the Bank account that is debited, instead the debit entry is made in a Trade receivables account – remember that an increase in an asset such as a trade receivable is always a debit entry.

Sales account

Details	£	Details	£
		Bank	1,500
		Trade receivables	1,800

Trade receivables account

Details	£	Details	£
Sales	1,800		

Ben purchases a computer to help with the accounting process at a cost of £1,000 and pays for this by cheque

Cash goes out of the business, so credit the Bank account.

An asset such as a computer that will be owned for some time by the business – known as a NON-CURRENT ASSET – has been purchased so a debit is required in a Non-current asset account. Remember that increases in assets are always debit entries.

Bank account

Details	£	Details	£
Capital	10,000	Purchases	1,000
Sales	1,500	Rent	600
		Non-current asset	1,000

Non-current asset account

Details	£	Details	£
Bank	1,000		

Ben buys computer disks and other stationery for £200 by cheque

Cash goes out of the business, so credit the Bank account.

The stationery and disks are an expense to the business so a Stationery account will be opened and debited.

Bank account

Details	£	Details	£
Capital	10,000	Purchases	1,000
Sales	1,500	Rent	600
		Non-current asset	1,000
		Stationery	200

Stationery account

Details	£	Details	£
Bank	200		

Ben transfers £500 from the business to his own bank account for his own living expenses

Cash goes out of the business, so credit the Bank account.

This is the owner taking money out of the business which is known as DRAWINGS, so a Drawings account is debited.

Bank account

Details	£	Details	£
Capital	10,000	Purchases	1,000
Sales	1,500	Rent	600
		Non-current asset	1,000
		Stationery	200
		Drawings	500

Drawings account

Details	£	Details	£
Bank	500		

Ben pays his trade payable £1,500 by cheque

Cash goes out of the business, so credit the Bank account.

The money is being paid to his trade payable therefore it is reducing his liability to that trade payable. The Trade payables account is debited to reflect this.

Bank account

Details	£	Details	£
Capital	10,000	Purchases	1,000
Sales	1,500	Rent	600
		Non-current asset	1,000
		Stationery	200
		Drawings	500
		Trade payables	1,500

Trade payables account

Details	£	Details	£
Bank	1,500	Purchases	2,000

Ben's credit customer pays £1,750 by cheque

This is cash being received into the business so the Bank account is debited.

The credit entry is to the Trade receivables account, as this receipt is reducing the amount that the trade receivable owes the business.

Bank account

Details	£	Details	£
Capital	10,000	Purchases	1,000
Sales	1,500	Rent	600
Trade receivables	1,750	Non-current asset	1,000
		Stationery	200
		Drawings	500
		Trade payables	1,500

Trade receivables account

Details	£	Details	£
Sales	1,800	Bank	1,750

> Ben agrees with his credit customer that, as it paid so quickly, Ben would deduct £50 from the amount owed as settlement discount

There is no cash being received into or paid out from the business so the Bank account is not affected. There is a credit entry to the Trade receivables account, as the settlement discount reduces the amount owed to Ben by the customer. The debit entry is made to a special expense ledger account, called DISCOUNTS ALLOWED.

Discounts allowed

Details	£	Details	£
Trade receivables	50		

Trade receivables account

Details	£	Details	£
Sales	1,800	Bank	1,750
		Discounts allowed	50

Task 2

For each of the following transactions, state which account should be debited and which account credited by using the account names from the picklist:

(a)   Purchase of goods on credit

Account name	Debit	Credit

(b)   Sale of goods on credit

Account name	Debit	Credit

(c)   Receipt of money for sale of goods on credit

Account name	Debit	Credit

(d) Payment of a trade payable

Account name	Debit	Credit

Picklist:
Bank
Trade payables
Trade receivables
Sales
Purchases

BALANCING THE LEDGER ACCOUNTS

Once all of the accounting entries have been put into the ledger accounts for a period then it is likely that the owner or managers of a business will want to know certain things such as how much is there in the bank account, how many sales have there been in the period, how much do we owe our trade payables at the end of the period etc?

These questions can be answered by balancing the ledger accounts.

HOW IT WORKS

We will illustrate the balancing process by using Ben Charles's ledger accounts for his initial period of trading. Let's start with the Bank account.

Bank account

Details	£	Details	£
Capital	10,000	Purchases	1,000
Sales	1,500	Rent	600
Trade receivables	1,750	Non-current asset	1,000
		Stationery	200
		Drawings	500
		Trade payables	1,500
	———		———
	———		———

Step 1   Total both the debit and the credit columns, making a note of the totals for each.

Debit column total £13,250
Credit column total £4,800

Step 2 Put the largest of the two totals as the column total for both the debit and credit columns, leaving at least one empty line at the bottom of each column.

Bank account

Details	£	Details	£
Capital	10,000	Purchases	1,000
Sales	1,500	Rent	600
Trade receivables	1,750	Non-current asset	1,000
		Stationery	200
		Drawings	500
		Trade payables	1,500
	13,250		13,250

Step 3 At the bottom of the column with the smaller actual total, put in the figure that makes the column total add to the larger figure. In this case, in the credit column, put in £(13,250 – 4,800) = £8,450. This is called the BALANCE CARRIED DOWN (Bal c/d).

Bank account

Details	£	Details	£
Capital	10,000	Purchases	1,000
Sales	1,500	Rent	600
Trade receivables	1,750	Non-current asset	1,000
		Stationery	200
		Drawings	500
		Trade payables	1,500
		Balance c/d	8,450
	13,250		13,250

Step 4 Show this balancing figure on the opposite side of the account below the total and describe it as the BALANCE BROUGHT DOWN (Bal b/d).

Bank account

Details	£	Details	£
Capital	10,000	Purchases	1,000
Sales	1,500	Rent	600
Trade receivables	1,750	Non-current asset	1,000
		Stationery	200
		Drawings	500
		Trade payables	1,500
		Balance c/d	8,450
	13,250		13,250
Balance b/d	8,450		

The brought down balance is showing us that we have an asset (a debit balance) of £8,450 of cash in the bank account.

Now we will balance all of the other accounts for Ben Charles in the same way. Note that if we include dates in the ledger accounts, the date of the balance brought down is one day after the date of the balance carried down.

Capital account

Details	£	Details	£
		Bank	10,000

When an account has only one entry, like the capital account, there is no need for the balancing exercise as this single entry is the balance ie, a credit balance of £10,000.

Purchases account

Details	£	Details	£
Bank	1,000		
Trade payables	2,000	Balance c/d	3,000
	3,000		3,000
Balance b/d	3,000		

This shows that purchases totalled £3,000 in the period.

Trade payables account

Details	£	Details	£
Bank	1,500	Purchases	2,000
Balance c/d	500		
	2,000		2,000
		Balance b/d	500

This shows that Ben still owes his trade payable £500 at the end of the period.

Rent account

Details	£	Details	£
Bank	600		

This shows that the rent expense for the period was £600.

Sales account

Details	£	Details	£
		Bank	1,500
Balance c/d	3,300	Trade receivables	1,800
	3,300		3,300
		Balance b/d	3,300

This shows that sales totalled £3,300 in the period.

Trade receivables account

Details	£	Details	£
Sales	1,800	Bank	1,750
		Discounts allowed	50
		Balance c/d	0
	1,800		1,800
Balance b/d	0		

This shows that Ben's trade receivable owes nothing at the end of the period.

Non-current asset account

Details	£	Details	£
Bank	1,000		

This is simply the balance on the non-current asset account showing that the business has a non-current asset that cost £1,000.

Stationery account

Details	£	Details	£
Bank	200		

The stationery expense in the period was £200.

Drawings account

Details	£	Details	£
Bank	500		

This shows that the owner's drawings for the period totalled £500.

Discounts allowed

Details	£	Details	£
Trade receivables	50		

This shows us that the total expense of discounts allowed in the period was £50.

Task 3

Balance the following ledger account, showing clearly the balances carried down and brought down.

Trade receivables

Details	£	Details	£
Sales	2,600	Bank	1,800
Sales	1,400	Bank	1,200
Sales	3,700	Bank	2,000
Sales	1,300		
Total		Total	

What does the balance represent?

The amount owed by trade receivables

The amount owed to trade receivables

DOUBLE ENTRY AND THE ACCOUNTING EQUATION

We saw above that the accounting equation is closely linked with the dual effect and therefore double entry.

ASSETS minus LIABILITIES equals CAPITAL

So let's see if the accounting equation holds true for Ben Charles now that we have done all the double entry for the period and know the balances on all his ledger accounts.

HOW IT WORKS

Bearing in mind that the capital side of the accounting equation comprises initial capital plus income less purchases, expenses and drawings, we can slot all the balances into place:

Assets	£	Liabilities	£	Capital	£
Bank	8,450	Trade payables	500	Capital	10,000
Trade receivables	0			Purchases	(3,000)
Non-current asset	1,000			Rent	(600)
				Sales	3,300
				Stationery	(200)
				Drawings	(500)
				Discounts allowed	(50)
Total assets	9,450	Total liabilities	500	Total capital	8,950

We can see that the accounting equation holds:

> ASSETS minus LIABILITIES equals CAPITAL
>
> £9,450 minus £500 equals £8,950

We can be confident, therefore, that we have followed the rules of double entry properly.

CAPITAL AND REVENUE EXPENDITURE

Most of the payments that a business makes, both cash and credit transactions, are for purchases of items for manufacture or resale, or wages, or for expenses of the business. These are called REVENUE EXPENDITURE because they are deducted from revenue or income in order to calculate the profit made by the business in a single period such as a year. They are essentially short-term in nature, being purchased and used up all within the period.

Remember though that Ben Charles bought a computer which he planned to use in the business for some time. When a business buys an asset which is for long-term use in the business over a number of periods, such as machinery, property, cars, fixtures and fittings, and computers, these are known as NON-CURRENT ASSETS. The expenditure on these non-current assets is known as CAPITAL EXPENDITURE.

CAPITAL AND REVENUE INCOME

A similar distinction can be made in relation to income. Sales of goods and services, on credit and for cash, are short-term (made and paid within one period only) and are classified as REVENUE INCOME. Other types of REVENUE INCOME include interest received from the bank, commission receipts and rental income. The only type of CAPITAL INCOME that you need to be aware of is income received when a non-current asset such as machinery is sold.

Task 4

Identify whether each of these items is capital expenditure, revenue expenditure, capital income or revenue income.

	Revenue expenditure	Revenue income	Capital expenditure	Capital income
Sale of goods to credit customers				
Cash sales				
Sale of delivery van				
Purchase of goods for resale				
Purchase of building				
Purchase of coffee for office from petty cash				

DOUBLE ENTRY FOR CREDIT SALES IN GENERAL LEDGER

The example of Ben Charles shows us most of the double entries in the general ledger that need to be made for credit sales transactions (which we processed in Chapter 4). In addition, you should note that the double entry for a credit note to a customer is the reverse of that for an invoice, but instead of reversing the sale in the ledger account for sales, the entry is made in a special SALES RETURNS LEDGER ACCOUNT.

The following table summarises the double entries in the general ledger for credit sales transactions:

Transaction	Ledger account to DEBIT	Ledger account to CREDIT
Invoice for a credit sale	Trade receivables	Sales
Credit note for a return	Sales returns	Trade receivables
Cash received	Bank OR Cash	Trade receivables
Settlement discount allowed	Discounts allowed (an expense account)	Trade receivables

DOUBLE ENTRY FOR CREDIT PURCHASES IN GENERAL LEDGER

Again the example of Ben Charles shows us most of the double entries in the general ledger that need to be made for credit purchases transactions (which we processed in Chapter 5). In addition, you should note that:

- The double entry for a credit note from a supplier is the reverse of that for an invoice, but instead of reversing the purchase in the ledger account for purchases, the entry is made in a special PURCHASES RETURNS LEDGER ACCOUNT.

- The double entry for a settlement discount that a supplier has let the business deduct is the opposite of the entry made in relation to discounts allowed, with the credit entry being in the DISCOUNTS RECEIVED LEDGER ACCOUNT.

The following table summarises the double entries in the general ledger for credit purchases transactions:

Transaction	Ledger account to DEBIT	Ledger account to CREDIT
Invoice for a purchase	Purchases	Trade payables
Credit note for a return	Trade payables	Purchases returns
Cash paid	Trade payables	Bank OR Cash
Settlement discount received	Trade payables	Discounts received (an income account)

TYPES OF LEDGER

The ledger accounts that we have been considering so far in this chapter are all kept together in one LEDGER or book. This is known as the GENERAL LEDGER (or sometimes nominal ledger or main ledger).

There are also two other types of ledger, known as the SUBSIDIARY LEDGERS. These are the SALES LEDGER and the PURCHASES LEDGER.

- The sales ledger is a collection of ledger accounts for each individual trade receivable of the business.

- The purchases ledger is a collection of ledger accounts for each individual trade payable of the business.

We have already come across the sales ledger and purchases ledger in previous chapters. We will look at how these subsidiary ledgers and the general ledger interact, and how in practice transactions are recorded in these ledgers, in this and the following chapters.

HOW IT WORKS

A business which is not registered for VAT has three credit customers, A, B and C. The following transactions occur with them during a period.

Sales to credit customers:

	Invoice number	£
A	78346	400
B	78347	600
C	78348	500

The double entry in the general ledger for a sale on credit is:

- To credit the Sales account (if the business was registered for VAT the VAT account would also be credited)

- To debit what we have so far called the Trade receivables account, but which in practice and in the assessment is called the SALES LEDGER CONTROL ACCOUNT (because it reflects the total of all the individual credit customer accounts in the sales ledger)

Therefore the double entry in the general ledger will be as follows (note that under 'details' you include the name of the account that takes the other side of the entry).

General ledger

Sales account

Details	£	Details	£
		Sales ledger control	400
		Sales ledger control	600
		Sales ledger control	500

Sales ledger control account

Details	£	Details	£
Sales	400		
Sales	600		
Sales	500		

However, this sales ledger control account gives no detail of the individual trade receivables and how much is due from each of them. To rectify this, an account is held for each trade receivable in the sales ledger. This is in the form of a ledger account with the same debit and credit entries that are used in the general ledger. The big difference is that the sales ledger is a subsidiary ledger: there is no double entry taking place. The accounts in the sales ledger are not part of the double entry system of the general ledger but completely separate 'memorandum' accounts. They just give information. As a result, under 'details' we include the day book and document number rather than the name of the other side of the transaction.

The entries in the sales ledger for these three trade receivables would be as follows:

Sales ledger

A's account

Details	£	Details	£
SDB – 78346	400		

B's account

Details	£	Details	£
SDB – 78347	600		

C's account

Details	£	Details	£
SDB – 78348	500		

Now suppose that £300 is received from A and £250 from C, both via BACS. We will look at the entries for these receipts in the general ledger and in the sales ledger.

In the general ledger, money in means a debit to the Bank account and therefore a credit to the Sales ledger control account. In the sales ledger the individual accounts will also be credited with the amounts received.

General ledger

Bank account

Details	£	Details	£
Sales ledger control	300		
Sales ledger control	250		

Sales ledger control account

Details	£	Details	£
Sales	400	Bank	300
Sales	600	Bank	250
Sales	500		

Sales ledger

A's account

Details	£	Details	£
SDB – 78346	400	Bank – BACS	300

B's account

Details	£	Details	£
SDB – 78347	600		

C's account

Details	£	Details	£
SDB – 78348	500	Bank – BACS	250

Task 5

A credit customer James Daniels buys goods from your business on credit for £1,000 including VAT and later pays £800 by cheque. Record these transactions in his account in the sales ledger.

James Daniels

Details	£	Details	£

HOW IT WORKS

The same principles apply when dealing with trade payables in the purchases ledger. The double entry for purchases on credit and money paid to trade payables takes place in the general ledger in the PURCHASES LEDGER CONTROL ACCOUNT, and then each individual trade payable account in the purchases ledger is also updated.

Suppose that our business has three credit suppliers, D, E and F.

The following transactions take place with these suppliers:

Purchases on credit	D – invoice 67532	£200
	E – invoice 736	£350
	F – invoice 24425	£100
Payments made	D – BACS	£100
	E – cheque	£250

These transactions must now be recorded in the general ledger and the purchases ledger.

General ledger

Purchases account

Details	£	Details	£
Purchases ledger control	200		
Purchases ledger control	350		
Purchases ledger control	100		

Purchases ledger control account

Details	£	Details	£
Bank	100	Purchases	200
Bank	250	Purchases	350
		Purchases	100

Bank account

Details	£	Details	£
		Purchases ledger control	100
		Purchases ledger control	250

Purchases ledger

D's account

Details	£	Details	£
CB – BACS	100	PDB – 67532	200

E's account

Details	£	Details	£
CB – cheque	250	PDB – 736	350

F's account

Details	£	Details	£
		PDB – 24425	100

CHAPTER OVERVIEW

- The principles behind double entry bookkeeping are that:

  - Every transaction has two effects on a business

  - The owner is a separate entity from the business itself

  - The accounting equation (assets minus liabilities equals capital) is always true

- The two effects of each transaction are recorded in ledger accounts with a debit entry in one account and a credit entry in another account

- If money is paid out of the business then the Bank or Cash account is credited. Money coming into the business is debited to the Bank or Cash account

- Increases in assets and expenses are recorded on the debit side of their accounts, decreases on the credit side

- Increases in liabilities and income are recorded on the credit side of their accounts, decreases on the debit side

- Money paid into the business by the owner is recorded on the credit side of a capital account, and money or goods taken out of the business by the owner are recorded on the debit side of a drawings account

- Balancing the ledger accounts enables the business to determine key business information such as the balance on the bank account, sales for a period and how much is owed to trade payables

- The general ledger is the complete set of ledger accounts of a business

- The sales ledger and purchases ledger are subsidiary ledgers (not part of the general ledger) which contain a ledger account for each individual trade receivable or trade payable. They do not form part of the double entry system

- In the general ledger the sales ledger control account and the purchases ledger control account only contain total figures in relation to trade receivables (for sales, sales returns, receipts and discounts allowed) and trade payables (for purchases, purchases returns, payments and discounts received)

Keywords

Double entry bookkeeping – a system of accounting where the two effects of each transaction are recorded

Separate entity concept – the owner of a business is a completely separate entity to the business itself

Accounting equation – assets minus liabilities equals capital

Dual effect – every transaction a business undertakes has two effects on the business

Assets – something that a business owns

Liabilities – something that a business owes

Capital – the amount owed by the business to its owner as a separate entity

Income – what the business earns when it makes sales of goods or services to other parties

Expenses – what the business spends to purchase goods or services for the company

Ledger accounts – the accounts in which each transaction is recorded – there will be a ledger account for each type of transaction such as sales and purchases and for every type of asset and liability

General ledger – this is where the double entry takes place for all of the transactions of the business

Debit – the debit side of a ledger account is the left hand side

Credit – the credit side of a ledger account is the right hand side

Drawings – the money or goods that the owner takes out of the business

Non-current asset – an asset which is for long-term use in the business eg machinery

Discounts allowed ledger account – expense account which records settlement discounts deducted by credit customers

Balance brought down – in the ledger account the term used to describe the balancing figure that makes the column with the smaller figure total the larger figure

Balance carried down – used on the opposite side of the account, the balancing figure is described as the balance carried down

Capital expenditure – on assets used in the long term ie in more than one period (non-current assets)

Capital income – from sales of assets used in the long term

Revenue expenditure – payments for day-to-day running costs and purchases, including wages and interest paid to the bank

Revenue income – receipts from sales and other short-term income such as interest from the bank, rent and commission

Sales returns ledger account – used to record customer returns

Purchases returns ledger account – used to record returns of goods to suppliers

Discounts received ledger account – ledger account which records settlement discount deducted by the business when making payments to credit suppliers

Subsidiary ledgers – the sales ledger and purchases ledger, which are memorandum ledgers that are not part of the general ledger, contain a ledger account for each individual trade receivable or trade payable. Not part of the double entry system

Sales ledger control account – a general ledger account for trade receivables, representing the total of all the accounts in the sales ledger. Part of the double entry system

Purchases ledger control account – a general ledger account for trade payables, representing the total of all the accounts in the purchases ledger. Part of the double entry system

TEST YOUR LEARNING

Test 1

Identify the general ledger accounts that are debited and credited for each of the following transactions.

	Debit	Credit
Money paid into the business by the owner		
Purchases on credit		
Purchases of machinery for use in the business, paid for by cheque		
Sales on credit		
Money taken out of the business by the owner		

Test 2

The following account is in the general ledger at the close of day on 30 June.

(a) Insert the balance carried down together with date and details.
(b) Insert the totals.
(c) Insert the balance brought down together with date and details.

Sales ledger control account

Date	Details	Amount £	Date	Details	Amount £
1/6	Balance b/d	1,209	28/6	Bank	3,287
30/6	Sales	6,298	30/6	Sales returns	786
	Total			Total	

Test 3

The following transactions all took place on 30 November and have been entered into the Sales Day Book as shown below. No entries have yet been made into the ledger system.

Sales Day Book

Date 20XX	Details	Invoice number	Gross £	VAT £	Net £
30 Nov	Fries & Co	23907	2,136	356	1,780
30 Nov	Hussey Enterprises	23908	3,108	518	2,590
30 Nov	Todd Trading	23909	3,720	620	3,100
30 Nov	Milford Ltd	23910	2,592	432	2,160
	Totals		11,556	1,926	9,630

What will be the entries in the general ledger?

General ledger

Account name	Amount £	Debit ✓	Credit ✓	Details in account

Test 4

The following transactions all took place on 30 November and have been entered into the Purchases Day Book as shown below. No entries have yet been made into the ledger system.

Purchases Day Book

Date 20XX	Details	Invoice number	Gross £	VAT £	Net £
30 Nov	Lindell Co	24577	2,136	356	1,780
30 Nov	Harris Rugs	829	5,256	876	4,380
30 Nov	Kinshasa Music	10/235	2,796	466	2,330
30 Nov	Calnan Ltd	9836524	2,292	382	1,910
	Totals		12,480	2,080	10,400

What will be the entries in the general ledger?

General ledger

Account name	Amount £	Debit ✓	Credit ✓	Details in account

chapter 7:
MAINTAINING THE CASH BOOK

chapter coverage 📖

The Cash Book is the main book of prime entry as it is vital for any business to ensure control over its cash, both when it is held on the premises (such as by a shop) and when it is in the bank account. Maintaining a Cash Book so that there is tight control of recording is therefore vital. The topics covered are:

- ✍ The three-column Cash Book
- ✍ The Cash Book and double entry
- ✍ Using the three-column Cash Book
- ✍ Making entries in the three-column Cash Book
- ✍ Primary records for the Cash Book
- ✍ Writing up and maintaining the Cash Book
- ✍ Totalling and posting the Cash Book
- ✍ Balancing the Cash Book

THE THREE-COLUMN CASH BOOK

As well as money held in its bank account, many businesses – especially retailers – have cash from cash (ie non-credit) sales settled in notes and coin. They may use some of the notes and coin to make purchases in cash, and may also only bank the notes and coin occasionally, say on one day of the week. Having 'cash in hand' on the business's premises like this may cause security risks, but what we are more interested in here is that the recording of cash as it comes in and goes out – and also of any cheques that come in in respect of cash or credit sales – must be complete, and for this we use the Cash Book.

We looked at the layout of the Cash Book in Chapter 3 and identified that it is a book of prime entry along with the Sales and Sales Returns Day Books and the Purchases and Purchases Returns Day Books. As a reminder, here is the receipts side of the Cash Book that we considered:

Date	Details	Ref	Discount allowed £	Cash £	Bank £	VAT £	Cash sales £	Trade receivables £	Sundry income £
9 May	Cash sale			90.00		15.00	75.00		
10 May	Grigsons Ltd	SL21			127.20			127.20	
10 May	Hall & Co	SL05	10.00	93.60				93.60	

This is often referred to as a THREE COLUMN CASH BOOK as there are three key columns: Discount allowed, Cash and Bank. A two-column format is also possible, which would have columns just for Discount allowed and Bank – cash as such would be recorded completely separately.

Having a Cash Book that contains columns for both Cash and Bank allows businesses to record all transactions properly and, therefore, have control over them.

THE CASH BOOK AND DOUBLE ENTRY

The Cash Book is arguably the most important day book in the business and it differs from the Sales Day Book etc in two key ways:

- It has two total columns (for Cash and for Bank) plus a memorandum column (for discount allowed and received) while the Sales Day book etc has only one total column (for Gross or Total) and no memorandum column.

- The Cash Book can be – and usually is in practice – **both** a book of prime entry **and** part of the double entry system in the general ledger. It is both the Cash account and the Bank account in the general ledger as it has a column for each.

The Cash Book as both book of prime entry and general ledger for Cash and Bank

When the Cash Book is both a book of prime entry and part of the double entry system in the general ledger:

- The **receipts side** of the Cash Book is the **debit side** of the Cash and Bank general ledger accounts:

  - Receipts that are entered in the Cash Book are themselves the DEBIT entries for the Cash account or the Bank account in the general ledger.

  - Instead of both debit and credit entries being posted from the Cash Book, only CREDIT entries in respect of actual receipts are posted to the general ledger from the Cash Book.

  - The exception to this is that amounts in the Discount allowed column, which is a memorandum column, are posted as both debit entries (to the Discount allowed general ledger account) and credit entries (to the Trade receivables general ledger account).

- The **payments side** of the Cash Book is the **credit side** of the Cash and Bank general ledger accounts:

  - Payments that are entered in the Cash Book are themselves the CREDIT entries for the Cash account or the Bank account in the general ledger.

  - Only DEBIT entries in respect of actual payments need to be posted from the Cash Book to the general ledger.

  - The exception to this is that amounts in the Discount received column, which is a memorandum column, are posted as both

BPP LEARNING MEDIA

debit entries (to the Trade payables general ledger account) and credit entries (to the Discount received general ledger account).

This is how the double entry works when the Cash Book acts as both a book of prime entry and the Cash and Bank general ledger accounts:

Cash Book – Debit side

Discount allowed £	Cash £	Bank £	VAT £	Cash sales £	Trade receivables £	Sundry income £
Post DEBIT to Discount allowed in GL Post CREDIT to Sales ledger control in GL	= DEBIT side of GL account for Cash	= DEBIT side of GL account for Bank	Post CREDIT entries to relevant GL accounts			

Cash Book – Credit side

Discount received £	Cash £	Bank £	VAT £	Cash purchases £	Trade payables £	Petty cash £	Expenses £
Post DEBIT to Purchases ledger control in GL Post CREDIT to Discount received in GL	= CREDIT side of GL account for Cash	= CREDIT side of GL account for Bank	Post DEBIT entries to relevant GL accounts				

The Cash Book as a book of prime entry only

If the Cash Book is just acting as a book of prime entry there are also general ledger accounts for Cash and for Bank. Both debit and credit postings need to be made from both the receipts and the payments sides of the Cash Book.

This is how the double entry works when the Cash Book acts only as a book of prime entry:

Cash Book – Debit side

Discount allowed £	Cash £	Bank £	VAT £	Cash sales £	Trade receivables £	Sundry income £
Post DEBIT to Discount allowed in GL Post CREDIT to Sales ledger control in GL	Post DEBIT to Cash account in GL	Post DEBIT to Bank account in GL	Post CREDIT entries to relevant GL accounts			

Cash Book – Credit side

Discount received £	Cash £	Bank £	VAT £	Cash purchases £	Trade payables £	Petty cash £	Sundry £
Post DEBIT to Purchases ledger control in GL Post CREDIT to Discount received in GL	Post CREDIT to Cash account in GL	Post CREDIT to Bank account in GL	Post DEBIT entries to relevant GL accounts				

USING THE THREE-COLUMN CASH BOOK

Having a Cash Book that contains columns for both Cash and Bank (as well as discounts) allows businesses to record all transactions properly and, therefore, have control over them.

When there are **transfers between the Cash account and the Bank account** the format makes it easy to ensure they are fully reflected in the double entry system.

- In the Cash column on the DEBIT side we record receipts of cash from cash sales and (rarely) from credit customers, and analyse these as usual so that the relevant CREDIT entries can be posted to the general ledger and the sales ledger.

- In the Cash column on the CREDIT side we record:
    - Payments of cash as cash purchases or (rarely) to credit suppliers, and analyse these as usual so the relevant DEBIT entries can be posted to the general ledger and the purchases ledger

191

- **Payments of cash into the Bank account** – the corresponding debit entry for this in the general ledger is in the Bank column on the DEBIT side of the Cash Book

- In the Bank column on the DEBIT side we record the banking of cash from the Cash account. This has been analysed when received in the debit side of the Cash account, so no further analysis is needed – it is simply a transfer from one general ledger account to another.

- In the Bank column on the CREDIT side we record:

  - Payments of amounts from the bank account on cash (non-credit) purchases, to credit suppliers and for other expenses such as salaries, and analyse these as usual so the relevant DEBIT entries can be posted to the general ledger and the purchases ledger

  - Withdrawals of cash into petty cash or the Cash account – the corresponding debit entry for this in the general ledger is in Petty Cash (which we will come back to in Chapter 10) or the Cash column on the DEBIT side of the Cash Book

MAKING ENTRIES IN THE THREE-COLUMN CASH BOOK

Before we can complete the double entry from the Cash Book of course we must first record transactions in it as a book of prime entry. All receipts and payments must be separately recorded and then analysed.

Using the three column Cash Book means that we record separately:

- Receipts of and payments out of cash by the business
- Receipts into and payments out of the business's bank account

Note that the cash transactions that are recorded in the Cash Book are **not** those related to petty cash.

HOW IT WORKS

Zoe runs her own business and is registered for VAT. She banks all her cash at the end of each day. Zoe makes the following transactions in one day:

- Receives a cheque for £450 from Antoine, a credit customer

- Sells some goods to Bazzer for £282 cash including VAT

- Buys some goods for resale from a market for £56.40 including VAT and pays in cash

- Sends a cheque for £60 to Charlie, a credit supplier

- Pays Desmond, a credit supplier, £200 in cash, taking advantage of a £10 settlement discount

- Receives an automated payment from Ellie, a credit customer, into the bank account for £750. Ellie has taken £30 settlement discount

- Makes a payment of £40 by standing order for business rates

- Banks the remaining cash at the end of the day

Let's take each transaction in turn.

- **Receives a cheque for £450 from Antoine, a credit customer**

This is treated as a receipt into the Bank account since we assume the cheque is paid directly into the bank, so the amount should be recorded in the **Bank** column of the Cash Book (debit side) and analysed to Trade receivables.

Cash Book – Debit side

Details	Discount allowed £	Cash £	Bank £	VAT £	Cash sales £	Trade receivables £	Sundry income £
Antoine			450.00			450.00	

- **Sells some goods to Bazzer for £282 cash including VAT**

This is not a receipt straight into the bank account so it is recorded in the **Cash** column, and analysed to sales (£282 × 100/120 = £235) and VAT (£282 × 20/120 = £47)

Cash Book – Debit side

Details	Discount allowed £	Cash £	Bank £	VAT £	Cash sales £	Trade receivables £	Sundry income £
Antoine			450.00			450.00	
Bazzer		282.00		47.00	235.00		

- **Buys some goods for resale from a market for £56.40 including VAT and pays in cash**

This cash comes out of the amount of cash that Zoe has received from Bazzer so it is recorded in the **Cash** column of the credit side of the Cash Book, and analysed to purchases (£56.40 × 100/120 = £47.00) and VAT (£56.40 × 20/120 = £9.40).

Cash Book – Credit side

Details	Discount received £	Cash £	Bank £	VAT £	Cash purchases £	Trade payables £	Petty cash £	Expenses £
Market		56.40		9.40	47.00			

- **Sends a cheque for £60 to Charlie, a credit supplier**

Writing out a cheque means that the money will come straight out of Zoe's bank account and will bypass the cash system entirely. Thus it is recorded in the **Bank** column.

Cash Book – Credit side

Details	Discount received £	Cash £	Bank £	VAT £	Cash purchases £	Trade payables £	Petty cash £	Expenses £
Market		56.40		9.40	47.00			
Charlie			60.00			60.00		

- **Pays Desmond, a credit supplier, £200 in cash, taking advantage of a £10 settlement discount**

This is again a payment out of the cash that Zoe has collected in the day. By taking a £10 settlement discount she pays £200 in cash to settle a debt of £210. We record this in the **Cash** column on the credit side and analyse it to Trade payables. We record the discount in the **Discount received** column.

Cash Book – Credit side

Details	Discount received £	Cash £	Bank £	VAT £	Cash purchases £	Trade payables £	Petty cash £	Expenses £
Market		56.40		9.40	47.00			
Charlie			60.00			60.00		
Desmond	10.00	200.00				200.00		

- **Receives an automated payment from Ellie, a credit customer, into the bank account for £750. Ellie has taken £30 settlement discount**

The automated payment means that the money comes straight into Zoe's bank account and bypasses the cash system entirely. Thus it is recorded in the **Bank** column on the debit side and analysed to Trade receivables. We record the discount in the **Discount allowed** column.

Cash Book – Debit side

Details	Discount allowed £	Cash £	Bank £	VAT £	Cash sales £	Trade receivables £	Sundry income £
Antoine			450.00			450.00	
Bazzer		282.00		47.00	235.00		
Ellie	30.00		750.00			750.00	

- **Makes a payment of £40 by standing order for business rates**

A standing order payment means that the money comes straight out of Zoe's bank account and again bypasses the cash system entirely. Thus it is recorded in the **Bank** column on the credit side and analysed in the Expenses column.

Cash Book – Credit side

Details	Discount received £	Cash £	Bank £	VAT £	Cash purchases £	Trade payables £	Petty cash £	Expenses £
Market		56.40		9.40	47.00			
Charlie			60.00			60.00		
Desmond	10.00	200.00				200.00		
Rates			40.00					40.00

- **Banks all the cash that it holds at the end of the day**

To calculate and record this we follow a three-step process:

Step 1   Calculate a balance on Zoe's cash account by totalling the Cash columns on both sides and deducting the cash on the credit side from the cash on the debit side (£282.00 – £256.40 = £25.60).

Cash Book – Debit side

Details	Discount allowed £	Cash £	Bank £	VAT £	Cash sales £	Trade receivables £	Sundry income £
Antoine			450.00			450.00	
Bazzer		282.00		47.00	235.00		
Ellie	30.00		750.00			750.00	
Total		**282.00**					

Cash Book – Credit side

Details	Discount received £	Cash £	Bank £	VAT £	Cash purchases £	Trade payables £	Petty cash £	Expenses £
Market		56.40		9.40	47.00			
Charlie			60.00			60.00		
Desmond	10.00	200.00				200.00		
Rates			40.00					40.00
Total		256.40						
Balance		25.60						

Step 2   Keep the amount of the cash balance in the **Cash** column on the credit side as the 'Banking' amount, since it is a payment of the balance of cash out of the Cash account and into the Bank account. This reduces the Cash balance to zero. (For clarity, you should also delete the total calculated in both Cash columns.)

Cash Book – Credit side

Details	Discount received £	Cash £	Bank £	VAT £	Cash purchases £	Trade payables £	Petty cash £	Expenses £
Market		56.40		9.40	47.00			
Charlie			60.00			60.00		
Desmond	10.00	200.00				200.00		
Rates			40.00					40.00
~~Total~~		~~256.40~~						
~~Balance~~ Banking		25.60						

Step 3   Enter the same amount in the **Bank** column on the debit side as it is a receipt into the bank account.

Cash Book – Debit side

Details	Discount allowed £	Cash £	Bank £	VAT £	Cash sales £	Trade receivables £	Sundry income £
Antoine			450.00			450.00	
Bazzer		282.00		47.00	235.00		
Ellie	30.00		750.00			750.00	
~~Total~~		~~282.00~~					
Banking			25.60				

PRIMARY RECORDS FOR THE CASH BOOK

Most businesses like Zoe's do not record each transaction immediately in the Cash Book. Instead they maintain PRIMARY RECORDS which are financial documents that are used to update the Cash Book on a regular basis. These primary records include:

For receipts	For payments
Remittance advice notes from credit customers	Remittance advice notes sent to credit suppliers
Receipts issued to non-credit customers paying in cash, by cheque or debit card, by credit card or by automated payment (usually till receipts or automated emails if it is an online sale)	Receipts issued by non-credit suppliers paid in cash, by cheque or debit card, by credit card or by automated payment (usually till receipts)
Paying-in slip stubs	Cheque book stubs
Automated receipts – bank statement and remittance advice note from customers	Automated payments – bank giro credit forms, and automated payments BACS and CHAPS), standing order and direct debit schedules, plus remittance advices sent to suppliers
Bank statements issued by the bank	

WRITING UP AND MAINTAINING THE CASH BOOK

We are now ready to go through the full process of writing up and maintaining the Cash Book from primary records, including:

- Cash and Bank balances brought forward
- Writing up transactions from primary records
- Making the entry for banking cash received
- Identifying the postings from the Cash Book
- Casting and cross-casting the Cash Book
- Calculating and carrying down the balances for Cash and for Bank

HOW IT WORKS

We will use examples of receipts and payments that Southfield Electrical received and made during the week ended 28 September 20XX. Before we start it may be useful for you to see the Cash Book as it will eventually be written up:

Cash Book – Debit side

Details	Ref	Discount allowed £	Cash £	Bank £	VAT £	Cash sales £	Trade receivables £
Bal b/f			900.00	12,940.00			
Dagwell	SL15	14.02		336.50			336.50
Polygon	SL03			158.20			158.20
Hayward				227.40	37.90	189.50	
G Thomas	SL30	11.23		269.43			269.43
Whitehill	SL24	28.07		673.58			673.58
Weller	SL18			225.49			225.49
Cash sale			75.60		12.60	63.00	
Treseme	SL42	40.00		2,910.00			2,910.00
Banking				200.00			
Totals		93.32	975.60	17,940.60	50.50	252.50	4,573.20
Bal b/d			**507.70**	**13,615.56**			

Cash Book – Credit side

Details	Cheque number	Ref	Discount received £	Cash £	Bank £	VAT £	Cash purchases £	Trade payables £
Seeban	003102	PL46	67.62		1,284.90			1,284.90
Electric	003103	PL13			440.00			440.00
Comtec	003104	PL19	34.23		650.37			650.37
Chiller	003105	PL03			849.37			849.37
Cash purchase				267.90		44.65	223.25	
Cash purchase	003106				500.40	83.40	417.00	
Benham	STO	PL12			400.00			400.00
Gas	DD	PL04			200.00			200.00
Banking				200.00				
Bal c/d				**507.70**	**13,615.56**			
Totals			101.85	~~467.90~~ 975.60	~~4,325.04~~ 17,940.60	128.05	640.25	3,824.64

Southfield Electrical started the week with £900.00 held in cash and £12,940.00 held in the bank account. As we saw in Chapter 6 brought down (or 'brought forward' or 'b/f' balances of assets) are shown on the DEBIT side of a general ledger account, that is on the RECEIPTS side of the Cash Book.

Cash Book – Debit side

Details	Ref	Discount allowed £	Cash £	Bank £	VAT £	Cash sales £	Trade receivables £
Bal b/f			900.00	12,940.00			

Receipts of cheques and cash for the week, together with information on settlement discounts taken as set out in the customer's remittance advice notes, were as follows:

CASH AND CHEQUES RECEIVED	
	£
Dagwell Enterprises, cheque	336.50 (£14.02 discount taken)
Polygon Stores, cheque	158.20
Peter Hayward, cheque	227.40 including VAT
(customer without credit account)	
G Thomas & Co, cheque	269.43 (£11.23 discount taken)
Whitehill Superstores, cheque	673.58 (£28.07 discount taken)
Weller Enterprises, cheque	225.49
John Cooper, cash	75.60 including VAT
(customer without credit account)	

Customer codes (being the sales ledger account codes) are as follows:

Polygon Stores	SL03
Dagwell Enterprises	SL15
Weller Enterprises	SL18
Whitehill Superstores	SL24
G Thomas	SL30
Treseme Ltd	SL42

A remittance advice from Treseme Ltd indicates a receipt of £2,910.00 with discount taken of £40. This is to be received directly into the bank account by automated payment on 28 September.

Cheques completed and sent in the week together with supplier codes (purchase ledger account codes), and till receipts for cash purchases made, were as follows:

CHEQUES SENT

Cheque number	Payee	Supplier code	Amount £	Discount £
003102	Seeban	PL46	1,284.90	67.62
003103	Elec. North Ltd	PL13	440.00	
003104	Comtec Ltd	PL19	650.37	34.23
003105	Chiller Supplies	PL03	849.37	

TILL RECEIPTS FOR CASH PURCHASES

P J Harvey (inc VAT)	Cash purchase paid in cash	267.90
W G Supplies (inc VAT)	Cash purchase paid by cheque 003106	500.40

The relevant information from the business's automated payments schedules is as follows:

25th of each month	Benham District Council – business rates PL12
	£400.00 Standing order
27th of each month	English Gas – gas bill PL04
	£200.00 Direct debit

Finally the paying-in slip stub shows that £200.00 of cash physically held by Southfield at the end of the week was paid into the bank account on the Friday afternoon. All the cheques received were banked individually on the day of receipt using the paying-in book.

We can now complete both sides of the Cash Book.

As regards **receipts**:

- The receipt of cash by Southfield is entered in the Cash column (we are not including dates for reasons of space).

- The receipts of cheques by Southfield are entered individually in the Bank column.

- The automated payment received is entered in the Bank column.

- Each receipt is then analysed.

- The payment of cash into the bank account is recorded in the Cash column on the credit side and the Bank column on the debit side.

Cash Book – Debit side

Details	Ref	Discount allowed £	Cash £	Bank £	VAT £	Cash sales £	Trade receivables £
Bal b/f			900.00	12,940.00			
Dagwell	SL15	14.02		336.50			336.50
Polygon	SL03			158.20			158.20
Hayward				227.40	37.90	189.50	
G Thomas	SL30	11.23		269.43			269.43
Whitehill	SL24	28.07		673.58			673.58
Weller	SL18			225.49			225.49
Cash sale			75.60		12.60	63.00	
Treseme	SL42	40.00		2,910.00			2,910.00
Banking				200.00			

Remember that when cash sales are made to non-credit customers the VAT element must be analysed out:

Peter Hayward   VAT = £227.40 × 20/120   =   £37.90
John Cooper   VAT = £75.60 × 20/120   =   £12.60

As regards **payments**:

- The cheques, standing order and direct debit payments will be entered in the Bank column on the credit side. Each payment then needs to be analysed.

- The purchase made in cash will be entered in the Cash column on the credit side. The payment then needs to be analysed.

- The payment of cash into the bank account is recorded in the Cash column on the credit side.

Cash Book – Credit side

Details	Cheque number	Ref	Discount received £	Cash £	Bank £	VAT £	Cash purchases £	Trade payables £
Seeban	003102	PL46	67.62		1,284.90			1,284.90
Electric	003103	PL13			440.00			440.00
Comtec	003104	PL19	34.23		650.37			650.37
Chiller	003105	PL03			849.37			849.37
Cash purchase				267.90		44.65	223.25	
Cash purchase	003106				500.40	83.40	417.00	
Benham	STO	PL12			400.00			400.00
Gas	DD	PL04			200.00			200.00
Banking				200.00				

The cash purchases include VAT so must be analysed out into the VAT column:

P J Harvey (cash paid)   VAT = £267.90 × 20/120   =   £44.65

W G Supplies (cheque paid)   VAT = £500.40 × 20/120   =   £83.40

TOTALLING AND POSTING THE CASH BOOK

At this stage the Cash Book should be totalled. This totalling process is also sometimes known as CASTING. When casting any day book it is very easy to make errors in your additions. Therefore it is always advisable to CROSS CAST the day book as well. This means adding the analysis column totals to ensure that it adds back to the total column – if it does not then an error has been made. Once the day book has been cast and cross-cast the relevant amounts can be posted to the general ledger.

HOW IT WORKS

We cast each column and ensure that, for each side of the Cash Book, the analysis columns added together are the same as the totals for the two Cash and Bank columns, **ignoring any balance brought forward.**

> Step 1   Cast each column in the debit side of the Cash Book.

Cash Book – Debit side

Details	Ref	Discount allowed £	Cash £	Bank £	VAT £	Cash sales £	Trade receivables £
Bal b/f			900.00	12,940.00			
Dagwell	SL15	14.02		336.50			336.50
Polygon	SL03			158.20			158.20
Hayward				227.40	37.90	189.50	
G Thomas	SL30	11.23		269.43			269.43
Whitehill	SL24	28.07		673.58			673.58
Weller	SL18			225.49			225.49
Cash sale			75.60		12.60	63.00	
Treseme	SL42	40.00		2,910.00			2,910.00
Banking				200.00			
Totals		93.32	975.60	17,940.60	50.50	252.50	4,573.20

Step 2 Cross-cast the debit entries for the week in the Cash Book, making sure:

- Both the brought forward balances and the banking figure are deducted from the Cash and Bank totals

- The discounts allowed column is not included

	£
Cash total	975.60
Less cash balance b/f	(900.00)
Bank receipts total	17,940.60
Less: bank balance b/f	(12,940.00)
receipt of cash and cheques banked	(200.00)
	4,876.20
VAT	50.50
Cash sales	252.50
Trade receivables	4,573.20
	4,876.20

Step 3 Cast each column in the Cash Book on the credit side.

Cash Book – Credit side

Details	Cheque number	Ref	Discount received £	Cash £	Bank £	VAT £	Cash purchases £	Trade payables £
Seeban	003102	PL46	67.62		1,284.90			1,284.90
Electric	003103	PL13			440.00			440.00
Comtec	003104	PL19	34.23		650.37			650.37
Chiller	003105	PL03			849.37			849.37
Cash purchase				267.90		44.65	223.25	
Cash purchase	003106				500.40	83.40	417.00	
Benham	STO	PL12			400.00			400.00
Gas	DD	PL04			200.00			200.00
Banking				200.00				
Totals			101.85	467.90	4,325.04	128.05	640.25	3,824.64

Step 4 Cross-cast the entries for the week in the Cash Book on the credit side, making sure:

- Any brought forward balances (there are none here) and the banking figure are deducted from the Cash and Bank totals

- The discount received column is not included

	£
Cash total	467.90
Less payment of cash and cheques into bank	(200.00)
Bank total	4,325.04
	4,592.94
VAT	128.05
Cash purchases	640.25
Trade payables	3,824.64
	4,592.94

Step 5   Make the postings from the analysis columns of the debit side of the Cash Book. Remember that the Cash Book here is both a book of prime entry and a general ledger account. Therefore on the **receipts** side of the Cash Book:

- Entries in the Cash and the Bank columns are themselves the **debit** entries in the general ledger

- The analysis columns are posted to the **credit** sides of the relevant general ledger accounts (individual entries in the Trade receivables column are also credited to each relevant account in the sales ledger)

- The discount allowed column total is:

    – **Debited** to Discount allowed
    – **Credited** to the Sales ledger control account

Cash Book – Debit side

		Discount allowed £	Cash £	Bank £	VAT £	Cash sales £	Trade receivables £
Totals		93.32	975.60	17,940.60	50.50	252.50	4,573.20
General ledger	Debit	Discount allowed					
	Credit	Sales ledger control			VAT	Sales	Sales ledger control

Step 6   Make the postings from the analysis columns of the **credit** side of the Cash Book:

- Entries in the Cash and the Bank columns are themselves the **credit** entries in the general ledger

- The analysis columns are posted to the **debit** sides of the relevant general ledger accounts (individual entries in the Trade payables column are also debited to each relevant account in the purchases ledger)

- The discount received column total is:

  - **Debited** to the Purchases ledger control account
  - **Credited** to Discount received

Cash Book – Credit side

		Discount received £	Cash £	Bank £	VAT £	Cash purchases £	Trade payables £
Totals		101.85	467.90	4,325.04	128.05	640.25	3,824.64
General ledger	Debit	Purchases ledger control			VAT	Purchases	Purchases ledger control
	Credit	Discount received					

BALANCING THE CASH BOOK

In the three-column Cash Book there are only two balances: for the Cash account (cash in hand on the premises) and for the Bank account.

The procedure for finding the balances on the Cash Book is the same as for any other general ledger account. Let us look first at the Bank columns:

Step 1   For the totals on the two Bank columns, deduct the lower total from the higher total

Step 2   Write in this difference as the balance carried down in the column with the lower total

Step 3   Amend the total in that column so it casts properly

Step 4   Enter the balance in the Bank column on the other side as the balance brought down

Unless it has a nil balance, the Bank column may have either a debit or a credit balance brought down:

- A **debit balance** brought down means that the business has an **asset** at the bank, that is it has a **positive bank balance**

- A **credit balance** brought down means that the business has a **liability** to the bank, that is it has a negative or **overdrawn bank balance,** or **overdraft**

The same procedure applies for the Cash columns, but note that as we are dealing with actual notes and coin on the premises, there will only ever be either no balance for the Cash columns, or a debit balance.

HOW IT WORKS

Returning to Southfield Electrical Ltd you need to write in the closing balances on the Cash Book at 28 September 20XX.

- For the Bank columns, the debit side total (£17,940.60) is greater than the credit side (£4,325.04), so the balance of £13,615.56 is carried down from the credit side to the debit side, where it is a **debit balance**.

- For the Cash columns, the debit side total (£975.60) is greater than the credit side (£467.90), so the balance of £507.70 is carried down from the credit side to the debit side, where it is again a **debit balance**.

Cash Book – Debit side

Details	Ref	Discount allowed £	Cash £	Bank £	VAT £	Cash sales £	Trade receivables £
Bal b/f			900.00	12,940.00			
Dagwell	SL15	14.02		336.50			336.50
Polygon	SL03			158.20			158.20
Hayward				227.40	37.90	189.50	
G Thomas	SL30	11.23		269.43			269.43
Whitehill	SL24	28.07		673.58			673.58
Weller	SL18			225.49			225.49
Cash sale			75.60		12.60	63.00	
Treseme	SL42	40.00		2,910.00			2,910.00
Banking				200.00			
Totals		93.32	975.60	17,940.60	50.50	252.50	4,573.20
Bal b/d			**507.70**	**13,615.56**			

Cash Book – Credit side

Details	Cheque number	Ref	Discount received £	Cash £	Bank £	VAT £	Cash purchases £	Trade payables £
Seeban	003102	PL46	67.62		1,284.90			1,284.90
Electric	003103	PL13			440.00			440.00
Comtec	003104	PL19	34.23		650.37			650.37
Chiller	003105	PL03			849.37			849.37
Cash purchase				267.90		44.65	223.25	
Cash purchase	003106				500.40	83.40	417.00	
Benham	STO	PL12			400.00			400.00
Gas	DD	PL04			200.00			200.00
Banking				200.00				
Bal c/d				**507.70**	**13,615.56**			
Totals			101.85	~~467.90~~ 975.60	~~4,325.04~~ 17,940.60	128.05	640.25	3,824.64

It is worth making a double check that the Cash balance is correct as follows:

	£
Balance brought forward	900.00
Cash receipt from cash sale	75.60
Cash paid for cash purchase	(267.90)
Cash banked	(200.00)
Cash balance	507.70

CHAPTER OVERVIEW

- A three-column Cash Book includes a Cash column and a Bank column on each side and enables a business to fully record all transactions involving cash or the bank account

- The Cash Book (debit side) is written up from cheques and cash received plus automated receipts

- The Cash Book (credit side) is written up from the cheques and cash paid and from the list of automated payments, including standing order and direct debit payments

Keywords

Cash Book – name given to the Cash and Bank general ledger accounts, both the debit (receipts) and the credit (payments) sides

Three-column Cash Book – An analysed Cash Book where the first column is the Discounts column, the second is the Cash column and the third column is the Bank column

Primary records – receipts, invoices, remittances and other documents which are retained and used to update the Cash Book on a regular basis

Casting – an accounting term for adding up a column of figures

Cross cast – adding up the totals of a number of columns to check that they add back to the overall total

TEST YOUR LEARNING

Test 1

You work for Natural Productions. One of your duties is to write up the Cash Book. Natural Productions makes sales on credit to a number of credit customers and also has some cash sales from a small shop attached to the factory.

The cash and cheques received for the last week in January 20XX are given below. Note that all cheques are received from customers who have an account in the sales ledger.

23 Jan	£545.14 cheque from Hoppers Ltd – settlement discount £16.86
23 Jan	£116.70 cheque from Superior Products
24 Jan	£128.46 cash from cash sales including VAT
24 Jan	£367.20 automated payment from Esporta Leisure – settlement discount £11.36
25 Jan	£86.40 cash from cash sales including VAT
27 Jan	£706.64 cheque from Body Perfect – settlement discount £21.86
27 Jan	£58.80 cash from cash sales including VAT
27 Jan	£267.90 automated payment from Langans Beauty

You are required to:

(a) Record these receipts in the Cash Book given below
(b) Total the Cash Book and check that it cross-casts

Cash Book – Debit side

Date	Details	Discount allowed £	Cash £	Bank £	VAT £	Cash sales £	Trade receivables £

Test 2

What is the double entry required for discount allowed to customers?

Debit

Credit

Test 3

Most of the payments by Natural Productions are to credit suppliers but there are some cash purchases of materials from small suppliers which include VAT.

The cheque payments and cash purchases (all of which include VAT) for the week ending 27 January 20XX are given below:

Date	Cheque number	Supplier	Amount £	Discount £
23 Jan	002144	Trenter Ltd	1,110.09	28.47
23 Jan		Cash purchase	105.60	
24 Jan	002145	W J Jones	246.75	
24 Jan	002146	P J Phillips	789.60	
24 Jan		Cash purchase	125.40	
25 Jan	002147	Packing Supplies	305.45	8.04
26 Jan	002148	O & P Ltd	703.87	18.72
27 Jan		Cash purchase	96.00	

You are required to:

(a) Record these payments in the analysed Cash Book (credit side) given below

(b)   Total the credit side of the Cash Book and check that it cross-casts

Cash Book – Credit side

Date	Details	Cheque No	Discount received £	Cash £	Bank £	VAT £	Cash purchases £	Trade payables £

Test 4

At the beginning of the week ending 27 January 20XX Natural Productions had cash of £142.60 and an overdraft of £1,290.00. At the end of the week it banked cash of £50.00. With reference to your answers to Tests 1 and 3, what are the Cash and Bank balances at the end of the week?

Cash	£	
Bank	£	

Test 5

There are five payments to be entered in Isdain Co's Cash Book.

Till receipts from suppliers for Isdain Co's cash purchases

Supplier: Klimt Supplies	Supplier: Patel Trading	Supplier: TWE Ltd
Received cash with thanks for goods bought.	Received cash with thanks for goods bought.	Received cash with thanks for goods bought.
Net £75 VAT £15 Total £90	Net £285 VAT £57 Total £342	Net £83 (No VAT)

Stubs from Isdain Co's cheque book

Payee: Western Industries (Purchases ledger account PL725) £4,278 (Note: We have taken £80 settlement discount) Cheque number 256387	Payee: Mountebank Co For marketing leaflets (Isdain Co has no credit account with this supplier) £564 including VAT Cheque number 256388

(a) Enter the details of the three till receipts from suppliers and two cheque book stubs into the credit side of the Cash Book shown below. Total each column.

Cash Book – Credit side

Details	Discounts £	Cash £	Bank £	VAT £	Cash purchases £	Trade payables £	Marketing expenses £
Balance b/f			3,295				
Klimt Supplies							
Patel Trading							
TWE Ltd							
Western Industries							
Mountebank Co							
Total							

There are two automated payments received from credit customers to be entered in the Cash Book:

Vantage Ltd   £1,278

Marbles Co   £2,183 (this customer has taken a £15 discount)

(b) Enter the above details into the debit side of the Cash Book and total each column.

Cash Book – Debit side

Details	Discounts £	Cash £	Bank £	Trade receivables £
Balance b/f		792		
Vantage Ltd				
Marbles Co				
Total				

(c) Using your answers to (a) and (b) above, calculate the cash balance.

£ _____

(d)   Using your answers to (a) and (b) above, calculate the bank balance.

£	

(e)   Is the bank balance calculated in (d) above a debit or credit balance?

	✓
Debit	
Credit	

chapter 8:
DOUBLE ENTRY FOR SALES AND TRADE RECEIVABLES

chapter coverage 📖

In this chapter we look at posting details of credit and cash sales, sales returns and cash received into the accounting records. The topics covered are:

✍ Books of prime entry and the ledgers

✍ Posting the Sales Day Book

✍ Posting the Sales Returns Day Book

✍ Posting the Cash Book

BOOKS OF PRIME ENTRY AND THE LEDGERS

In Chapter 6 we looked at double entry bookkeeping in the general ledger and the sales and purchases ledgers for the transactions of a business. In those examples we entered each individual transaction directly into the ledger accounts, and using double entry principles this meant that each transaction was in fact entered twice in the general ledger.

In practice, this would be impractical and therefore a step is built into the process before the ledger account entries are made.

The first stage of the accounting process is to enter details of transaction documents into the BOOKS OF PRIME ENTRY, which we saw in Chapter 3.

TRANSACTION DOCUMENTS → BOOKS OF PRIME ENTRY → LEDGER ACCOUNTS

Three books of prime entry are relevant for sales and trade receivables:

- Invoices in respect of credit sales for a period are initially recorded in the Sales Day Book (SDB).

- Credit notes in respect of credit sales are recorded in the Sales Returns Day Book (SRDB).

- All receipts (including some that are not related to sales) and also discounts allowed are recorded in the debit side of the Cash Book (CB).

Both the general ledger and the sales ledger are affected by transactions involving credit sales and trade receivables, though it is only the general ledger that is part of the double entry system.

POSTING THE SALES DAY BOOK

The next stage of the accounting process is to transfer the details from the book of prime entry – we will look at the Sales Day Book first – to the accounting records, in this case:

- The general ledger (so we will be **debiting Trade receivables** and **crediting Sales**); and

- The sales ledger (where we will just be debiting the individual customer ledger accounts – the sales ledger is **not** part of the double entry bookkeeping system).

It is common to refer to the process of transferring data into the ledgers as POSTING to the ledgers from the day books.

SALES INVOICES

SALES DAY BOOK

ACCOUNTING RECORDS

GENERAL LEDGER   SALES LEDGER

In order to do this the Sales Day Book must first be cast and cross-cast. The day book used in Chapter 3 has now been cast.

Date 20XX	Customer	Invoice number	Customer code	Gross £	VAT £	Net £
1 May	Grigsons Ltd	10356	SL 21	199.20	33.20	166.00
1 May	Hall & Co	10357	SL 05	103.60	15.60	88.00
1 May	Harris & Sons	10358	SL 17	120.00	20.00	100.00
2 May	Jaytry Ltd	10359	SL 22	309.60	51.60	258.00
	Totals			732.40	120.40	612.00

As we saw in Chapter 7 in the case of the Cash Book, when casting any day book it is very easy to make errors in your additions. Therefore it is always advisable to cross cast as well. In the case of day books other than the Cash Book, this means adding the net total to the VAT to ensure that it adds back to the total of the gross amounts – if it does not then an error has been made in the casting (£612.00 + £120.40 = £732.40).

Posting to the general ledger

Now we want to post the totals from the Sales Day Book into the general ledger. Remember the general ledger is where the double entry takes place so let us consider the double entry required here. The Sales Day Book represents the sales on credit that have been made by the business so:

- **Gross** is the amount that the customer must pay to the business – the net total plus VAT. Therefore this is the amount of the trade receivable so the gross column total is a **debit** entry in the total trade receivables account in the general ledger, which as we saw in Chapter 6 is called the SALES LEDGER CONTROL ACCOUNT (SLCA).

- **Net total** is the total of credit sales – the business makes no profit out of charging VAT as it is paid over to HM Revenue and Customs (HMRC), therefore the VAT is excluded from the sales total. This net total column total must be a **credit** entry in the ledger account for SALES.

- **VAT total** is the amount of VAT that is owed as a liability to HMRC and as such is a **credit** entry in the VAT ledger account.

General ledger

Sales ledger control account (SLCA)

Details	£	Details	£
Sales*	732.40		

Sales account

Details	£	Details	£
		SLCA	612.00

VAT account

Details	£	Details	£
		Sales*	120.40

While there are three different entries for these transactions, as always in double entry the total of the debit entries must equal the total of the credit entries:

DEBIT		£732.40
CREDITS	£612.00 + £120.40 =	£732.40

* Note that in general in the Details we include the name of the other account to be debited or credited. In the case of the sales ledger control account however the other side of the entry is split between two accounts, Sales and VAT. In this case we include the name of the primary or linking transaction, Sales, under Details in the SLCA. The same is true in the VAT account, where again we include the name of the linking transaction, Sales, under Details.

Task 1

Identify the general ledger accounts that the following totals from the Sales Day Book will be posted to and whether they are a debit or a credit entry:

	Account name	Debit	Credit
Gross			
VAT			
Net			

Posting to the sales ledger

So far we have completed the double entry in the general ledger for credit sales, but it is vitally important that we go on to post the gross amounts to the individual trade receivable accounts in the SALES LEDGER, which is the collection of ledger accounts for individual credit customers. It is not part of the double entry system and is known as a SUBSIDIARY LEDGER.

Step 1   Find the individual customer's account in the sales ledger using the customer code in the reference column of the Sales Day Book.

Step 2   Enter the invoice total of the invoice, including VAT, on the debit side of the customer's account.

You will remember that we completed the following entries for the four invoices in the Sales Day Book in the sales ledger accounts in Chapter 3. You can assume the invoice in the last ledger account, Sukie Ltd, was posted three days ago.

Sales ledger

	Grigsons Ltd			SL 21
Details	£	Details		£
SDB – 10356	199.20			

	Hall & Co			SL 05
Details	£	Details		£
SDB – 10357	103.60			

	Harris & Sons			SL 17
Details	£	Details		£
SDB – 10358	120.00			

Jaytry Ltd   SL 22

Details	£	Details	£
SDB – 10359	309.60		

Sukie Ltd   SL 39

Details	£	Details	£
SDB – 10350	1,673.00		

Remember that in the sales ledger we use the details from the book of prime entry (the invoice number from the SDB in this case) as this makes it easier to trace the source of the transaction.

A useful double check at this point is that the total of all the postings we made to the sales ledger (ignore the Sukie Ltd posting) is the same as the single debit posting to the sales ledger control account from the Sales Day Book:

	Debit entries £	
Grigsons Ltd	199.20	
Hall & Co	103.60	Sales ledger
Harris & Sons	120.00	
Jaytry Ltd	309.60	
Sales ledger control	732.40	General ledger

POSTING THE SALES RETURNS DAY BOOK

We have already considered the preparation of credit notes for valid and authorised sales returns, and their entry into the Sales Returns Day Book. Now we will look at posting the Sales Returns Day Book to the general and sales ledgers.

First of all it needs to be cast and the totals cross cast.

Date 20XX	Customer	Credit note number	Customer code	Gross £	VAT £	Net £
4 May	Grigsons Ltd	CN668	SL 21	72.00	12.00	60.00
5 May	Harris & Sons	CN669	SL 17	96.00	16.00	80.00
	Totals			168.00	28.00	140.00

Again, remember to check that the column totals cross cast to the total of the credit note totals (£140.00 + £28.00 = £168.00).

Posting to the general ledger

In the general ledger the three column totals must be entered into the ledger accounts. The double entry is the reverse of that for a sale on credit, but let's consider the logic behind each entry:

- **Gross** As the customers have returned these goods they will no longer have to pay for them, so we must deduct the total of the gross amounts. As trade receivables are decreased, this total is a **credit** entry in the sales ledger control account.

- **Net total** is the total of sales returns for the period which is effectively the reverse of a sale. Therefore a **debit** entry is required in the SALES RETURNS LEDGER ACCOUNT (not the sales account – we keep these separate).

- **VAT** As these returned goods have not been sold the VAT is no longer due to HMRC. Therefore a **debit** entry is made in the VAT account.

General ledger

Sales ledger control account

Details	£	Details	£
Sales	732.40	Sales returns	168.00

Sales returns account

Details	£	Details	£
SLCA	140.00		

VAT account

Details	£	Details	£
Sales returns	28.00	Sales	120.40

Again note that:

- The total of the two new debit entries is equal to the new credit entry: £140.00 + £28.00 = £168.00

- In both the SLCA and the VAT account we include the linking transaction 'Sales returns' under Details, while in the sales returns account we include 'SLCA'

Posting to the sales ledger

We have completed the double entry in the general ledger for sales returns from credit customers, so now we must enter each individual credit note in the relevant customer's account in the sales ledger. The amount to be used is the gross amount and the trade receivable's account must be credited with this figure to show that the customer no longer owes this amount.

Grigsons Ltd			SL 21
Details	£	Details	£
SDB – 10356	199.20	SRDB – CN668	72.00

Harris & Sons			SL 17
Details	£	Details	£
SDB – 103568	120.00	SRDB – CN669	96.00

Again a useful double check is that the total of all the postings to the sales ledger from the Sales Returns Day Book is the same as the single credit posting to the sales ledger control account:

	Credit entries £	
Grigsons Ltd	72.00	Sales ledger
Harris & Sons	96.00	
Sales ledger control	168.00	General ledger

Task 2

A credit note for £200 plus VAT has been issued to a customer. How much will be entered in the sales ledger control account in the general ledger and the customer's account in the sales ledger, and will these entries be debits or credits?

	Amount £	Debit ✓	Credit ✓
Sales ledger control account (general ledger)			
Customer's account (sales ledger)			

Posting an analysed Sales Day Book

Where an organisation analyses its net sales into geographical area or product family, posting to the general ledger is the same except that there will be a posting to more than one sales account.

HOW IT WORKS

Analysed Sales Day Book

Date 20XX	Customer	Invoice number	Customer code	Gross £	VAT £	Net £	North £	South £	East £	West £
1/6	AB Ltd	936	SL23	120.00	20.00	100.00		100.00		
1/6	CD & Co	937	SL03	240.00	40.00	200.00			200.00	
2/6	EF Ltd	938	SL45	64.80	10.80	54.00	54.00			
3/6	GH Ltd	939	SL18	144.00	24.00	120.00				120.00
4/6	IJ Bros	940	SL25	72.00	12.00	60.00		60.00		
				640.80	106.80	534.00	54.00	160.00	200.00	120.00

The posting of this Sales Day Book in the general ledger requires a separate sales account for each area as follows:

Sales ledger control account

Details	£	Details	£
Sales	640.80		

VAT account

Details	£	Details	£
		Sales	106.80

Sales account – North

Details	£	Details	£
		SLCA	54.00

Sales account – South

Details	£	Details	£
		SLCA	160.00

Sales account – East

Details	£	Details	£
		SLCA	200.00

Sales account – West

Details	£	Details	£
		SLCA	120.00

You can again check that all of the credit entries do add up to the total of the debit entry £(106.80 + 54.00 + 160.00 + 200.00 + 120.00) = £640.80.

The posting of the debit entries to the sales ledger are unaffected as it is the individual invoice totals that are posted to the sales ledger.

POSTING THE CASH BOOK

We have looked at the Cash Book in some detail in Chapter 7, where we saw that it is the book of prime entry for the initial recording of receipts of cash in hand and into the business's bank account. We also saw how the Cash Book is posted to the general ledger depending on whether it acts only as a book of prime entry or as general ledger accounts for Cash and Bank in addition.

As with the Sales Day Book, the Cash Book is posted to the general ledger. Only some – not all – transactions are also posted to the sales ledger.

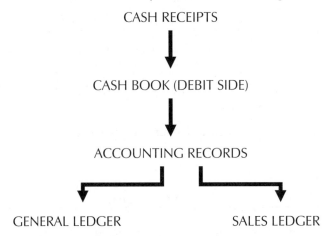

We shall use the following Cash Book (debit side) as an example. In order to do this the Cash Book must first be cast.

Date	Details	Ref	Discounts allowed £	Cash £	Bank £	VAT £	Cash sales £	Trade receivables £	Sundry £
10 May	Grigsons Ltd	SL 21			127.20			127.20	
10 May	Sukie Ltd	SL 39	22.00		1,651.00			1,651.00	
10 May	Cash sale			360.00		60.00	300.00		
10 May	Capital introduced				1,000.00				1,000.00
	Totals		22.00	360.00	2,778.20	60.00	300.00	1,778.20	1,000.00

Having studied Chapter 7 you will understand straightaway that the Cash Book does **not** cross-cast to the totals of the Cash and Bank columns: £(60.00 + 22.00 + 300.00 + 1,778.20 + 1,000.00) = £3,160.20, while £(360.00 + 2,778.20) = £3,138.20. The difference is £(3,160.20 − 3,138.20) = £22.00. This is the amount of the settlement discounts allowed, which is not received as cash so it is not included in the total cash receipt from Sukie Ltd shown in the 'bank' column.

Posting to the general ledger

If the Cash Book is acting only as a book of prime entry, all the totals are posted either to the debit or the credit side of an account in the general ledger, except for the settlement discounts allowed total which is posted twice:

- The debit entry is to the Discounts allowed expense account.
- The credit entry is to the Sales ledger control account.

Posting the Cash Book is therefore a more complicated task than posting the Sales Day Book.

HOW IT WORKS

We can now make the postings to the general ledger, which contains accounts for Cash and for Bank since the Cash Book is a book of prime entry only.

Note that for the debit entry in the Bank account we have included 'Bank receipts' under Details. Unlike with the Sales and Sales Returns Day Books, there are more than two other accounts which receive the other side of this entry (ie Sales and Capital), and the transactions are not linked. For the sake of neatness therefore we have used the catch-all 'Bank receipts' as a narrative here.

General ledger

Cash account

Details	£	Details	£
Cash sales	360.00		

Bank account

Details	£	Details	£
Bank receipts	2,778.20		

Sales ledger control account

Details	£	Details	£
Sales	732.40	Sales returns	168.00
		Bank (receipt)	1,778.20
		Bank (discount allowed)	22.00

Sales account

Details	£	Details	£
		SLCA	612.00
		Cash	300.00

Sales returns account

Details	£	Details	£
SLCA	140.00		

VAT account

Details	£	Details	£
Sales returns	28.00	Sales	120.40
		Cash	60.00

Discounts allowed account

Details	£	Details	£
Bank (SLCA)	22.00		

Capital account

Details	£	Details	£
		Bank	1,000.00

A useful double check is that the debit and credit postings marked 'Cash' or 'Bank' in the ledger accounts balance each other out (although you should note that usually the discounts allowed posting would not be marked Bank but would instead just contain the details of the two opposing accounts, Discounts allowed and SLCA):

Ledger account	Debit entries £	Credit entries £
Cash	360.00	
Bank	2,778.20	
Sales ledger control		1,778.20
Sales ledger control		22.00
Sales		300.00
VAT		60.00
Discounts allowed	22.00	
Capital		1,000.00
	3,160.20	3,160.20

Posting to the sales ledger

We also need to enter each credit sales-related receipt and the settlement discount in the customers' accounts in the sales ledger. The amount for the receipt is the amount in the 'Trade receivables' column and this must be entered in the **credit** side of the customer's ledger account as it is a reduction in how much the customer owes us. The amount for settlement discount allowed is the amount in the 'Discounts allowed' column and again must be entered on the **credit** side of the customer's account as it reduces the amount owed.

Remember that no debit entries are made as the sales ledger is not part of the double entry system. In addition, we do not post all the receipts in the Cash Book to the sales ledger: the two cash sales amounts (for the net sale and the related VAT) and the capital receipt are **not** posted to the sales ledger.

Sales ledger

Grigsons Ltd			SL 21
Details	£	Details	£
SDB – 10356	199.20	SRDB – CN668	72.00

Sukie Ltd			SL 39
Details	£	Details	£
SDB – 10350	1,673.00	CB – receipt	1,651.00
		CB – discounts allowed	22.00

Task 3

You have been handed the Sales Day Book and Sales Returns Day Books and the debit side of the Cash Book for Mr Chapter, plus relevant ledger accounts from his general and sales ledgers. The Cash Book is a book of prime entry only.

Total each day book, and then post each one to the ledgers.

Sales Day Book

Customer	Invoice number	Customer code	Gross £	VAT £	Net £
Trissom Ltd	124	SL 09	1,190.00	190.00	1,000.00
Miley & Co	125	SL 22	540.00	90.00	450.00
Totals					

Sales Returns Day Book

Customer	Credit note number	Customer code	Gross £	VAT £	Net £
Trissom Ltd	07	SL 09	238.00	38.00	200.00
Miley & Co	08	SL 22	36.00	6.00	30.00
Totals					

Cash Book – Debit side

Details	Ref	Discount allowed £	Cash £	Bank £	VAT £	Cash sales £	Trade receivables £
Trissom Ltd	SL 09	40.00		912.00			912.00
Miley & Co	SL 22			504.00			504.00
Cash sale			240.00		40.00	200.00	
Totals							

General ledger

Cash account

Details	£	Details	£

Bank account

Details	£	Details	£

Sales ledger control account

Details	£	Details	£

Sales account

Details	£	Details	£

Sales returns account

Details	£	Details	£

VAT account

Details	£	Details	£

Discounts allowed account

Details	£	Details	£

Sales ledger

Trissom Ltd   SL 09

Details	£	Details	£

Miley & Co   SL 22

Details	£	Details	£

The Cash Book as part of the general ledger

As we saw in Chapter 7, in many businesses the Cash Book is treated as **both** a book of prime entry **and** as part of the general ledger. This means that for receipts the Cash Book is itself the debit side of the Cash and the Bank general ledger accounts (the credit side of the account is the payments side of the Cash Book). The effect of this is that:

- There is no need to post debit entries for the total receipts from the Cash Book shown in the Cash and Bank columns.

- There is no Cash or Bank general ledger account.

- Credit entries, and both entries in respect of discounts allowed, are posted from the Cash Book as usual.

Task 4

The Cash Book for a business acts as both a book of prime entry and as part of the general ledger. Total receipts for the last month are as follows:

Details	Discounts allowed £	Cash £	Bank £	VAT £	Cash sales £	Trade receivables £
Totals	65.00	220.00	5,016.50	20.00	100.00	5,116.50

What entries will be posted to the general ledger (tick debit or credit for each entry)?

Account name	Amount £	Debit ✓	Credit ✓

CHAPTER OVERVIEW

- The first stage of the accounting process is to enter details of transactions into the books of prime entry eg Sales and Sales Returns Day Books and Cash Book

- The second stage of the accounting process is to transfer details from the books of prime entry to the accounting records ie the general ledger and sales ledger

- The Sales Day Book must be totalled and the totals entered into the ledger accounts in the general ledger

- The gross amount of each individual sales invoice must also be entered into the individual trade receivable's account in the sales ledger

- The Sales Returns Day Book must also be totalled and posted to the general ledger and the sales ledger

- The Cash Book must be totalled and posted to the general ledger

- Each receipt in the Trade receivables column of the Cash Book must also be entered into the individual trade receivable's account in the sales ledger

- The discounts allowed column in the Cash Book must have both a debit and a credit posting in the general ledger, and each individual entry must be credited to a trade receivable's account in the sales ledger

Keywords

Posting – transferring data from the books of prime entry (day books) into the ledgers

Sales ledger control account – a general ledger account for trade receivables, representing the total of all the accounts in the sales ledger

Subsidiary ledgers – ledgers that are not part of the general ledger and which contain a ledger account for each individual trade receivable or trade payable. Not part of the double entry system

Sales returns ledger account – used to record customer returns

TEST YOUR LEARNING

Test 1

From the Sales Day Book and Sales Returns Day Book below, make the relevant entries in the general ledger and sales ledger accounts.

Sales Day Book

Date	Customer	Invoice number	Customer code	Gross £	VAT £	Net £
21/9	Dagwell Enterprises	56401	SL15	948.60	158.10	790.50
21/9	G Thomas & Co	56402	SL30	3,537.60	589.60	2,948.00
21/9	Polygon Stores	56403	SL03	1,965.60	327.60	1,638.00
21/9	Weller Enterprises	56404	SL18	1,152.00	192.00	960.00
				7,603.80	1,267.30	6,336.50

Sales Returns Day Book

Date	Customer	Credit note number	Customer code	Gross £	VAT £	Net £
21/9	Whitehill Superstores	08650	SL37	356.40	59.40	297.00
23/9	Dagwell Enterprises	08651	SL15	244.80	40.80	204.00
				601.20	100.20	501.00

General ledger

Sales ledger control account

Details	£	Details	£

Sales account

Details	£	Details	£

Sales returns account

Details	£	Details	£

VAT account

Details	£	Details	£

Sales ledger

Dagwell Enterprises SL 15

Details	£	Details	£

G Thomas & Co SL 30

Details	£	Details	£

Polygon Stores SL 03

Details	£	Details	£

Weller Enterprises SL 18

Details	£	Details	£

Whitehill Superstores   SL 37

Details	£	Details	£

Test 2

Post the Cash Book below to the general ledger and sales ledger. Note the Cash Book is itself part of the general ledger.

Cash Book

Date	Details	Ref	Discounts allowed £	Cash £	Bank £	VAT £	Cash sales £	Trade receivables £
30/6	Cash sales			372.00		62.00	310.00	
30/6	H Henry	SL0115			146.79			146.79
30/6	P Peters	SL0135	6.85		221.55			221.55
30/6	K Kilpin	SL0128			440.30			440.30
30/6	Cash sales			300.76		50.12	250.64	
30/6	B Bennet	SL0134			57.80			57.80
30/6	S Shahir	SL0106	3.55		114.68			114.68
			10.40	672.76	981.12	112.12	560.64	981.12

General ledger

VAT account   GL 562

Details	£	Details	£

Sales account   GL 049

Details	£	Details	£

Sales ledger control account   GL 827

Details	£	Details	£

Discounts allowed account   GL 235

Details	£	Details	£

Sales ledger

H Henry   SL 0115

Details	£	Details	£

P Peters   SL 0135

Details	£	Details	£

K Kilpin   SL 0128

Details	£	Details	£

B Bennet   SL 0134

Details	£	Details	£

S Shahir   SL 0106

Details	£	Details	£

Test 3

Post the Cash Book below to the general ledger and sales ledger. The Cash Book is **not** part of the general ledger.

Cash Book

Date	Details	Ref	Discounts allowed £	Cash £	Bank £	VAT £	Cash sales £	Trade receivables £
20/5	G Gonpipe	SL55			332.67			332.67
20/5	Cash sales			672.00		112.00	560.00	
20/5	J Jimmings	SL04	6.70		127.37			127.37
20/5	N Nutely	SL16	17.70		336.28			336.28
20/5	T Turner	SL21			158.35			158.35
20/5	Cash sales			336.90		56.15	280.75	
20/5	R Ritner	SL45	38.90		739.10			739.10
			63.30	1,008.90	1,693.77	168.15	840.75	1,693.77

General ledger codes

Cash	050
Bank	100
Sales	110
Discounts allowed	280
Sales ledger control	560
VAT	710

General ledger

Cash **GL 050**

Details	£	Details	£

Bank **GL 100**

Details	£	Details	£

VAT account **GL 710**

Details	£	Details	£

Sales account **GL 110**

Details	£	Details	£

Sales ledger control account **GL 560**

Details	£	Details	£

Discounts allowed account **GL 280**

Details	£	Details	£

Sales ledger

G Gonpipe **SL 55**

Details	£	Details	£

J Jimmings   SL 04

Details	£	Details	£

N Nutely   SL 16

Details	£	Details	£

T Turner   SL 21

Details	£	Details	£

R Ritner   SL 45

Details	£	Details	£

Test 4

The following transactions all took place on 30 November and have been entered into the Sales Day Book as shown below. No entries have yet been made into the ledger system.

Sales Day Book

Date 20XX	Details	Invoice number	Gross £	VAT £	Net £
30 Nov	Fries & Co	23907	2,136	356	1,780
30 Nov	Hussey Enterprises	23908	3,108	518	2,590
30 Nov	Todd Trading	23909	3,720	620	3,100
30 Nov	Milford Ltd	23910	2,592	432	2,160
	Totals		11,556	1,926	9,630

Make the required entries in the general ledger.

VAT account

Details	£	Details	£

Sales account

Details	£	Details	£

Sales ledger control account

Details	£	Details	£

chapter 9:
DOUBLE ENTRY FOR PURCHASES AND TRADE PAYABLES

chapter coverage 📖

In this chapter we look at posting credit and cash purchases, purchases returns and cash paid into the ledgers. The topics covered are:

✎ Books of prime entry and the ledgers

✎ Posting the Purchases Day Book

✎ Posting the Purchases Returns Day Books

✎ Posting the Cash Book

BOOKS OF PRIME ENTRY AND THE LEDGERS

As with sales and trade receivables, the first stage of the accounting process for purchases and trade payables is to enter details of transaction documents into the relevant books of prime entry:

TRANSACTION   ➡   BOOKS OF   ➡   LEDGER
DOCUMENTS   PRIME ENTRY   ACCOUNTS

Three books of prime entry are relevant for purchases and trade payables:

- Invoices for purchases on credit that are received in a period are initially recorded in the Purchases Day Book.

- Credit notes received in respect of credit purchases are recorded in the Purchases Returns Day Book.

- All payments (including some that are not related to purchases) plus settlement discounts received from suppliers are recorded in the Cash Book.

Both the general ledger and the purchases ledger are affected by transactions involving credit purchases and trade payables, though it is only the general ledger that is part of the double entry system.

POSTING THE PURCHASES DAY BOOK

The next stage of the accounting process is to transfer details from the books of prime entry to the accounting records. We will look at the Purchases Day Book first.

The Purchases Day Book needs to be posted to:

- The general ledger (so we will be **crediting Trade payables** and **debiting Purchases** or some other **Expense**)

- The purchases ledger (where we will just be crediting the individual supplier ledger accounts – the purchases ledger is **not** part of the double entry bookkeeping system)

HOW IT WORKS

As with sales, we must first cast and cross cast the Purchases Day Book.

Date 20XX	Supplier	Invoice number	Supplier code	Gross £	VAT £	Purchases £	Telephone £	Stationery £
1 May	Haley Ltd	33728	PL 25	60.00	10.00			50.00
1 May	JJ Bros	242G	PL 14	1,440.00	240.00	1,200.00		
1 May	B Tel	530624	PL 06	154.00	24.00		130.00	
1 May	Shipley & Co	673	PL 59	4,800.00	800.00	4,000.00		
	Totals			6,454.00	1,074.00	5,200.00	130.00	50.00

The total of the analysis columns – in this case, for purchases, telephone and stationery – plus the VAT must add back to the total of the invoice totals – if not then an error has been made in the casting: £(5,200.00 + 130.00 + 50.00 + 1,074.00) = £6,454.00.

Posting to the general ledger

Now we want to post the totals into the general ledger. The Purchases Day Book represents the purchases on credit that have been made by the business so:

- **Gross** is the amount that the business must pay to the supplier – the net total plus VAT. Therefore this is the amount of the trade payable, so the invoice total column total is a **credit** entry in the purchases ledger control account (PLCA) in the general ledger.

- The **VAT total** is the amount of VAT that is reclaimable from HMRC (ie it is an asset) and as such is a **debit** entry in the VAT ledger account.

- ■ The **purchases, telephone** and **stationery** totals are the cost to the business of the goods it has acquired and the expenses it has incurred – the business does not suffer VAT as a cost as it is paid back by HM Revenue and Customs, so VAT is excluded from the purchases and expenses totals. The totals in these columns must be **debit** entries in the relevant general ledger accounts.

General ledger

Purchases ledger control account

Details	£	Details	£
		Purchases*	6,454.00

* Several accounts (purchases, telephone and stationery) take the other side of this entry. For the sake of neatness we have just included one under Details, namely Purchases.

Purchases account

Details	£	Details	£
PLCA	5,200.00		

Telephone account

Details	£	Details	£
PLCA	130.00		

Stationery account

Details	£	Details	£
PLCA	50.00		

VAT account

Details	£	Details	£
Purchases	1,074.00		

Under Details in the VAT account we include the linking transaction of Purchases, as we saw in Chapter 8.

While there are five different entries for these transactions, as always in double entry the total of the debit entries must equal the total of the credit entries:

DEBIT   £(5,200.00 + 130.00 + 50.00 + 1,074.00) £6,454.00

CREDITS   £6,454.00

Task 1

Identify the general ledger accounts that the following totals from the Purchases Day Book will be posted to, and whether they are a debit or a credit entry:

	Account name	Debit ✓	Credit ✓
Gross			
VAT			
Purchases			

Posting to the purchases ledger

We have completed the double entry in the general ledger for credit purchases, so we now need to post the invoice totals to the individual payable accounts in the PURCHASES LEDGER, which is the collection of ledger accounts for individual credit suppliers. It is not part of the double entry system and, like the sales ledger, is known as a subsidiary ledger.

Step 1   Find the individual supplier's account in the purchases ledger using the supplier code.

Step 2   Enter the invoice total of the invoice (ie including VAT) on the credit side of the supplier's account.

Purchases ledger

Haley Ltd			PL 25
Details	£	Details	£
		PDB – 33728	60.00

JJ Bros			PL 14
Details	£	Details	£
		PDB – 242G	1,440.00

B Tel			PL 06
Details	£	Details	£
		PDB – 530824	154.00

Shipley & Co			PL 59
Details	£	Details	£
		PDB – 673	4,800.00

A useful double check at this point is that the total of all the postings we have just made to the purchases ledger is the same as the single credit posting to the purchases ledger control account from the Purchases Day Book:

	Credit entries £	
Haley Ltd	60.00	
JJ Bros	1,440.00	Purchases ledger
B Tel	154.00	
Shipley & Co	4,800.00	
Purchases ledger control	6,454.00	General ledger

POSTING THE PURCHASES RETURNS DAY BOOK

We have already considered the preparation of credit notes for valid and authorised purchases returns, and their entry into the Purchases Returns Day Book. Now we will look at posting the Purchases Returns Day Book to the general and purchases ledgers.

HOW IT WORKS

First of all, it needs to be cast and the totals cross cast.

Date 20XX	Supplier	Credit note number	Supplier code	Gross £	VAT £	Purchases £	Telephone £	Stationery £
4 May	Haley Ltd	CN783	PL25	24.00	4.00			20.00
5 May	JJ Bros	C52246	PL14	69.60	11.60	58.00		
				93.60	15.60	58.00		20.00

Again remember to check that the column totals do cross cast to the total of the credit note totals (£20.00 + £58.00 + £15.60 = £93.60).

Posting to the general ledger

In the general ledger the column totals must be entered into the ledger accounts. The double entry is the reverse of that for a purchase on credit, but let's consider the logic behind each entry:

- **Gross** – As the business has returned these goods to suppliers it will no longer have to pay for them, so we must deduct the total column for the credit note totals. As trade payables are decreased, this total is a **debit** entry in the purchases ledger control account.

- **VAT total** – As the cost of these returned goods has not been incurred the VAT is no longer reclaimable from HMRC. Therefore a **credit** entry is made in the VAT account.

The **purchases** and **stationery** totals are the reduction in the cost to the business of the goods it has returned – again VAT is excluded.

- The total in the purchases column is a **credit** entry in the purchases returns account.

- The total in the stationery column is a **credit** entry in the stationery returns account.

General ledger

Purchases ledger control account

Details	£	Details	£
Purchases returns*	93.60	Purchases	6,454.00

* Again for the sake of neatness we have included just one named linked account here even though there are two (stationery returns as well as purchases returns) plus VAT that take the other side of the entry.

Purchases returns account

Details	£	Details	£
		PLCA	58.00

Stationery returns account

Details	£	Details	£
		PLCA	20.00

VAT account

Details	£	Details	£
Purchases	1,074.00	Purchases returns	15.60

Again, note that the total of the three credit postings is equal to the debit posting: £58.00 + £20.00 + £15.60 = £93.60.

Posting to the purchases ledger

We have completed the double entry in the general ledger for purchases returns to credit suppliers, so now we must enter each individual credit note in the supplier's account in the purchases ledger. The amount to be used is the credit note total and the trade payable's account must be **debited** with this figure to show that the business no longer owes the supplier this amount.

Purchases ledger

Haley Ltd   PL 25

Details	£	Details	£
PRDB – CN783	24.00	PDB – 33728	60.00

JJ Bros   PL 14

Details	£	Details	£
PRDB – C52246	69.60	PDB – 242G	1,440.00

Again, a useful double check is that the total of all the postings to the purchases ledger from the Purchases Returns Day Book is the same as the single debit posting to the purchases ledger control account.

	Debit entries £	
Haley Ltd	24.00	Purchases ledger
JJ Bros	69.60	
Purchases ledger control	93.60	General ledger

Task 2

A credit note for £600 plus VAT has been received from a supplier. How much will be entered in the purchases ledger control account in the general ledger and the supplier's account in the purchases ledger, and will this entry be a debit or a credit?

	Amount £	Debit	Credit
Purchases ledger control account (general ledger)			
Supplier's account (purchases ledger)			

POSTING THE CASH BOOK

As with the Purchases and Purchases Returns Day Book, the Cash Book is posted to the general ledger. Some – but not all – transactions are also posted to the purchases ledger.

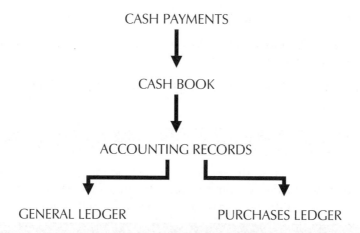

CASH PAYMENTS

CASH BOOK

ACCOUNTING RECORDS

GENERAL LEDGER   PURCHASES LEDGER

HOW IT WORKS

In order to post payments from the Cash Book to the ledgers it must first be cast and cross cast.

Date	Details	Ref	Discounts received £	Cash £	Bank £	VAT £	Cash purchases £	Trade payables £	Petty cash £	Sundry £
10 May	Haley Ltd	PL 25			36.00			36.00		
10 May	Shipley & Co	PL 59	200.00		4,600.00			4,600.00		
10 May	Cash purchase			204.00		34.00	170.00			
10 May	Drawings			300.00						300.00
10 May	Petty cash				150.00				150.00	
	Totals		200.00	504.00	4,786.00	34.00	170.00	4,636.00	150.00	300.00

You will see straightaway that the Cash Book does **not** cross cast to the total of the Cash and Bank totals £(504.00 + 4,786.00 = 5,290.00) since the £200.00 discount received has to be ignored: £(34.00 + 170.00 + 4,636.00 + 150.00 + 300.00) = £5,290.00.

Posting to the general ledger

All the other totals in the Cash Book are posted either to the debit or the credit side of an account in the general ledger, but the settlement discounts received total is posted twice:

- The debit entry is to the Purchases ledger control account.

- The credit entry is to the Discounts received account, which is a type of income account.

Posting the Cash Book is therefore a slightly more complicated task than posting the Purchases Day Book.

HOW IT WORKS

The easiest way to see how the postings are made in the general ledger is to show the relevant general ledger account name beneath each Cash Book total, with an indication of whether the posting is a debit entry or a credit entry:

Date	Details	Discounts received £	Cash £	Bank £	VAT £	Cash purchases £	Trade payables £	Petty cash £	Sundry £
	Totals	200.00	504.00	4,786.00	34.00	170.00	4,636.00	150.00	300.00
General ledger account	Debit entry	Purchases ledger control			VAT	Purchases	Purchases ledger control	Petty cash	Drawings
	Credit entry	Discounts received	Cash	Bank					

We can then make the postings to the general ledger:

General ledger

Cash account

Details	£	Details	£
		Cash payments*	504.00

Bank account

Details	£	Details	£
		Bank payments*	4,786.00

*As in Chapter 8, because there are a number of unlinked accounts which take the opposing entries, we have used a catch-all narrative under Details here (Cash payments or Bank payments).

Purchases ledger control account

Details	£	Details	£
Purchases returns	93.60	Purchases	6,454.00
Bank	4,636.00		
Discounts received	200.00		

Purchases account

Details	£	Details	£
PLCA	5,200.00		
Cash	170.00		

Purchases returns account

Details	£	Details	£
		PLCA	58.00

Telephone account

Details	£	Details	£
PLCA	130.00		

Stationery account

Details	£	Details	£
PLCA	50.00		

Stationery returns account

Details	£	Details	£
		PLCA	20.00

VAT account

Details	£	Details	£
Purchases	1,074.00	Purchases returns	15.60
Cash	34.00		

Discounts received account

Details	£	Details	£
		PLCA	200.00

Petty cash account*

Details	£	Details	£
Bank	150.00		

Drawings account

Details	£	Details	£
Cash	300.00		

*Note we shall see more about petty cash, the Petty Cash Book and the petty cash account in the general ledger in Chapter 10.

A useful double check is that the most recent debit and credit postings in the ledger accounts balance each other out:

Ledger account	Debit entries £	Credit entries £
Cash		504.00
Bank		4,786.00
Purchases ledger control (payments)	4,636.00	
Purchases ledger control (discounts received)	200.00	
Purchases	170.00	
VAT	34.00	
Discounts received		200.00
Petty cash	150.00	
Drawings	300.00	
	5,490.00	5,490.00

Posting to the purchases ledger

We also need to enter each credit purchases-related payment and the settlement discount in the suppliers' accounts in the purchases ledger. The amount for the payment is the amount in the 'Trade payables' column and this must be entered in the **debit** side of the purchases ledger account as it is a reduction in how much the business owes. The amount for settlement discount received is the amount from the Discounts received column in the Cash Book and again must be entered on the **debit** side of the supplier's account as it reduces the amount owed.

Remember that no credit entries are made as the purchases ledger is not part of the double entry system. In addition, we do not post the two cash purchases amounts (for the net purchase and the related VAT) nor the petty cash or drawings payments to the purchases ledger.

Purchases ledger

Haley Ltd   **PL 25**

Details	£	Details	£
PRDB – CN783	24.00	PDB – 33728	60.00
CB – payment	36.00		

Shipley & Co   **PL 59**

Details	£	Details	£
CB – payment	4,600.00	PDB – 673	4,800.00
CB – discount	200.00		

Task 3

You have been handed the unanalysed Purchases and Purchases Returns Day Books and the credit side of the Cash Book for Mr Chapter, plus relevant ledger accounts from his general and purchases ledgers.

Total each day book and then post each one to the ledgers.

Purchases Day Book

Supplier	Invoice number	Supplier code	Gross £	VAT £	Net £
Rawley Ltd	7869	PL 54	3,000.00	500.00	2,500.00
Jipsum plc	323980	PL 02	3,808.00	608.00	3,200.00
Totals					

Purchases Returns Day Book

Supplier	Credit note number	Supplier code	Gross £	VAT £	Net £
Rawley Ltd	CN627	PL 54	96.00	16.00	80.00
Jipsum plc	CN08	PL 02	476.00	76.00	400.00
Totals					

Cash Book

Details	Ref	Discounts received £	Cash £	Bank £	VAT £	Cash purchases £	Trade payables £
Rawley Ltd	PL 54			2,904.00			2,904.00
Jipsum plc	PL 02	140.00		3,192.00			3,192.00
Cash purchase			720.00		120.00	600.00	
Totals							

General ledger

Cash account

Details	£	Details	£

Bank account

Details	£	Details	£

Purchases ledger control account

Details	£	Details	£

Purchases account

Details	£	Details	£

Purchases returns account

Details	£	Details	£

VAT account

Details	£	Details	£

Discounts received account

Details	£	Details	£

Purchases ledger

Rawley Ltd   PL 54

Details	£	Details	£

Jipsum plc   PL 02

Details	£	Details	£

The Cash Book as part of the general ledger

The Cash Book for payments is a book of prime entry that records cash going out of the business's cash in hand and bank account. The example we have seen so far in this chapter is of a Cash Book that is just a book of prime entry: postings from it are always to the credit side of the Cash and the Bank ledger accounts in the general ledger, with debit entries being posted to the purchases ledger control account, purchases, VAT etc.

Where the Cash Book is treated as **both** a book of prime entry **and** part of the general ledger, the Cash Book for payments is itself the credit side of general ledger accounts for Cash and for Bank. The effect of this is that:

- There is no need to post credit entries for the total columns from the Cash Book.

- There are no Cash or Bank general ledger accounts.

- Debit entries from the Cash Book, plus both entries for discounts received, are posted as usual.

Task 4

The Cash Book for a business is both a book of prime entry and part of the general ledger. Total payments for the last month are as follows:

Details	Discounts received £	Cash £	Bank £	VAT £	Cash purchases £	Trade receivables £
Totals	109.00	386.00	2,911.65	48.00	240.00	3,009.65

What entries will be posted to the general ledger (tick debit or credit for each entry)?

Account name	Amount £	Debit ✓	Credit ✓

CHAPTER OVERVIEW

- The first stage of the accounting process is to enter details of transactions into the books of prime entry eg Purchases and Purchases Returns Day Books and Cash Book – credit side

- The second stage is to transfer details from the books of prime entry to the accounting records ie the general ledger and purchases ledger

- The Purchases Day Book must be totalled and the totals entered into the ledger accounts in the general ledger

- The gross amount of each individual purchase invoice must be entered into the individual trade payable's account in the purchases ledger

- The Purchases Returns Day Book must be totalled and posted to the general ledger and the purchases ledger

- The Cash Book – credit side must be totalled and posted to the general ledger (only debit entries, plus the debit and credit discount entries, if the Cash Book is part of the general ledger as well as a book of prime entry)

- Each cash payment in the trade payables column of the Cash Book must be entered into the individual trade payable's account in the purchases ledger

- The discounts received column in the Cash Book must have both a debit and a credit posting in the general ledger

Keywords

Purchases ledger control account – total trade payables account in the general ledger

Purchases ledger – collection of ledger accounts for individual credit suppliers (not part of the double entry system – a subsidiary ledger)

TEST YOUR LEARNING

Test 1

From the Purchases Day Book and Purchases Returns Day Book below, make the relevant entries in the general ledger and purchases ledger accounts.

Purchases Day Book

Date	Supplier	Invoice number	Supplier code	Gross £	VAT £	Net £
16/10	Herne Industries	46121	PL15	864.00	144.00	720.00
15/10	Bass Engineers	663211	PL13	460.80	76.80	384.00
12/10	Southfield Electrical	56521	PL20	2,008.80	334.80	1,674.00
				3,333.60	555.60	2,778.00

Purchases Returns Day Book

Date	Supplier	Credit note number	Supplier code	Gross £	VAT £	Net £
20/10	Southfield Electrical	08702	PL20	120.00	20.00	100.00
20/10	Herne Industries	4502	PL15	132.00	22.00	110.00
				252.00	42.00	210.00

General ledger

Purchases ledger control account

Details	£	Details	£

Purchases account

Details	£	Details	£

Purchases returns account

Details	£	Details	£

VAT account

Details	£	Details	£

Purchases ledger

Herne Industries   PL 15

Details	£	Details	£

Bass Engineers   PL 13

Details	£	Details	£

Southfield Electrical   PL 20

Details	£	Details	£

Test 2

Post from the Cash Book below to the general ledger and purchases ledger accounts. The Cash Book is **not** part of the double entry system.

Details	Ref	Discounts received £	Cash £	Bank £	VAT £	Cash purchases £	Trade payables £	Sundry £
P Products Ltd	PL23			241.58			241.58	
Jason Bros	PL36	6.86		336.29			336.29	
P Taylor			255.24		42.54	212.70		
R R Partners	PL06	4.19		163.47			163.47	
Troyde Ltd	PL14			183.57			183.57	
O L Simms			119.40		19.90	99.50		
F Elliott	PL20	8.15		263.68			263.68	
G L Finance	GL400			200.00				200.00
		19.20	374.64	1,388.59	62.44	312.20	1,188.59	200.00

General ledger

VAT account   GL 100

Details	£	Details	£

Purchases account   GL 200

Details	£	Details	£

Purchases ledger control account   GL 300

Details	£	Details	£

Loan account   GL 400

Details	£	Details	£

Discounts received   GL 500

Details	£	Details	£

Cash   GL 550

Details	£	Details	£

Bank   GL 600

Details	£	Details	£

Purchases ledger

R R Partners   PL 06

Details	£	Details	£

Troyde Ltd — PL 14

Details	£	Details	£

F Elliott — PL 20

Details	£	Details	£

P Products Ltd — PL 23

Details	£	Details	£

Jason Bros — PL 36

Details	£	Details	£

Test 3

The following transactions all took place on 30 November and have been entered into the Purchases Day Book as shown below. No entries have yet been made into the ledger system.

Purchases Day Book

Date 20XX	Details	Invoice number	Gross £	VAT £	Net £
30 Nov	Lindell Co	24577	2,136	356	1,780
30 Nov	Harris Rugs	829	5,256	876	4,380
30 Nov	Kinshasa Music	10/235	2,796	466	2,330
30 Nov	Calnan Ltd	9836524	2,292	382	1,910
	Totals		12,480	2,080	10,400

Make the required entries in the general ledger.

VAT account

Details	£	Details	£

Purchases account

Details	£	Details	£

Purchases ledger control account

Details	£	Details	£

chapter 10:
ACCOUNTING FOR PETTY CASH

chapter coverage 📖

In this chapter we consider all the procedures necessary for dealing with and accounting for petty cash. The topics covered are:

- ✍ The petty cash system
- ✍ Petty cash claims
- ✍ An imprest system for petty cash
- ✍ Petty cash vouchers
- ✍ Petty Cash Book
- ✍ VAT
- ✍ Writing up the Petty Cash Book
- ✍ Reconciling the Petty Cash Book with petty cash
- ✍ Topping-up petty cash: restoring the imprest
- ✍ Posting the Petty Cash Book – receipts side
- ✍ Posting the Petty Cash Book – payments side

THE PETTY CASH SYSTEM

We have seen that the Cash Book is the book of prime entry for both cash received from cash sales and trade receivables and money held in the business's bank account. The payments of most organisations will usually be from the bank account by cheque, debit card or automated payment, since businesses generally try to avoid paying out for expenses in notes and coin received from cash sales. Instead the common practice is to bank cash and cheques as soon as possible, as we have seen.

However most businesses need to access small amounts of notes and coin on occasion to make various small payments. It is convenient to have an amount specifically set aside for this purpose rather than to hope there is cash from cash sales available whenever it is needed. This readily available amount of notes and coin is known as PETTY CASH ('small' cash).

Petty cash is used to:

- Make low value cash purchases

- Reimburse employees immediately for valid business expenses they have paid for from their own money on the business's behalf

Examples of typical reasons for needing cash for purchases might include:

- Purchase of stationery or small items (eg milk, coffee) required in the office

- Postage payments

- Payment of casual, non-payroll wages, eg the window cleaner

- Payment of taxi and bus fares needed for business travel by relevant staff

It would be inappropriate to draw up a cheque or authorise an automated payment each time these types of expense are incurred so, instead, a small amount of cash is kept for these purposes, known as the PETTY CASH FLOAT.

In outline, the petty cash system is operated by the PETTY CASHIER who:

- Writes out a cheque for a certain amount of cash to be withdrawn from the bank account

- Collects this amount as notes and coin from the bank

- Places the cash in a lockable PETTY CASH BOX

- Physically looks after the petty cash box

- Deals with all PETTY CASH CLAIMS

- Ensures that every payment from petty cash has a valid PETTY CASH VOUCHER

- Writes up the PETTY CASH BOOK, which is the book of prime entry for petty cash

- Regularly checks that the amount of notes and coin in the petty cash box is correct

- Tops up the amount of notes and coin in the petty cash box so there is always money available

PETTY CASH CLAIMS

Before looking at the details of recording and accounting for petty cash we will consider the overall process of an employee being reimbursed for expenditure by making a claim for petty cash.

HOW IT WORKS

Your name is P Norris and you work in the accounts department of Southfield Electrical. You have been asked to go out to the local shop, called Corner Stores, to buy more coffee for the office kitchen. This is how the petty cash claim process would work:

you go to the shop and buy a jar of coffee
with your own money for £3.59

you return to the office with the coffee
and a shop till receipt for £3.59

you go to the petty cashier and fill out a petty cash voucher
with the shop receipt attached

you take the petty cash voucher to the person who told you
to buy the coffee for authorisation

you take the authorised petty cash voucher to the petty cashier
and you are given £3.59 in return

the petty cashier puts the petty cash voucher in the petty cash box
and eventually records this in the petty cash book

We will now consider this system in more detail.

AN IMPREST SYSTEM FOR PETTY CASH

An IMPREST SYSTEM for petty cash is a common method of dealing with petty cash as it provides a fairly simple way of controlling the cash and payments.

The principle of an imprest system is that when the system is set up a certain sum of cash, say £100, is put into the petty cash box. This is the IMPREST AMOUNT. In order for any money to be paid out of the petty cash box a valid, authorised petty cash voucher must be created. These vouchers, once the money that they represent has been paid out, are also kept in the petty cash box. Therefore, at any point in time, the amount of cash in the box plus the total of the vouchers should equal the imprest amount:

| CASH | + | VOUCHERS | = | £100 |

At the end of a period of time (such as a week or month, or when the cash falls below a certain level) the cash in the petty cash box is topped up to the imprest amount. This is done by withdrawing cash from the organisation's bank account (by writing a cheque payable to cash and presenting this at the bank). The amount needed to top-up the petty cash box to the imprest amount is the total of the vouchers for the period:

	£
Imprest amount at start of period	100.00
Petty cash paid out = vouchers	(64.00)
Cash remaining in box	36.00
Cash withdrawn from bank to restore imprest amount	64.00
Cash at start of next period = imprest amount	100.00

Other non-imprest petty cash systems may be used by some organisations where, for example, a fixed amount is paid into the petty cash box at the start of each week or month.

PETTY CASH VOUCHERS

The key internal document for the proper functioning of a petty cash system is the PETTY CASH VOUCHER. This must be completed by the petty cashier and authorised before any cash can be paid out of the petty cash box.

The petty cash voucher for your coffee purchase from Corner Stores is given below:

PETTY CASH VOUCHER

Number: *0463* Date: *1 June XX*

Details	Amount
Coffee for office kitchen	*3 - 59*
Net	*3 - 59*
VAT	—
Total	*3 - 59*

Claimed by: *P. Norris*
Authorised by: *J. Smith*

There are a number of important points to note about this petty cash voucher:

- It is prepared by the petty cashier in response to a request from an employee who has a valid receipt – in this case it would be a till receipt – for expenditure to be reimbursed.

- It has a sequential number entered by the petty cashier – '0463' – which ensures that all petty cash vouchers are accounted for.

- The details of the expense are clear – 'coffee for office kitchen' – and a till receipt (from the shop) should be attached.

- The amount of the expense is shown both net of VAT and gross, with VAT at 20% separated out where appropriate – in this case there is no charge for VAT because the purchase was of food (see later in the chapter).

- The voucher is signed by you, the employee claiming the petty cash – 'P Norris'.

- Most importantly the voucher is authorised by an appropriate member of staff – 'J Smith'.

If money had been taken out of the box by you and taken to Corner Stores to pay for the purchase, so you did not have to pay out your own cash at all, then the petty cash voucher would be completed in the same way, except that instead of 'Claimed by P Norris' it would be marked 'Paid to Corner Stores'. The till receipt would need to be authorised and attached in both cases.

Task 1

Stationery has been purchased for £4.00 plus VAT at 20%. Insert the amount that will be included as the total figure on the petty cash voucher.

£

PETTY CASH BOOK

Once payments have been made out of the petty cash box and petty cash vouchers have been placed back in the box, they must be recorded in the Petty Cash Book, which is the book of prime entry for petty cash. As for the Cash Book, as well as being a book of prime entry the Petty Cash Book may also itself be the Petty cash general ledger account and, therefore, part of the double entry system:

- The Petty Cash Book DEBIT side is for receipts of notes and coin into petty cash.

- The Petty Cash Book CREDIT side is for payments of notes and coin from petty cash.

This is what a typical Petty Cash Book might look like:

Petty Cash Book

Debit side RECEIPTS			Credit side PAYMENTS								
							ANALYSIS COLUMNS				
Date	Details	Total £	Date	Details	Voucher number	Total £	VAT £	Travel £	Post £	Stationery £	Office supplies £

Note the following points about this layout:

- The receipts (debit) side of the Petty Cash Book is not analysed, as all that will be recorded here is the receipt of cash from the bank into the petty cash box.

- The total on the payments (credit) side is analysed into the types of petty cash expenditure incurred by the organisation (there may well be more or fewer columns than are illustrated here).

- The payments side includes an analysis column for VAT as this must be analysed out if any of the payments include a VAT element (see below).

VAT

If a payment is made out of the petty cash box for an item that has had VAT charged on it:

- The total amount paid out (the gross amount) is recorded in the Total column.

- The VAT paid is analysed in the VAT column.

- The net of VAT amount is analysed in the relevant analysis column (eg Stationery, Office supplies) – there is no separate Net column.

The VAT laws are fairly complex but for the purposes of writing-up the Petty Cash Book the following guidelines should help. There is no VAT on:

- Postage costs
- Bus or rail fares
- Food or drink

Where the seller is registered for VAT there is VAT on:

- Stationery
- Taxi fares

When goods are purchased in a shop a till receipt is given to the customer. When a claim for petty cash is made this receipt is used to determine any VAT on the purchase. Very often this till receipt shows only the total price of the goods and the VAT is not analysed out. However, the VAT can be reclaimed from HM Revenue and Customs, provided the following are shown on the till receipt:

- The total is less than £250
- The retailer's name, address and VAT registration number
- The date of supply and a description of the goods

In this instance the VAT can be calculated from the total amount (using the 20/120 or 1/6 VAT fraction) and recorded in the Petty Cash Book.

In an assessment you may assume that a valid till receipt for VAT is held unless you are specifically told otherwise.

HOW IT WORKS

A typical till receipt for a pack of printer paper is shown below:

```
F G SMITH
VAT 446 7265 31

1 Manchester Road
London, W1 3PZ

PAPER          3.60
TOTAL          3.60

CASH           5.00
CHANGE         1.40

CASHIER 2
10.26AM 8/12/XX
```

- The receipt contains the shop's name, address and VAT registration number.
- The receipt shows the total cost of the paper as £3.60.
- The receipt contains a date and description of the goods purchased.
- The cash given to pay for it was £5.00 and the change was £1.40.
- The total includes VAT so the amount of the VAT must be calculated using the VAT fraction (rounding down the VAT if necessary):

  £3.60 × 20/120 (or 1/6) = £0.60
- The net amount of the paper is therefore:

  £3.60 – 0.60 = £3.00

Task 2

A taxi fare of £9.36 has been paid from petty cash. The receipt issued by the taxi driver is dated and contains his VAT registration number and name and address, and includes VAT.

Calculate:

The VAT included in this fare

£	

The net amount of the fare

£	

WRITING UP THE PETTY CASH BOOK

At regular intervals the petty cashier will write up the Petty Cash Book from the petty cash vouchers that have been kept in the petty cash box, and will then file the vouchers in numerical sequence. When the petty cash float is reimbursed or 'topped-up' to the imprest amount there will also be an entry in the receipts side of the Petty Cash Book for the cash paid in.

HOW IT WORKS

One of your duties at Southfield Electrical is to write up the Petty Cash Book each week. At the start of the week, 4 October, the petty cash box was empty and the imprest amount of £100.00 was withdrawn from the bank in cash and placed in the petty cash box.

The petty cash vouchers for the week show the following details:

Voucher 0465	Stationery costing £5.64 including VAT
Voucher 0466	Train fare of £15.80 (no VAT)
Voucher 0467	Postage costs of £15.60 (no VAT)
Voucher 0468	Coffee for the office costing £3.85 (no VAT)
Voucher 0469	Copy paper £7.50 including VAT
Voucher 0470	Postage costs of £8.30 (no VAT)
Voucher 0471	Envelopes costing £2.82 including VAT
Voucher 0472	Train fare of £12.30 (no VAT)

The Petty Cash Book will now be written up.

Petty Cash Book

Debit side RECEIPTS			Credit side PAYMENTS								
								ANALYSIS COLUMNS			
Date	Details	Total £	Date	Details	Voucher number	Total £	VAT £	Travel £	Post £	Stationery £	Office supplies £
4/10	Cash	100.00	8/10	Stationery	465	5.64	0.94			4.70	
			8/10	Train fare	466	15.80		15.80			
			8/10	Postage	467	15.60			15.60		
			8/10	Coffee	468	3.85					3.85
			8/10	Copy paper	469	7.50	1.25			6.25	
			8/10	Postage	470	8.30			8.30		
			8/10	Envelopes	471	2.82	0.47			2.35	
			8/10	Train fare	472	12.30		12.30			

Once the petty cash vouchers have been written up in the Petty Cash Book they are filed in numerical sequence. The Petty Cash Book is then totalled and balanced.

Step 1   Total the total receipts column and underline it.

Step 2   Total the total payments column but do not underline the total.

Step 3   Total each of the payments analysis columns and rule them off. Cross-cast these totals to ensure that they add back to the total of the total payments column.

Step 4   Put the receipts total as the final total in the payments column and calculate the difference between the receipts total and the total payments total – this is the balance on the Petty Cash Book that should be carried down (c/d) from the payments side and brought down (b/d) as the opening balance on the receipts side.

Petty Cash Book

Debit side RECEIPTS			Credit side PAYMENTS					ANALYSIS COLUMNS			
Date	Details	Total £	Date	Details	Voucher number	Total £	VAT £	Travel £	Post £	Stationery £	Office supplies £
4 Oct	Cash	100.00	8 Oct	Stationery	465	5.64	0.94			4.70	
			8 Oct	Train fare	466	15.80		15.80			
			8 Oct	Postage	467	15.60			15.60		
			8 Oct	Coffee	468	3.85					3.85
			8 Oct	Copy paper	469	7.50	1.25			6.25	
			8 Oct	Postage	470	8.30			8.30		
			8 Oct	Envelopes	471	2.82	0.47			2.35	
			8 Oct	Train fare	472	12.30		12.30			
						71.81	2.66	28.10	23.90	13.30	3.85
				Balance c/d		28.19					
		100.00				100.00					
Balance b/d		28.19									

RECONCILING THE PETTY CASH BOOK WITH PETTY CASH

Whenever a balance is calculated on the Petty Cash Book it is usual to ensure that it agrees with the actual amount of cash in the petty cash box at that time. This is done by counting the cash, totalling it on a PETTY CASH SCHEDULE and checking that it agrees to the balance on the Petty Cash Book – a process known as RECONCILIATION.

HOW IT WORKS

Having written up and balanced the Petty Cash Book, one of your duties at Southfield Electrical is to reconcile the balance with the contents of the petty cash box.

Step 1 Empty the petty cash box and list out the notes and coins it contains on the petty cash schedule (there will not be any petty cash vouchers as you have just written them all up in the Petty Cash Book and filed them away).

Step 2 Calculate the total of the notes and coins.

Step 3 Enter the balance calculated on the Petty Cash Book and sign the schedule to show that the total and the balance reconcile.

PETTY CASH SCHEDULE		Date: 8/10/XX
	In petty cash box	
Denomination	Number	£
£20	0	0.00
£10	1	10.00
£5	2	10.00
£2	3	6.00
£1	1	1.00
50p	2	1.00
20p	0	0.00
10p	1	0.10
5p	1	0.05
2p	1	0.02
1p	2	0.02
Total		28.19
Balance per Petty Cash Book		£28.19
Amounts reconcile?		Yes
Signature		P Norris

When the reconciliation of the cash in the petty cash box to the vouchers is carried out and the two amounts do not agree back to the imprest amount, it is clear that something has gone wrong with the system or procedure.

Too little cash in the petty cash box

If the reconciliation shows that there is not enough cash in the petty cash box then there are a number of possible reasons for this:

- Probably the most obvious is that cash has been removed from the petty cash box without being supported by an authorised petty cash voucher.

- Too much cash may have been given to a petty cash claimant and not noticed by either the petty cashier or the claimant.

- A petty cash voucher may be missing – this can be checked as the petty cash vouchers should be sequentially numbered.

- A top-up has been recorded but the cash was not placed in the petty cash box.

Too much cash in the petty cash box

If the reconciliation shows that there is more cash in the petty cash box than there should be, this could also be for a number of possible reasons:

- Too little cash may have been given to a petty cash claimant and not noticed by either the petty cashier or the claimant.

- A petty cash voucher has been placed in the petty cash box but no cash has yet been paid out.

- The amount paid into the petty cash box at the start of the period brought it up to an amount that was greater than the imprest amount.

- Some cash has been placed in the petty cash box and this has not been recorded.

Task 3

The petty cash box is totalled and reconciled at the end of the week and it is discovered that there are petty cash vouchers totalling £103.69 and actual cash of £36.31. The imprest amount is £150. Does the petty cash reconcile with the vouchers?   Yes/No

If not, suggest possible reasons why not.

These matters must be fully investigated and rectified before the next stage in the process – topping-up the petty cash – can be performed.

TOPPING-UP PETTY CASH: RESTORING THE IMPREST

The final stage in the process is to bring the petty cash amount back to the imprest amount and to record this in the Petty Cash Book.

HOW IT WORKS

We have already seen that to bring the petty cash amount back to the imprest amount the cash required is the total of all of the petty cash vouchers. Therefore, in this case, £71.81 in cash is required. To obtain a cheque for this amount to be withdrawn as cash from the bank account, a CHEQUE REQUISITION FORM must be completed, as shown below:

CHEQUE REQUISITION FORM

Southfield Electrical

Requested by: _Petty cashier_   **Date:** _8 Oct XX_

Payable to: _Cash_

Amount: _£71.81_

Send to: _Petty cashier_

Reason: _Petty cash imprest_

Invoice/receipt attached: _____

Other documentation: _____

Authorised by: _____   **Date:** _____

The cheque requisition form will now be authorised by a more senior person in the accounts department and a cheque written out made payable to 'Cash' of £71.81. This will be presented at the bank, together with an extended form of the petty cash schedule listing the denominations of notes and coin that the petty cashier would like the bank to hand over. The mix of notes and coin will be decided by the petty cashier based on:

- What is in the box already
- Their experience of how often each denomination is used

An extended petty cash schedule is set out next.

PETTY CASH SCHEDULE				Date: 8/10/XX
	In petty cash box		Required in top-up	
Denomination	Number	£	Number	£
£20	0	0.00	2	40.00
£10	1	10.00	2	20.00
£5	2	10.00	1	5.00
£2	3	6.00	1	2.00
£1	1	1.00	3	3.00
50p	2	1.00	1	0.50
20p	0	0.00	5	1.00
10p	1	0.10	3	0.30
5p	1	0.05	0	0.00
2p	1	0.02	0	0.00
1p	2	0.02	1	0.01
Total		28.19		71.81
Balance per Petty Cash Book		£28.19		
Amounts reconcile?		Yes		
Signature		P Norris		

When the cash is obtained from the bank and put into the petty cash box it will contain £100 in notes and coin as follows:

PETTY CASH SCHEDULE			Date: 8/10/XX			
	In petty cash box		Top-up		Final	
Denomination	Number	£	Number	£	Number	£
£20	0	0.00	2	40.00	2	40.00
£10	1	10.00	2	20.00	3	30.00
£5	2	10.00	1	5.00	3	15.00
£2	3	6.00	1	2.00	4	8.00
£1	1	1.00	3	3.00	4	4.00
50p	2	1.00	1	0.50	3	1.50
20p	0	0.00	5	1.00	5	1.00
10p	1	0.10	3	0.30	4	0.40
5p	1	0.05	0	0.00	1	0.05
2p	1	0.02	0	0.00	1	0.02
1p	2	0.02	1	0.01	3	0.03
Total		28.19		71.81		100.00

The receipts (debit) side of the Petty Cash Book will be written up to show the receipt of the top-up cash:

Petty Cash Book

Debit side RECEIPTS			Credit side PAYMENTS				ANALYSIS COLUMNS				
Date	Details	Total £	Date	Details	Voucher number	Total £	VAT £	Travel £	Post £	Stationery £	Office supplies £
4 Oct	Cash	100.00	8 Oct	Stationery	465	5.64	0.94			4.70	
			8 Oct	Train fare	466	15.80		15.80			
			8 Oct	Postage	467	15.60			15.60		
			8 Oct	Coffee	468	3.85					3.85
			8 Oct	Copy paper	469	7.50	1.25			6.25	
			8 Oct	Postage	470	8.30			8.30		
			8 Oct	Envelopes	471	2.82	0.47			2.35	
			8 Oct	Train fare	472	12.30		12.30			
						71.81	2.66	28.10	23.90	13.30	3.85
			Balance c/d			28.19					
		100.00				100.00					
Balance b/d		28.19									
8 Oct	Bank	71.81									

280

The Petty Cash Book now has an opening balance of £100.00 (£28.19 + £71.81), the imprest amount, ready for the start of the following week.

Task 4

A business has a petty cash system with an imprest amount of £50.00. During the week petty cash was paid out of the petty cash box totalling £41.30 and the remaining balance in the box was £8.70. How much cash is required to bring the petty cash box back to the imprest amount?

£ [   ]

POSTING THE PETTY CASH BOOK – RECEIPTS SIDE

The receipts side of the Petty Cash Book is the book of prime entry for the initial recording of receipts of cash from the business's bank account into the petty cash box.

Receipts into the Petty Cash Book are posted only to the general ledger, not to the sales ledger.

PETTY CASH RECEIPTS

↓

PETTY CASH BOOK

↓

ACCOUNTING RECORDS

↓

GENERAL LEDGER

HOW IT WORKS

As there are so few receipts into petty cash the receipts side of the Petty Cash Book rarely needs casting and cross casting. Instead it is posted straight to the general ledger.

The receipt of cash into the petty cash box is actually an internal transfer between the Bank ledger account and the Petty cash ledger account (sometimes called the Petty cash control account).

- The **debit** side of the transaction is posted from the Petty Cash Book to the Petty cash account in the general ledger.

Petty cash

Details	£	Details	£
Bank	150.00		

- The **credit** side of the transaction is included in the posting from the Cash Book in relation to payments to the Bank ledger account – as we saw in Chapter 9.

Bank

Details	£	Details	£
		Petty cash	150.00

The Petty Cash Book as part of the general ledger

As with the main Cash Book, in many businesses the Petty Cash Book is treated as **both** a book of prime entry **and** as part of the general ledger. This means that the receipts side of the Petty Cash Book is itself the debit side of the Petty cash general ledger account. The effect of this is that:

- There is no need to post a debit entry for the total receipts column from the Petty Cash Book (remember the credit entry is in the credit side of the Cash Book in the Bank column)

- There is no Petty cash general ledger account

POSTING THE PETTY CASH BOOK – PAYMENTS SIDE

Here is the payments side of a Petty Cash Book:

Petty Cash Book (payments side)

Date	Details	Voucher number	Total £	VAT £	Postage £	Stationery £	Office cleaning £
10 May	Stationery – Lara Moschetta	067	48.00	8.00		40.00	
10 May	Post office – stamps	068	15.00		15.00		
10 May	Green Clean – window cleaning	069	30.00				30.00

This shows that:

- The business has reimbursed one employee, Lara Moschetta, for £48.00 of expenditure on stationery that Lara paid herself. Both the net amount and the VAT are recorded in the Petty Cash Book.

- Money has been taken out of the petty cash box to make a purchase of postage stamps at the Post Office (no VAT).

- Money has also been taken out of the petty cash box to pay the business's window cleaner (no VAT).

The Petty Cash Book is posted only to the general ledger, not to the purchases ledger.

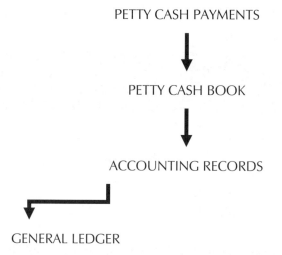

HOW IT WORKS

In order to do this the Petty Cash Book must first be cast and cross cast.

Petty Cash Book (payments side)

Date	Details	Voucher number	Total £	VAT £	Postage £	Stationery £	Other £
10 May	Stationery – Lara Moschetta	067	48.00	8.00		40.00	
10 May	Post office – stamps	068	15.00		15.00		
10 May	Green Clean – window cleaning	069	30.00				30.00
	Totals		93.00	8.00	15.00	40.00	30.00

Posting to the general ledger

The total column in the payments side of the Petty Cash Book is posted to the debit side of the Petty cash account in the general ledger, and each of the totals of the analysis columns is posted to the debit side of the general ledger account that bears the same name.

HOW IT WORKS

The easiest way to see how the postings are made in the general ledger is to show the relevant general ledger account name beneath each Petty Cash Book total, with an indication of whether the posting is a debit entry or a credit entry:

Petty Cash Book (payments side)

Date	Details	Voucher number	Total £	VAT £	Postage £	Stationery £	Office cleaning £
	Totals		93.00	8.00	15.00	40.00	30.00
	General ledger	Debit entry		VAT	Postage	Stationery	Office cleaning
		Credit entry	Petty cash				

Note that the petty cash account is the one that we updated above with the receipt of £150 cash from the Bank account.

We can now make the postings to the general ledger:

General ledger

Petty cash

Details	£	Details	£
Bank	150.00	Petty cash payments*	93.00

*Because there are a number of unlinked accounts which take the opposing entries, we have used a catch-all narrative under Details here (Petty cash payments).

Postage account

Details	£	Details	£
Petty cash	15.00		

Office cleaning account

Details	£	Details	£
Petty cash	30.00		

Stationery account

Details	£	Details	£
Petty cash	40.00		

VAT account

Details	£	Details	£
Petty cash	8.00		

A useful double check is that the new debit and credit postings in the ledger accounts balance each other out:

Ledger account	Debit entries £	Credit entries £
Petty cash		93.00
Postage	15.00	
Office cleaning	30.00	
Stationery	40.00	
VAT	8.00	
	93.00	93.00

The Petty Cash Book as part of the general ledger

If the Petty Cash Book is **both** a book of prime entry **and** part of the general ledger, the payments side of the Petty Cash Book is itself the credit side of a general ledger account.

The effect of this is that:

- There is no need to post a credit entry for the total column from the Petty Cash Book payments side.

- There is no Petty cash account in the general ledger.

- Debit entries for payments from the Petty Cash Book are posted as usual.

In fact it is normal practice for the Petty Cash Book to be not only the book of prime entry for petty cash vouchers but also part of the double entry in the general ledger. Other than writing up the Petty Cash Book, the only necessary entries are therefore to debit the various expense accounts with the totals of the analysis columns on the credit side of the Petty Cash Book, and to credit Bank with the amount of the top-up entered on the debit side of the Petty Cash Book.

CHAPTER OVERVIEW

- Most businesses will require small amounts of cash on the premises for the purchase of low value items and the reimbursement of employees for business expenses

- This cash is known as the petty cash float and is kept in the petty cash box by the petty cashier

- If an employee incurs a business expense and pays for it themselves then this can be reclaimed by presenting evidence of the expense to the petty cashier, who prepares the petty cash voucher, has the voucher authorised and then reimburses the employee for the amount spent out of the petty cash float

- An imprest system for petty cash is where the petty cash box is always topped-up to the same amount, the imprest amount, at the end of each week or month

- Claims can only be paid by the petty cashier if they are supported by a properly authorised petty cash voucher plus a receipt

- The petty cash vouchers must then be written up in the Petty Cash Book

- The Petty Cash Book has a receipts (debit) side and a payments (credit) side and is normally part of the general ledger as well as being a book of prime entry – the payments side is analysed into columns for VAT and all of the types of petty cash expense that the organisation normally deals with

- When the petty cash vouchers have been written up into the Petty Cash Book it must then be totalled and balanced

- The amount of notes and coin in the petty cash box is counted and reconciled to the balance on the Petty Cash Book using a petty cash schedule

- The petty cash box must be reimbursed back to the imprest amount by means of a receipt of note and coin taken out from the bank, and this is recorded on the receipts (debit) side of the Petty Cash Book

- The double entry for the cash being paid into the petty cash box is a credit entry in the Bank account and a debit entry in the Petty Cash Book

- The analysed payments side of the Petty Cash Book is posted to the general ledger by debiting the VAT and analysis column totals to the relevant accounts in the general ledger

- If the Petty Cash Book is just a book of prime entry and not part of the double entry system then a separate Petty cash account must be kept in the general ledger to record the receipts into the petty cash box and the total payments made; the VAT and analysis amounts are posted as usual

Keywords

Petty cash float – the amount of cash held in the petty cash box at any one time

Petty cash box – a secure lockable box in which the petty cash float and petty cash vouchers are kept

Petty cashier – the person in the organisation who is responsible for the petty cash

Petty cash voucher – the document that must be completed and authorised before any cash can be paid out to an employee from the petty cash box

Petty cash claims – a claim from an employee for reimbursement from the petty cash box

Petty Cash Book – the primary record used to record the petty cash vouchers and any money paid into the petty cash box

Petty cash control account – the general ledger account for petty cash when the Petty Cash Book acts only as a book of prime entry

Imprest system – a petty cash system whereby the petty cash box is always topped-up to the same amount at the end of each week or month

Imprest amount – the amount to which the petty cash float is topped-up at the end of a period of time

Petty cash schedule – a list of the different denominations of notes and coin contained in the petty cash float. It can be extended to include an analysis of the actual notes and coin that the organisation wants the bank to provide as the top-up

Reconciliation – the process by which a check is carried out that two amounts agree

Cheque requisition form – an internal document used to request a cheque to be raised

TEST YOUR LEARNING

Test 1

Complete the following explanation of how an imprest petty cash system works by selecting the appropriate choices in each case.

1.1 An imprest petty cash system is one where the amount of the topped-up petty cash float at the start of each period is:

Always the same

Sometimes the same

Never the same

1.2 Amounts that have been paid out for authorised expenditure are represented in the petty cash box by:

Notes and coin

Petty cash vouchers

Till receipts

1.3 At the end of the period the total of the

| Notes and coin |
| Petty cash vouchers |
| Till receipts |

in the petty cash box is the amount needed to restore the petty cash box to the imprest amount.

Test 2

A petty cash system is run on the basis of having £150 in the petty cash box at the start of each week. At the end of one week the total of the vouchers in the petty cash box was £89.46. For how much should the cheque requisition form be made out to restore the petty cash box to its imprest amount?

£

Test 3

The petty cash system in your organisation is run on an imprest system with an imprest amount of £150.00. The petty cash float at the start of the week beginning 20 October was £150.00 and eight petty cash vouchers were completed, authorised and paid on 24 October. The Petty Cash Book analyses payments into VAT, postage, travel, sundry office expenses, and miscellaneous expenses.

The details of the petty cash vouchers are given below:

Voucher 771   Train fare (no VAT) £14.00
Voucher 772   Postage (no VAT) £18.60
Voucher 773   Envelopes (VAT receipt) £16.80
Voucher 774   Window cleaner (no VAT receipt) £20.00
Voucher 775   Pens and paper (VAT receipt) £18.90
Voucher 776   Postage (no VAT) £5.46
Voucher 777   Taxi fare (VAT receipt) £9.60
Voucher 778   Rewritable CDs for computers (VAT receipt) £28.20

You are required to:

(a)   Write up the Petty Cash Book for these vouchers

(b)   Total and balance the Petty Cash Book, bringing down the balance

(c)   Record the amount of cash paid into the petty cash box to restore it to the imprest amount

Petty Cash Book

RECEIPTS			PAYMENTS								
Date	Details	Amount £	Date	Details	Voucher number	Total £	VAT £	Post £	Travel £	Sundry office £	Misc £
20 Oct	Bank	150.00									
						____	____	____	____	____	____
						____	____	____	____	____	____
		____	Balance c/d			____					
	Total	____		Total		____					
Balance b/d											
Cash top-up											

Test 4

This is a summary of petty cash payments made by a business.

Post Office paid	£12.60 (no VAT)
Motor Repair Workshop paid	£72.60 including VAT
Great Eastern Trains paid	£32.00 (no VAT)

Use the appropriate narrative from the picklist to complete the details column:

(a) Enter the above transactions in the Petty Cash Book.
(b) Total the Petty Cash Book and show the balance carried down.

Petty Cash Book

Debit side		Credit side					
Details	Amount £	Details	Amount £	VAT £	Postage £	Travel £	Motor expenses £
Balance b/d	180.00						

Picklist:

Amount
Balance b/d
Balance c/d
Details
Great Eastern Trains
Motor expenses
Motor Repair Workshop
Postage
Post Office
Travel
VAT

chapter 11:
INITIAL TRIAL BALANCE

chapter coverage 📖

Now that we have posted the books of prime entry to the general ledger, we complete this Text by extracting an initial trial balance, so we can be sure that the double entry is correct.

The topic covered is:

✎ The trial balance

✎ Balances to watch out for

THE TRIAL BALANCE

You will recall that in Chapter 6 we prepared and balanced the following ledger accounts for Ben Charles (remember we are now calling the trade receivables account the Sales ledger control account, and the trade payables account the Purchases ledger control account):

Bank

Details	£	Details	£
Capital	10,000	Purchases	1,000
Sales	1,500	Rent	600
Sales ledger control	1,750	Non-current assets	1,000
		Stationery	200
		Drawings	500
		Purchases ledger control	1,500
		Balance c/d	8,450
	13,250		13,250
Balance b/d	8,450		

Capital

Details	£	Details	£
		Bank	10,000

Purchases

Details	£	Details	£
Bank	1,000		
Purchases ledger control	2,000	Balance c/d	3,000
	3,000		3,000
Balance b/d	3,000		

Purchases ledger control

Details	£	Details	£
Bank	1,500	Purchases	2,000
Balance c/d	500		
	2,000		2,000
		Balance b/d	500

Rent

Details	£	Details	£
Bank	600		

Sales

Details	£	Details	£
		Bank	1,500
Balance c/d	3,300	Sales ledger control	1,800
			3,300
	3,300	Balance b/d	3,300

Sales ledger control

Details	£	Details	£
Sales	1,800	Bank	1,750
		Discount allowed	50
	1,800		1,800

Non-current assets

Details	£	Details	£
Bank	1,000		

Stationery

Details	£	Details	£
Bank	200		

Drawings

Details	£	Details	£
Bank	500		

Discounts allowed t

Details	£	Details	£
Sales ledger control	50		

Once all of the accounts have been balanced then a very useful exercise is often carried out. This is the preparation of an INITIAL TRIAL BALANCE.

The initial trial balance is simply a list of all of the debit and credit balances on each of the general ledger accounts. The purpose of the trial balance is that it forms a check on the accuracy of the entries in the ledger accounts. If the debits in the trial balance do not equal the credits then this indicates that there has been an error in the double entry.

HOW IT WORKS

Now we will complete Ben Charles's accounts for the period by preparing a trial balance.

Step 1   List the balance brought down on each account as a debit or credit as appropriate.

	Debits	Credits
	£	£
Bank	8,450	
Capital		10,000
Purchases	3,000	
Purchases ledger control		500
Rent	600	
Sales		3,300
Sales ledger control	0	
Non-current asset	1,000	
Stationery	200	
Drawings	500	
Discounts allowed	50	

Step 2 Total the debit column and the credit column and check that they are equal.

	Debits £	Credits £
Bank	8,450	
Capital		10,000
Purchases	3,000	
Purchases ledger control		500
Rent	600	
Sales		3,300
Sales ledger control	0	
Non-current asset	1,000	
Stationery	200	
Drawings	500	
Discounts allowed	50	
	13,800	13,800

Task 1

You have been handed the completed general ledger accounts for Mr Chapter, whom we saw in Chapters 8 and 9. Note that:

- Balances brought forward from the previous period have been added to some of the accounts
- The two sides of the Bank account have been combined
- There is an additional account, for capital

Balance these accounts and produce an initial trial balance.

General ledger

Cash account

Details	£	Details	£
Balance (b/f)	1,000.00	Cash payments	720.00
Cash receipts	240.00		

Bank account

Details	£	Details	£
Balance (b/f)	14,000.00	Bank payments	6,096.00
Bank receipts	1,416.00		

Sales ledger control account

Details	£	Details	£
Balance (b/f)	10,000.00	Sales returns	274.00
Sales	1,730.00	Bank	1,416.00
		Discounts allowed	40.00

Sales account

Details	£	Details	£
		Balance b/f	20,000.00
		SLCA	1,450.00
		Cash	200.00

Sales returns account

Details	£	Details	£
SLCA	230.00		

VAT account

Details	£	Details	£
Sales returns	44.00	Balance b/f	1,500.00
Purchases	1,108.00	Sales	280.00
Cash	120.00	Cash	40.00
		Purchases returns	92.00

Discounts allowed account

Details	£	Details	£
SLCA	40.00		

Purchases ledger control account

Details	£	Details	£
Purchases returns	572.00	Balance b/f	2,500.00
Bank	6,096.00	Purchases	6,808.00
Discounts received	140.00		

Purchases account

Details	£	Details	£
PLCA	5,700.00		
Cash	600.00		

Purchases returns account

Details	£	Details	£
		PLCA	480.00

Discounts received account

Details	£	Details	£
		PLCA	140.00

Capital account

Details	£	Details	£
		Balance b/f	1,000.00

Trial balance

	Debits £	Credits £
Cash		
Bank		
Sales ledger control		
Sales		
Sales returns		
VAT		
Discounts allowed		
Purchases ledger control		
Purchases		
Purchases returns		
Discounts received		
Capital		

BALANCES TO WATCH OUT FOR

When you are given a set of ledger accounts it is clear which side of the trial balance each balance should appear in: the same side as the **balance brought down** on the account.

However in your assessment you will be given a list of balances and required to identify from their names whether they are debit or credit balances. You should watch out for the following, which learners often get wrong:

Name of balance	Debit or credit balance?	Nature of balance
Inventory – of goods or materials held at any point in time	Debit	Asset
Bank overdraft	Credit	Liability
Bank OR Cash OR Petty Cash	Debit	Asset
Loan	Credit	Liability
VAT owed to HMRC	Credit	Liability
VAT owed by HMRC	Debit	Asset
Capital	Credit	Capital
Drawings	Debit	Reduction in capital
Bank interest paid or bank charges	Debit	Expense
Bank interest received	Credit	Income

CHAPTER OVERVIEW

- Ledger accounts are balanced by totalling both sides of the account, inserting the larger total at the bottom of both the debit and credit sides and putting in the figure that makes the smaller side of the account add back to this total. This is called the balance carried down and this balance is brought down on the other side of the account below the total

- A trial balance is prepared by listing all of the debit balances brought down and credit balances brought down and checking the totals of these balances to ensure that they agree

Keyword

Initial trial balance – a list of all of the debit and credit balances brought down on the ledger accounts

TEST YOUR LEARNING

Test 1

Calculate and carry down the closing balances on each of the following accounts.

VAT account

	£		£
Purchases	3,778	Balance b/f	2,116
Bank	2,116	Sales	6,145

Sales account

	£		£
		Balance b/f	57,226
		SLCA	42,895

Sales ledger control account

	£		£
Balance b/f	4,689	Bank	21,505
Sales	23,512	Discounts allowed	2,019

Purchases ledger control account

	£		£
Purchases returns	1,334	Balance b/f	2,864
Bank	13,446	Purchases	14,552
Discounts received	662		

BPP
LEARNING MEDIA

Test 2

Indicate whether each of the following balances would be shown as a debit balance or a credit balance in the trial balance.

	£	Debit balance ✓	Credit balance ✓
Discounts allowed	1,335		
Discounts received	1,013		
Purchases returns	4,175		
Sales returns	6,078		
Bank interest received	328		
Bank charges	163		

Test 3

Given below are the balances on the ledger accounts of Thames Traders at 30 November 20XX. Prepare the trial balance as at 30 November 20XX, including totals.

	£	Debits £	Credits £
Motor vehicles	64,000		
Office equipment	21,200		
Sales	238,000		
Purchases	164,000		
Cash	300		
Bank overdraft	1,080		
Petty cash	30		
Capital	55,000		
Sales returns	4,700		
Purchases returns	3,600		
Sales ledger control	35,500		
Purchases ledger control	30,100		
VAT (owed to HMRC)	12,950		
Telephone	1,600		
Electricity	2,800		
Wages	62,100		
Loan from bank	30,000		
Discounts allowed	6,400		
Discounts received	3,900		
Rent expense	12,000		
Totals			

Test 4

Below is a list of balances to be transferred to the trial balance as at 30 June.

Place the figures in the debit or credit column, as appropriate, and total each column.

Account name	Amount £	Debit £	Credit £
Advertising	3,238		
Bank overdraft	27,511		
Capital	40,846		
Cash	689		
Discount allowed	4,416		
Discount received	2,880		
Hotel expenses	2,938		
Inventory	46,668		
Loan from bank	39,600		
Miscellaneous expenses	3,989		
Motor expenses	7,087		
Motor vehicles	63,120		
Petty cash	720		
Purchases	634,529		
Purchases ledger control	110,846		
Purchases returns	1,618		
Rent and rates	19,200		
Sales	1,051,687		
Sales ledger control	405,000		
Sales returns	11,184		
Stationery	5,880		
Subscriptions	864		
Telephone	3,838		
VAT (owing to HM Revenue and Customs)	63,650		
Wages	125,278		
Totals			

ANSWERS TO CHAPTER TASKS

CHAPTER 1 Business documentation

1   A credit transaction   ✓

2   An invoice   ✓

3   A credit note   ✓

4   A remittance advice note   ✓

5   A petty cash voucher   ✓

6   PRE62   ✓

CHAPTER 2   Discounts and VAT

1

| Output tax is VAT on | sales |
| Input tax is VAT on | purchases |

2   £230 × 20/100 = £46

| £ | 46 |

3   £246 × 20/120 = £41.00

| £ | 41 |

4

	£
List price	2,400.00
Less discount £2,400.00 × 15/100	(360.00)
Net total	2,040.00
VAT: £2,040.00 × 20/100	408.00
Gross total	2,448.00

| £ | 2,448.00 |

5

	£
List price	2,400.00
Less trade discount £2,400.00 × 10/100	(240.00)
	2,160.00
Less bulk discount £2,160.00 × 12/100	(259.20)
Net total	1,900.80
VAT: £1,900.80 × 20/100	380.16
Gross total	2,280.96

£	2,280.96

6

	£
Net total	368.00
Less settlement discount	(11.04)
	356.96
Net total	368.00
VAT £356.96 × 20/100 (rounded down)	71.39
Gross total	439.39

£	439.39

CHAPTER 3   The books of prime entry

1

	£	Gross	VAT	Net
Goods total	1,236.00			✓
VAT	247.20		✓	
Total	1,483.20	✓		

2

An invoice is entered on the	left	side of the customer's account
A credit note is entered on the	right	side of the customer's account

£	24.00

3

Gross £	VAT £	Net £	Computers £	Printers £	Scanners £
1,560.00	260.00	1,300.00	800.00	300.00	200.00

4

An invoice is entered on the	right	side of the supplier's account
A credit note is entered on the	left	side of the supplier's account

£	**36.00**

5

Gross £	VAT £	Net £	Purchases £	Expenses £
1,980.00	330.00	1,650.00	1,650.00	

6

True   ✓

False

7   **Grigsons Ltd:** £199.20 invoice less credit note of £72.00 less receipt of £127.20 = £0

£	**0.00**

Hall & Co: £103.60 invoice less receipt of £93.60 less discount of £10.00 = £0

£	**0.00**

8

On any payments that are not payments to credit suppliers (trade payables)   ✓

9   **Haley Ltd:** £60.00 invoice less credit note of £24.00 less receipt of £36.00 = £0

£	**0.00**

B Tel: £154.00 invoice less payment of £144.00 less discount of £10.00 = £0

£	**0.00**

CHAPTER 4   Recording credit sales

1

The buyer of goods

2

Yes ✓

Working: £400 × 95% = £380 + £76 (VAT) = £456

CHAPTER 5   Recording credit purchases

1

| £ | 304 |

Working

	£
Net total	1,600.00
Less discount 5/100 × £1,600	(80.00)
	1,520.00
VAT £1,520.00 × 20/100	304.00

2   Discount = £800.00 × 3/100 =

| £ | 24 |

3

| 5 August |

Working

(9 + 30 – 3 – 31)

4

| 1 December |

Working

(23 + 10 – 2 – 30)

5

£	2,340

Working

£2,390 − (2.5/100 × £2,000)

CHAPTER 6   Double entry bookkeeping

1

(a) Purchase of goods on credit

Increase expense	✓
Increase sales	
Increase trade payable	✓
Increase trade receivable	

(b) Sale of goods on credit

Increase expense	
Increase sales	✓
Increase trade payable	
Increase trade receivable	✓

(c) Receipt of money for sale of goods on credit

Increase cash	✓
Decrease cash	
Decrease trade receivable	✓
Increase trade receivable	

(d) Payment to a trade payable for purchase of goods on credit

Increase cash	
Decrease cash	✓
Decrease trade payable	✓
Increase trade payable	

2

(a) Purchase of goods on credit

Account name	Debit	Credit
Purchases	✓	
Trade payables		✓

(b) Sale of goods on credit

Account name	Debit	Credit
Trade receivables	✓	
Sales		✓

(c) Receipt of money for sale of goods on credit

Account name	Debit	Credit
Bank	✓	
Trade receivables		✓

(d) Payment of a trade payable

Account name	Debit	Credit
Trade payables	✓	
Bank		✓

3

Trade receivables

Details	£	Details	£
Sales	2,600	Bank	1,800
Sales	1,400	Bank	1,200
Sales	3,700	Bank	2,000
Sales	1,300	Balance c/d	4,000
Total	9,000	Total	9,000
Balance b/d	4,000		

The amount owed by trade receivables	✓
The amount owed to trade receivables	

4

	Revenue expenditure	Revenue income	Capital expenditure	Capital income
Sale of goods to credit customers		✓		
Cash sales		✓		
Sale of delivery van				✓
Purchase of goods for resale	✓			
Purchase of building			✓	
Purchase of coffee for office from petty cash	✓			

5

James Daniels

	£		£
SDB	1,000	CB	800

CHAPTER 8   Double entry for sales and trade receivables

1

	Account name	Debit	Credit
Gross	Sales ledger control	✓	
VAT	VAT		✓
Net	Sales		✓

2

	Amount £	Debit	Credit
Sales ledger control account (general ledger)	240		✓
Customer's account (sales ledger)	240		✓

3

Sales Day Book

Customer	Invoice number	Customer code	Gross £	VAT £	Net £
Trissom Ltd	124	SL 09	1,190.00	190.00	1,000.00
Miley & Co	125	SL 22	540.00	90.00	450.00
Totals			1,730.00	280.00	1,450.00

Sales Returns Day Book

Customer	Credit note number	Customer code	Gross £	VAT £	Net £
Trissom Ltd	07	SL 09	238.00	38.00	200.00
Miley & Co	08	SL 22	36.00	6.00	30.00
Totals			274.00	44.00	230.00

Cash Book – Debit side

Details	Ref	Discounts allowed £	Cash £	Bank £	VAT £	Cash sales £	Trade receivables £
Trissom Ltd	SL 09	40.00		912.00			912.00
Miley & Co	SL 22			504.00			504.00
Cash sale			240.00		40.00	200.00	
Totals		40.00	240.00	1,416.00	40.00	200.00	1,416.00

General ledger

Cash account

Details	£	Details	£
Cash receipts	240.00		

Bank account

Details	£	Details	£
SLCA	1,416.00		

Sales ledger control account

Details	£	Details	£
Sales	1,730.00	Sales returns	274.00
		Bank	1,416.00
		Discounts allowed	40.00

Sales account

Details	£	Details	£
		SLCA	1,450.00
		Cash	200.00

Sales returns account

Details	£	Details	£
SLCA	230.00		

VAT account

Details	£	Details	£
Sales returns	44.00	Sales	280.00
		Sales	40.00

Discounts allowed account

Details	£	Details	£
SLCA	40.00		

Sales ledger

Trissom Ltd   SL 09

Details	£	Details	£
SDB – 124	1,190.00	SRDB – CN07	238.00
		CB – receipt	912.00
		CB – discounts allowed	40.00

Miley & Co   SL 22

Details	£	Details	£
SDB – 125	540.00	SRDB – CN08	36.00
		CB – receipt	504.00

4

Account name	Amount £	Debit ✓	Credit ✓
VAT	20.00		✓
Sales	100.00		✓
Sales ledger control account	65.00		✓
Sales ledger control account	5,116.50		✓
Discounts allowed	65.00	✓	

Remember that the 'Cash' and 'Bank' columns in the Cash Book are acting as the debit side of the Cash and Bank accounts in the general ledger, so no additional debit postings are required.

CHAPTER 9 Double entry for purchases and trade payables

1

	Account name	Debit ✓	Credit ✓
Gross	Purchases ledger control		✓
VAT	VAT	✓	
Purchases	Purchases	✓	

2

	Amount £	Debit ✓	Credit ✓
Purchases ledger control account (general ledger)	720	✓	
Supplier's account (purchases ledger)	720	✓	

3

Purchases Day Book

Supplier	Invoice number	Supplier code	Gross £	VAT £	Net £
Rawley Ltd	7869	PL54	3,000.00	500.00	2,500.00
Jipsum plc	323980	PL02	3,808.00	608.00	3,200.00
Totals			6,808.00	1,108.00	5,700.00

Purchases Returns Day Book

Customer	Credit note number	Customer code	Gross £	VAT £	Net £
Rawley Ltd	CN627	PL54	96.00	16.00	80.00
Jipsum plc	CN08	PL02	476.00	76.00	400.00
Totals			572.00	92.00	480.00

Cash Book

Details	Ref	Discounts received £	Cash £	Bank £	VAT £	Cash purchases £	Trade payables £
Rawley Ltd	PL54			2,904.00			2,904.00
Jipsum plc	PL02	140.00		3,192.00			3,192.00
Cash purchase			720.00		120.00	600.00	
Totals		140.00	720.00	6,096.00	120.00	600.00	6,096.00

General ledger

Cash account

Details	£	Details	£
		Cash payments	720.00

Bank account

Details	£	Details	£
		Bank payments	6,096.00

Purchases ledger control account

Details	£	Details	£
Purchases returns	572.00	Purchases	6,808.00
Bank	6,096.00		
Discounts received	140.00		

Purchases account

Details	£	Details	£
PLCA	5,700.00		
Cash	600.00		

Purchases returns account

Details	£	Details	£
		PLCA	480.00

VAT account

Details	£	Details	£
Purchases	1,108.00	Purchases returns	92.00
Purchases	120.00		

Discounts received account

Details	£	Details	£
		PLCA	140.00

Purchases ledger

Rawley Ltd   PL 54

Details	£	Details	£
PRDB – CN627	96.00	PDB – 7869	3,000.00
CB – payment	2,904.00		

Jipsum plc   PL 02

Details	£	Details	£
PRDB – CN08	476.00	PDB – 323980	3,808.00
CB – payment	3,192.00		
CB – discount	140.00		

4

Account name	Amount £	Debit ✓	Credit ✓
VAT	48.00	✓	
Purchases	240.00	✓	
Purchases ledger control account	109.00	✓	
Purchases ledger control account	3,009.65	✓	
Discounts received	109.00		✓

Remember that the Cash and Bank columns in the Cash Book are acting as the credit side of the Cash and Bank accounts in the general ledger, so no additional credit posting is required.

CHAPTER 10 Accounting for petty cash

1   £4.80   VAT   =   £4.00 × 1.2   =   £4.80

2   VAT   =   £9.36 × 20/120   =   £1.56

    Net amount   =   £9.36 – 1.56   =   £7.80

3   Petty cash vouchers plus cash should equal imprest amount

    £103.69 + £36.31 = £140, this is below the imprest amount of £150 (ie too little cash)

    Possible reasons:

    ▪   Cash has been removed from the petty cash box without being supported by an authorised petty cash voucher.

    ▪   Too much cash might have been given to a petty cash claimant and not noticed by either the petty cashier or the claimant.

    ▪   A petty cash voucher may be missing (check the sequential numbering).

    ▪   A top-up has been recorded but the cash was not placed in the petty cash box.

4   £41.30

CHAPTER 11   Initial trial balance

1

Cash account

Details	£	Details	£
Balance b/f	1,000.00	Cash payments	720.00
Cash receipts	240.00	Balance c/d	520.00
	1,240.00		1,240.00
Balance b/d	520.00		

Bank account

Details	£	Details	£
Balance b/f	14,000.00	Bank payments	6,096.00
Bank receipts	1,416.00	Balance c/d	9,320.00
	15,416.00		15,416.00
Balance b/d	9,320.00		

BPP
LEARNING MEDIA

Sales ledger control account

Details	£	Details	£
Balance b/d	10,000.00	Sales returns	274.00
Sales	1,730.00	Bank	1,416.00
		Discounts allowed	40.00
		Balance c/d	10,000.00
	11,730.00		11,730.00
Balance b/d	10,000.00		

Sales account

Details	£	Details	£
		Balance b/d	20,000.00
		SLCA	1,450.00
Balance c/d	21,650.00	Cash	200.00
	21,650.00		21,650.00
		Balance b/d	21,650.00

Sales returns account

Details	£	Details	£
SLCA	230.00		

VAT account

Details	£	Details	£
Sales returns	44.00	Balance b/d	1,500.00
Purchases	1,108.00	Sales	280.00
Cash	120.00	Cash	40.00
Balance c/d	640.00	Purchases returns	92.00
	1,912.00		1,912.00
		Balance b/d	640.00

Discounts allowed account

Details	£	Details	£
SLCA	40.00		

Purchases ledger control account

Details	£	Details	£
Purchases returns	572.00	Balance b/d	2,500.00
Bank	6,096.00	Purchases	6,808.00
Discounts received	140.00		
Balance c/d	2,500.00		
	9,308.00		9,308.00
		Balance b/d	2,500.00

Purchases account

Details	£	Details	£
PLCA	5,700.00		
Cash	600.00	Balance c/d	6,300.00
	6,300.00		6,300.00
Balance b/d	6,300.00		

Purchases returns account

Details	£	Details	£
		PLCA	480.00

Discounts received account

Details	£	Details	£
		PLCA	140.00

Capital account

Details	£	Details	£
		Balance b/d	1,000.00

Trial balance

	Debits £	Credits £
Cash	520.00	
Bank	9,320.00	
Sales ledger control	10,000.00	
Sales		21,650.00
Sales returns	230.00	
VAT		640.00
Discounts allowed	40.00	
Purchases ledger control		2,500.00
Purchases	6,300.00	
Purchases returns		480.00
Discounts received		140.00
Capital		1,000.00
	26,410.00	26,410.00

Answers to chapter tasks

CHAPTER 1   Business documentation

1

	Cash ✓	Credit ✓
Purchase of a van with an agreed payment date in one month's time		✓
Sale of goods by credit card in a shop	✓	
Purchase of computer disks by cheque	✓	
Purchase of computer disks which are accompanied by an invoice		✓
Sale of goods which are paid for by cheque	✓	

2

Sale of goods for cash	Till receipt
Return of goods purchased on credit	Credit note
Reminder to customer of how much it owes and why	Statement of account
Reimbursement of employee for expense by cash	Petty cash voucher
Indication of which amounts that are owed are being paid	Remittance advice note

3

- Where income is more than expenses a business makes a profit

- Where expenses are more than income a business makes a loss

- Bank loans and overdrafts are examples of liabilities

- Cash and trade receivables are examples of assets

- When a business owner contributes money to the business, this is known as capital

- When a business owner takes out money from the business, this is known as drawings

CHAPTER 2   Discounts and VAT

1   (400 × 30) – (400 × 30 × 5/100) = £11,400 before bulk discount

11,400 – (11,400 × 10/100) = £10,260 net total after bulk discount

£	10,260

2   (a)   VAT   =   £378.00 × 20% (20/100)

£	75.60

(b)   VAT   =   £378.00 × 20/120

£	63.00

Net total =   £378.00 – 63.00

£	315.00

3   (a)   VAT   =   £3,154.80 × 20/120 = £525.80

Net total   =   £3,154.80 – 525.80 = £2,629.00

(b)   VAT   =   £446.40 × 20/120 = £74.40

Net total   =   £446.40 – 74.40   = £372.00

(c)   VAT   =   £169.20 × 20/120 = £28.20

Net total   =   £169.20 – 28.20   = £141.00

Gross amount	VAT	Net amount
(a) £3,154.80	£525.80	£2,629.00
(b) £446.40	£74.40	£372.00
(c) £169.20	£28.20	£141.00

4 (a)

(i) Total cost before discount	23 × £56.00	£1,288.00
(ii) Trade discount	15% × £1,288.00	£193.20
(iii) Net total	£1,288.00 – £193.20	£1,094.80
(iv) VAT	20% × £1,094.80	£218.96
(v) Gross total		£1,313.76

(b)

(i) Total cost before discount	23 × £56.00	£1,288.00
(ii) Trade discount	15% × £1,288.00	£193.20
(iii) Net total		£1,094.80
(iv) VAT	20% × (1,094.80 – (3% × 1,094.80))	£212.39
(v) Gross total		£1,307.19

CHAPTER 3   The books of prime entry

1   Sales Day Book

Date	Customer	Invoice number	Customer code	Gross £	VAT (Net × 20%) £	Net £
1/6	J Jepson	44263	SL34	141.60	23.60	118.00
2/6	S Beck & Sons	44264	SL01	384.00	64.00	320.00
3/6	Penfold Ltd	44265	SL23	196.80	32.80	164.00
4/6	S Beck & Sons	44266	SL01	307.20	51.20	256.00
4/6	J Jepson	44267	SL34	172.80	28.80	144.00
Total				1,202.40	200.40	1,002.00

Sales Returns Day Book

Date	Customer	Credit note number	Customer code	Gross £	VAT (Net × 20%) £	Net £
2/6	Scroll Ltd	3813	SL16	21.60	3.60	18.00
5/6	Penfold Ltd	3814	SL23	20.16	3.36	16.80
Total				41.76	6.96	34.80

2   Purchases Day Book

Date	Supplier	Invoice number	Supplier code	Gross £	VAT £	Net £
6/6	YH Hill	224363	PL16	190.08	31.68	158.40
6/6	Letra Ltd	PT445	PL24	273.60	45.60	228.00
6/6	Coldstores Ltd	77352	PL03	189.60	31.60	158.00
Total				653.28	108.88	544.40

Purchases Returns Day Book

Date	Supplier	Credit note number	Supplier code	Gross £	VAT £	Net £
6/6	Letra Ltd	CN92	PL24	120.00	20.00	100.00
6/6	YH Hill	C7325	PL16	31.20	5.20	26.00
Total				151.20	25.20	126.00

3

Cash Book – receipts

Date	Details	Ref	Disc allowed £	Cash £	Bank £	VAT £	Cash sales £	Trade receivables £	Sundry income £
1/6	J Jepson	SL34	10.00		220.00			220.00	
3/6	Cash sale			72.00		12.00	60.00		

Cash Book – payments

Date	Details	Ref	Disc received £	Cash £	Bank £	VAT £	Cash purchases £	Trade payables £	Petty cash £	Expenses £
2/6	Letra Ltd	PL24	20.00		500.00			500.00		
2/6	Cash purchase			48.00		8.00	40.00			

CHAPTER 4 Recording credit sales

1

To inform the customer of the amount due for a sale	Invoice
To inform the supplier of the quantities required	Customer order
To inform the supplier that some of the delivery was not of the standard or type required	Returns note
To inform the customer of the quantity delivered	Delivery note
To inform the customer that the invoiced amount was overstated	Credit note

2 (a)

	£
Price before discount 23 × £56.00	1,288.00
Trade discount 15% × £1,288.00	(193.20)
Net	1,094.80
VAT 20% × £1,094.80	218.96
Gross	1,313.76

(b)

	£
Price before discount 23 × £56.00	1,288.00
Trade discount 15% × £1,288.00	(193.20)
Net	1,094.80
VAT 20% × (1,094.80 – (3% × 1,094.80))	212.39
or 1,094.80 × 0.97 × 0.2	
Gross	1,307.19

3 Errors on the invoice:

- It is not dated.
- There is no customer code.
- The calculation of the total price of the tumble dryers is incorrect.

- The calculation of the trade discount is incorrect.

- The VAT has been calculated without taking account of the settlement discount offered.

Corrected figures:

	£
Tumble dryers 21 × £180	3,780.00
Mixers	400.00
Goods total	4,180.00
Less 15% discount	(627.00)
Net total	3,553.00
VAT 20% × (3,553 – (5% × 3,553))	675.07
Invoice total	4,228.07

4   (a) and (b)

Date	Customer	Invoice number	Customer code	Gross £	VAT £	Net £
21/9	Dagwell Enterprises	56401	SL 15	948.60	158.10	790.50
21/9	G Thomas & Co	56402	SL 30	3,514.01	566.01	2,948.00
22/9	Polygon Stores	56403	SL 03	1,965.60	327.60	1,638.00
23/9	Weller Enterprises	56404	SL 18	1,144.32	184.32	960.00
	Totals			7,572.53	1,236.03	6,336.50

5   Cheque from Quinn Ltd – the remittance advice has been correctly totalled but there has been an error made in writing the cheque as the cheque is for £770.80 rather than £770.08.

Cheque from T T Peters – the remittance advice has been incorrectly totalled and the cheque total should have been for £1,191.02.

6   By a process of trial and error you can find the invoices and credit note that total to £226.79.

Invoice/credit note number	£
30234	157.35
30239	85.24
CN2381	(15.80)
Total	226.79

7   Sales ledger

Account name	Amount £	Left side of account ✓	Right side of account ✓	Details in account
Fries & Co	2,136	✓		SDB – 23907
Hussey Enterprises	3,108	✓		SDB – 23908
Todd Trading	3,720	✓		SDB – 23909
Milford Ltd	2,592	✓		SDB – 23910

8   Sales Day Book

Date 20XX	Details	Invoice number	Gross £	VAT £	Net £	Sales type 1 £	Sales type 2 £
30 Nov	Wright & Co	5627	12,000	2,000	10,000	10,000	
30 Nov	H Topping	5628	1,560	260	1,300		1,300
30 Nov	Sage Ltd	5629	600	100	500	500	
	Totals		14,160	2,360	11,800	10,500	1,300

9

Quantity of cases	Product code	Total list price £	Net amount after discount £	VAT £	Gross £

<table>
<tr><td colspan="6" align="center">Wendlehurst Trading
VAT Registration No. 876983479</td></tr>
<tr><td colspan="3">Stroll In Stores</td><td colspan="3">Customer account code: ST725
Delivery note number: 8973
Date: 1 Dec 20XX</td></tr>
<tr><td colspan="6" align="center">Invoice No: 624</td></tr>
<tr><td>Quantity of cases</td><td>Product code</td><td>Total list price £</td><td>Net amount after discount £</td><td>VAT £</td><td>Gross £</td></tr>
<tr><td>600/12 = 50</td><td>TIG300</td><td>500.00</td><td>425.00</td><td>81.60</td><td>506.60</td></tr>
</table>

10

<table>
<tr><td colspan="4" align="center">Wendlehurst Trading
VAT Registration No. 876983479</td></tr>
<tr><td colspan="4">To: Holroyda
Date: 30 Nov 20XX</td></tr>
<tr><td>Date 20XX</td><td>Details</td><td>Transaction amount £</td><td>Outstanding amount £</td></tr>
<tr><td>18 Nov</td><td>Invoice 5607</td><td>4,390</td><td>4,390</td></tr>
<tr><td>21 Nov</td><td>Invoice 5612</td><td>1,400</td><td>5,790</td></tr>
<tr><td>22 Nov</td><td>Credit note 524</td><td>– 160</td><td>5,630</td></tr>
<tr><td>29 Nov</td><td>Invoice 5616</td><td>980</td><td>6,610</td></tr>
<tr><td>30 Nov</td><td>Payment received – thank you</td><td>–4,000</td><td>2,610</td></tr>
</table>

CHAPTER 5   Recording credit purchases

1

To accompany goods being returned to a supplier	Returns note
To record for internal purposes the quantity of goods received	Goods received note
To request payment from a purchaser of goods	Invoice
To order goods from a supplier	Purchase order
To accompany payment to a supplier	Remittance advice note

2
- The invoice does not agree to the purchase order as only 70 Get Well cards were ordered. However when the credit note is taken into account the invoice quantity is correct minus the credit note quantity.

- The unit price on the credit note is only £0.25 whereas the invoice (and order) price is £0.33.

3

Purchases Day Book

Date	Supplier	Invoice number	Supplier code	Gross £	VAT £	Net £
16/10	Herne Industries	46121	PL15	864.00	144.00	720.00
15/10	Bass Engineers	663211	PL13	460.80	76.80	384.00
12/10	Southfield Electrical	56521	PL20	1,995.40	321.40	1,674.00
	Total			3,320.20	542.20	2,778.00

4

Purchases Returns Day Book

Date	Supplier	Credit note number	Supplier code	Gross £	VAT £	Net £
16/10	Southfield Electrical	08702	PL20	120.00	20.00	100.00
17/10	Herne Industries	4502	PL15	132.00	22.00	110.00
		Total		252.00	42.00	210.00

5 **Purchases ledger**

Account name	Amount £	Left side of account ✓	Right side of account ✓	Details in account
Lindell Co	2,136		✓	PDB 24577
Harris Rugs	5,256		✓	PDB 829
Kinshasa Music	2,796		✓	PDB 10/235
Calnan Ltd	2,292		✓	PDB 9836524

6 **Purchases Day Book**

Date 20XX	Details	Invoice number	Gross £	VAT £	Net £	Purchases £	Expenses £
30 Nov	Papford & Co	29000	3,180	530	2,650		2,650
30 Nov	Havelock Beauty	120/22	1,176	196	980	980	
30 Nov	Hareston Ltd	7638	9,384	1,564	7,820	7,820	
	Totals		13,740	2,290	11,450	8,800	2,650

7

	Yes ✓	No ✓
Has the correct purchase price of the printer paper been charged?	✓	
Has the correct trade discount been applied?		✓
What would be the VAT amount charged if the invoice was correct?	£	70.00
What would be the total amount charged if the invoice was correct?	£	420.00

CHAPTER 6   Double entry bookkeeping

1

	Debit	Credit
Money paid into the business by the owner	Bank	Capital
Purchases on credit	Purchases	Purchases ledger control
Purchases of machinery for use in the business, paid for by cheque	Non-current asset	Bank
Sales on credit	Sales ledger control	Sales
Money taken out of the business by the owner	Drawings	Bank

2

Sales ledger control

Date	Details	Amount £	Date	Details	Amount £
1/6	Balance b/d	1,209	28/6	Bank	3,287
30/6	Sales	6,298	30/6	Sales returns	786
			30/6	Balance c/d	3,434
	Total	7,507		Total	7,507
1/7	Balance b/d	3,434			

3   General ledger

Account name	Amount £	Debit ✓	Credit ✓	Details in account
Sales	9,630		✓	SLCA
VAT	1,926		✓	Sales
Sales ledger control	11,556	✓		Sales

4   **General ledger**

Account name	Amount £	Debit ✓	Credit ✓	Details in account
Purchases	10,400	✓		PLCA
VAT	2,080	✓		Purchases
Purchases ledger control	12,480		✓	Purchases

CHAPTER 7   Maintaining the Cash Book

1

Cash Book – Debit side

Date	Details	Discount allowed £	Cash £	Bank £	VAT £	Cash sales £	Trade receivables £
23 Jan	Hoppers Ltd	16.86		545.14			545.14
23 Jan	Superior Products			116.70			116.70
24 Jan	Cash sales		128.46		21.41	107.05	
24 Jan	Esporta Leisure (auto)	11.36		367.20			367.20
25 Jan	Cash sales		86.40		14.40	72.00	
27 Jan	Body Perfect	21.86		706.64			706.64
27 Jan	Cash sales		58.80		9.80	49.00	
27 Jan	Langans Beauty (auto)			267.90			267.90
		50.08	273.66	2,003.58	45.61	228.05	2,003.58

Cross-cast check:

	£
Trade receivables	2,003.58
Cash sales	228.05
VAT	45.61
Total	2,277.24
Cash receipts	273.66
Bank receipts	2,003.58
	2,277.24

2

Double entry for discount allowed:

DR Discount allowed account

CR Sales ledger control account

3

Cash Book – Credit side

Date	Details	Cheque No	Discount received £	Cash £	Bank £	VAT £	Cash purchases £	Trade payables £
23 Jan	Trenter Ltd	002144	28.47		1,110.09			1,110.09
23 Jan	Cash purchase			105.60		17.60	88.00	
24 Jan	W J Jones	002145			246.75			246.75
24 Jan	P J Phillips	002146			789.60			789.60
24 Jan	Cash purchase			125.40		20.90	104.50	
25 Jan	Packing Supp	002147	8.04		305.45			305.45
26 Jan	O & P Ltd	002148	18.72		703.87			703.87
27 Jan	Cash purchase			96.00		16.00	80.00	
			55.23	327.00	3,155.76	54.50	272.50	3,155.76

Cross-cast check:

	£
Trade payables	3,155.76
Cash purchases	272.50
VAT	54.50
Total	3,482.76
Cash payments	327.00
Cheque payments	3,155.76
	3,482.76

4

Cash balance:

Balance b/f	142.60
Cash received (128.46 + 86.40 + 58.80)	273.66
Cash paid	(327.00)
Cash banked	(50.00)
Balance c/d	39.26

Bank balance:

Balance b/f (overdraft)	(1,290.00)
Cheques paid	(3,155.76)
Automated payments received (367.20 + 267.90)	635.10
Cash banked	50.00
Cheques received and banked (545.14 + 116.70 + 706.64)	1,368.48
Balance c/d	(2,392.18)

5

(a) **Cash Book – Credit side**

Details	Discounts £	Cash £	Bank £	VAT £	Cash purchases £	Trade payables £	Marketing expenses £
Balance b/f			3,295				
Klimt Supplies		90		15	75		
Patel Trading		342		57	285		
TWE Ltd		83			83		
Western Industries	80		4,278			4,278	
Mountebank Co			564	94			470
Total	80	515	8,137	166	443	4,278	470

(b) **Cash Book – Debit side**

Details	Discounts £	Cash £	Bank £	Trade receivables £
Balance b/f		792		
Vantage Ltd			1,278	1,278
Marbles Co	15		2,183	2,183
Total	15	792	3,461	3,461

(c)   Cash balance £792 – £515

£	277

(d)   Bank balance £3.461 – £8,137

£	–4,676

(e)   Bank balance calculated in (d) above: credit balance

	✓
Debit	
Credit	✓

CHAPTER 8   Double entry for sales and trade receivables

1

General ledger

Sales ledger control account

Details	£	Details	£
Sales	7,603.80	Sales returns	601.20

Sales account

Details	£	Details	£
		SLCA	6,336.50

Sales returns account

Details	£	Details	£
SLCA	501.00		

VAT account

Details	£	Details	£
Sales returns	100.20	Sales	1,267.30

Sales ledger

Dagwell Enterprises   SL 15

Details	£	Details	£
SDB – Invoice 56401	948.60	SRDB – Credit note 08651	244.80

G Thomas & Co   SL 30

Details	£	Details	£
SDB – Invoice 56402	3,537.60		

Polygon Stores   SL 03

Details	£	Details	£
SDB – Invoice 56403	1,965.60		

Weller Enterprises — SL 18

Details	£	Details	£
SDB – Invoice 56404	1,152.00		

Whitehill Superstores — SL 37

Details	£	Details	£
		SRDB – Credit note 08650	356.40

2

General ledger

VAT account — GL 562

Details	£	Details	£
		Sales	112.12

Sales account — GL 049

Details	£	Details	£
		Cash	560.64

Sales ledger control account — GL 827

Details	£	Details	£
		Bank	981.12
		Discounts allowed	10.40

Discounts allowed account — GL 235

Details	£	Details	£
SLCA	10.40		

Sales ledger

H Henry — SL 0115

Details	£	Details	£
		CB – receipt	146.79

P Peters — SL 0135

Details	£	Details	£
		CB – receipt	221.55
		CB – discount	6.85

K Kilpin   SL 0128

Details	£	Details	£
		CB – receipt	440.30

B Bennet   SL 0134

Details	£	Details	£
		CB – receipt	57.80

S Shahir   SL 0106

Details	£	Details	£
		CB – receipt	114.68
		CB – discount	3.55

3

General ledger

Cash   GL 050

Details	£	Details	£
Cash receipts	1,008.90		

Bank   GL 100

Details	£	Details	£
Bank receipts	1,693.77		

VAT account   GL 710

Details	£	Details	£
		Sales	168.15

Sales account   GL 110

Details	£	Details	£
		Cash	840.75

Sales ledger control account   GL 560

Details	£	Details	£
		Bank	1,693.77
		Discounts allowed	63.30

Discounts allowed account GL 280

Details	£	Details	£
SLCA	63.30		

Sales ledger

G Gonpipe SL 55

Details	£	Details	£
		CB – receipt	332.67

J Jimmings SL 04

Details	£	Details	£
		CB – receipt	127.37
		CB – discount	6.70

N Nutely SL 16

Details	£	Details	£
		CB – receipt	336.28
		CB – discounts	17.70

T Turner SL 21

Details	£	Details	£
		CB – receipt	158.35

R Ritner SL 45

Details	£	Details	£
		CB – receipt	739.10
		CB – discount	38.90

4

VAT account

Details	£	Details	£
		Sales	1,926

Sales account

Details	£	Details	£
		SLCA	9,630

Sales ledger control account

Details	£	Details	£
Sales	11,556		

CHAPTER 9 Double entry for purchases and trade payables

1

General ledger

Purchases ledger control account

Details	£	Details	£
Purchases returns	252.00	Purchases	3,333.60

Purchases account

Details	£	Details	£
PLCA	2,778.00		

Purchases returns account

Details	£	Details	£
		PLCA	210.00

VAT account

Details	£	Details	£
Purchases	555.60	Purchases returns	42.00

Purchases ledger

Herne Industries   PL 15

Details	£	Details	£
Credit note 4502	132.00	Invoice 46121	864.00

Bass Engineers   PL 13

Details	£	Details	£
		Invoice 663211	460.80

Southfield Electrical   PL 20

Details	£	Details	£
Credit note 08702	120.00	Invoice 56521	2,008.80

2

General ledger

VAT account   GL 100

Details	£	Details	£
Bank	62.44		

Purchases account   GL 200

Details	£	Details	£
Bank	312.20		

Purchases ledger control account   GL 300

Details	£	Details	£
Bank	1,188.59		
Discounts received	19.20		

Loan account   GL 400

Details	£	Details	£
Bank	200.00		

Discounts received   GL 500

Details	£	Details	£
		PLCA	19.20

Cash   GL 550

Details	£	Details	£
		Cash payments	374.64

Bank   GL 600

Details	£	Details	£
		Bank payments	1,388.59

Purchases ledger

R R Partners — PL 06

Details	£	Details	£
CB	163.47		
CB – discount	4.19		

Troyde Ltd — PL 14

Details	£	Details	£
CB	183.57		

F Elliott — PL 20

Details	£	Details	£
CB	263.68		
CB – discount	8.15		

P Products Ltd — PL 23

Details	£	Details	£
CB	241.58		

Jason Bros — PL 36

Details	£	Details	£
CB	336.29		
CB – discount	6.86		

3

VAT account

Details	£	Details	£
Purchases	2,080.00		

Purchases account

Details	£	Details	£
PLCA	10,400.00		

Purchases ledger control account

Details	£	Details	£
		Purchases	12,480.00

CHAPTER 10   Accounting for petty cash

1

1.1 An imprest petty cash system is one where the amount of the topped up petty cash float at the start of each period is:

| Always the same |

1.2 Amounts that have been paid out for authorised expenditure are represented in the petty cash box by

| Petty cash vouchers |

1.3 At the end of the period the total of the

| Petty cash vouchers |

in the petty cash box is the amount needed to restore the petty cash box to the imprest amount.

2

| £ | 89.46 |

3

Petty Cash Book

RECEIPTS			PAYMENTS								
Date	Details	Amount £	Date	Details	Voucher number	Total £	VAT £	Post £	Travel £	Sundry office £	Misc £
20 Oct	Bank	150.00	24 Oct	Train fare	771	14.00			14.00		
			24 Oct	Postage	772	18.60		18.60			
			24 Oct	Envelopes	773	16.80	2.80			14.00	
			24 Oct	Window cleaner	774	20.00					20.00
			24 Oct	Pens/paper	775	18.90	3.15			15.75	
			24 Oct	Postage	776	5.46		5.46			
			24 Oct	Taxi fare	777	9.60	1.60		8.00		
			24 Oct	Computer discs	778	28.20	4.70			23.50	
						131.56	12.25	24.06	22.00	53.25	20.00
			Balance c/d			18.44					
	Total	150.00				150.00					
Balance b/d		18.44									
Bank top-up		131.56									

4

Petty Cash Book

Debit side		Credit side					
Details	Amount £	Details	Amount £	VAT £	Postage £	Travel £	Motor expenses £
Balance b/f	180.00	Post Office	12.60		12.60		
		Motor Repair Workshop	72.60	12.10			60.50
		Great Eastern Trains	32.00			32.00	
		Balance c/d	62.80				
	180.00		180.00	12.10	12.60	32.00	60.50

CHAPTER 11   Initial trial balance
1

VAT account

Details	£	Details	£
Purchases	3,778	Balance b/f	2,116
Bank	2,116	Sales	6,145
Balance c/d	2,367		
	8,261		8,261
		Balance b/d	2,367

Sales account

Details	£	Details	£
		Balance b/f	57,226
Balance c/d	100,121	SLCA	42,895
	100,121		100,121
		Balance b/d	100,121

Sales ledger control account

Details	£	Details	£
Balance b/f	4,689	Bank	21,505
Sales	23,512	Discounts allowed	2,019
		Balance c/d	4,677
	28,201		28,201
Balance b/d	4,677		

Purchases ledger control account

Details	£	Details	£
Purchases returns	1,334	Balance b/f	2,864
Bank	13,446	Purchases	14,552
Discounts received	662		
Balance c/d	1,974		
	17,416		17,416
		Balance b/d	1,974

2

	£	Debit balance ✓	Credit balance ✓
Discounts allowed	1,335	✓	
Discounts received	1,013		✓
Purchases returns	4,175		✓
Sales returns	6,078	✓	
Bank interest received	328		✓
Bank charges	163	✓	

3

	Debits £	Credits £
Motor vehicles	64,000	
Office equipment	21,200	
Sales		238,000
Purchases	164,000	
Cash	300	
Bank overdraft		1,080
Petty cash control	30	
Capital		55,000
Sales returns	4,700	
Purchases returns		3,600
Sales ledger control	35,500	
Purchases ledger control		30,100
VAT (owed to HMRC)		12,950
Telephone	1,600	
Electricity	2,800	
Wages	62,100	

	Debits £	Credits £
Loan from bank		30,000
Discounts allowed	6,400	
Discounts received		3,900
Rent expense	12,000	
Totals	374,630	374,630

4

Account name	Amount £	Debit £	Credit £
Advertising	3,238	3,238	
Bank overdraft	27,511		27,511
Capital	40,846		40,846
Cash	689	689	
Discount allowed	4,416	4,416	
Discount received	2,880		2,880
Hotel expenses	2,938	2,938	
Inventory	46,668	46,668	
Loan from bank	39,600		39,600
Miscellaneous expenses	3,989	3,989	
Motor expenses	7,087	7,087	
Motor vehicles	63,120	63,120	
Petty cash control	720	720	
Purchases	634,529	634,529	
Purchases ledger control	110,846		110,846
Purchases returns	1,618		1,618
Rent and rates	19,200	19,200	
Sales	1,051,687		1,051,687
Sales ledger control	405,000	405,000	
Sales returns	11,184	11,184	
Stationery	5,880	5,880	

Account name	Amount £	Debit £	Credit £
Subscriptions	864	864	
Telephone	3,838	3,838	
VAT (owing to HM Revenue and Customs)	63,650		63,650
Wages	125,278	125,278	
Totals		1,338,638	1,338,638

INDEX

Notes

Notes

Notes

Notes

Notes

REVIEW FORM

How have you used this Text?
(Tick one box only)

☐ Home study

☐ On a course_____

☐ Other _____

During the past six months do you recall seeing/receiving either of the following?
(Tick as many boxes as are relevant)

☐ Our advertisement in Accounting Technician

☐ Our Publishing Catalogue

Why did you decide to purchase this Text? *(Tick one box only)*

☐ Have used BPP Texts in the past

☐ Recommendation by friend/colleague

☐ Recommendation by a college lecturer

☐ Saw advertising

☐ Other _____

Which (if any) aspects of our advertising do you think are useful?
(Tick as many boxes as are relevant)

☐ Prices and publication dates of new editions

☐ Information on Text content

☐ Details of our free online offering

☐ None of the above

Your ratings, comments and suggestions would be appreciated on the following areas of this Text.

	Very useful	Useful	Not useful
Introductory section	☐	☐	☐
Quality of explanations	☐	☐	☐
How it works	☐	☐	☐
Chapter tasks	☐	☐	☐
Chapter overviews	☐	☐	☐
Test your learning	☐	☐	☐
Index	☐	☐	☐

	Excellent	Good	Adequate	Poor
Overall opinion of this Text	☐	☐	☐	☐

Do you intend to continue using BPP Products?   ☐ Yes   ☐ No

Please note any further comments and suggestions/errors on the reverse of this page. The Head of Programme for this edition can be emailed at: nisarahmed@bpp.com

Please return to: Nisar Ahmed, AAT Head of Programme, BPP Learning Media Ltd, FREEPOST, London, W12 8BR.

REVIEW FORM (continued)

TELL US WHAT YOU THINK

Please note any further comments and suggestions/errors below